T0321794

Formation Methods, Models, and Hardware Implementation of Pseudorandom Number Generators:

Emerging Research and Opportunities

Stepan Bilan
State Economy and Technology University of Transport, Ukraine

A volume in the Advances in Systems Analysis, Software Engineering, and High Performance Computing (ASASEHPC) Book Series

Published in the United States of America by
IGI Global
Engineering Science Reference (an imprint of IGI Global)
701 E. Chocolate Avenue
Hershey PA, USA 17033
Tel: 717-533-8845
Fax: 717-533-8661
E-mail: cust@igi-global.com
Web site: http://www.igi-global.com

Library of Congress Cataloging-in-Publication Data

Names: Bilan, Stepan, 1962-
Title: Formation methods, models, and hardware implementation of pseudorandom
  number generators : emerging research and opportunities / by Stepan Bilan.
Description: Hershey PA : Engineering Science Reference, [2018] | Includes
  bibliographical references.
Identifiers: LCCN 2017010712| ISBN 9781522527732 (hardcover) | ISBN
  9781522527749 (ebook)
Subjects: LCSH: Random number generators. | Cellular automata. |
  Computational complexity.
Classification: LCC QA298 .B55 2018 | DDC 004.01/51--dc23 LC record available at https://lccn.
loc.gov/2017010712

This book is published in the IGI Global book series Advances in Systems Analysis, Software Engineering, and High Performance Computing (ASASEHPC) (ISSN: 2327-3453; eISSN: 2327-3461)

British Cataloguing in Publication Data
A Cataloguing in Publication record for this book is available from the British Library.

All work contributed to this book is new, previously-unpublished material.
The views expressed in this book are those of the authors, but not necessarily of the publisher.

For electronic access to this publication, please contact: eresources@igi-global.com.

Advances in Systems Analysis, Software Engineering, and High Performance Computing (ASASEHPC) Book Series

ISSN:2327-3453
EISSN:2327-3461

Editor-in-Chief: Vijayan Sugumaran, Oakland University, USA

MISSION

The theory and practice of computing applications and distributed systems has emerged as one of the key areas of research driving innovations in business, engineering, and science. The fields of software engineering, systems analysis, and high performance computing offer a wide range of applications and solutions in solving computational problems for any modern organization.

The **Advances in Systems Analysis, Software Engineering, and High Performance Computing (ASASEHPC) Book Series** brings together research in the areas of distributed computing, systems and software engineering, high performance computing, and service science. This collection of publications is useful for academics, researchers, and practitioners seeking the latest practices and knowledge in this field.

COVERAGE

- Software engineering
- Engineering Environments
- Human-computer interaction
- Enterprise information systems
- Performance Modelling
- Computer System Analysis
- Distributed Cloud Computing
- Computer graphics
- Storage Systems
- Parallel Architectures

IGI Global is currently accepting manuscripts for publication within this series. To submit a proposal for a volume in this series, please contact our Acquisition Editors at Acquisitions@igi-global.com or visit: http://www.igi-global.com/publish/.

Titles in this Series

701 East Chocolate Avenue, Hershey, PA 17033, USA
Tel: 717-533-8845 x100 • Fax: 717-533-8661
E-Mail: cust@igi-global.com • www.igi-global.com

Table of Contents

Preface

Today we live in a world where computers are widely used. They are involved in practically all human affairs. A large number of universal and specialized computer systems were developed. They perform a variety of the different information processing tasks.

Modern computing systems use the digital form of the information presentation. This means that all the characters and numbers as binary codes, which represent the number in the binary notation, are represented.

In fact, today the modern computer systems are the systems of the digital data processing and they represent information as a sequence of numbers. Computer systems perform tasks of processing of the deterministic and nondeterministic numbers.

Sources of deterministic numbers are predefined and for solving of the exact calculations mainly are used. Sources of nondeterministic numbers are used for event simulation tasks, which cannot be predicted in advance. Among such tasks, have event simulation tasks in time. Each of their cannot be predicted in advance by the user because of the ignorance of all the processes that affect the event.

The random numbers sources have the most important meaning in such areas:

1. Information security.
2. Imitating modeling.
3. Computer games.
4. Training exercise machines.
5. Diagnostics of telecommunication systems.

Important is the unpredictability of the values of quantitative values for each of following event. Limitations or inability to find and select a random number of sources are coerces the specialists to create of the artificial sources of random numbers, which the pseudo-random number generator (PRNG) are called. They differ from natural sources so that we always can to repeat a sequence of numbers generated by a PRNG, if we know its initial installation.

At the same time the pseudo-random number generator have a number of limitations of the basic characteristics. The affiliation classes, structure, the number of states, and other parameters are influenced.

Today, there are many the pseudo-random number generator and new modifications are developed. One of the research directions in this field is the use of cellular automata (CA). This book focuses on the description of the new methods, models and tools for the PRNG building based on synchronous and asynchronous CA with different forms of coating. The main properties of the proposed PRNG are described and studied. Particular attention is paid to increasing the length of the repetition period of generated sequences and to improving the statistical properties of generators. To assess their behavior, known ENT and NIST tests were used, as well as graphic tests. With the help of these tests, the behavior of the generators was described and new properties of cellular automata were discovered that implement the proposed modes of operation and the selected local state transition functions of each cell.

The book is intended for professionals who conduct research and work in the field of information security and information technology. Also this book is aimed at researchers who conduct modeling of the dynamic behavior of various processes and objects. The material presented in the book will help bachelors, masters and graduate students who acquire knowledge in the field of information technology, computer engineering and computer science. Particularly the material of the book will be useful to developers of parallel processing systems, as well as real-time information protection systems when transmitting it via communication channels. The results presented in the book will help many researchers who use cellular automata in their work. The book contains a technique for conducting an experiment that will allow specialists to determine the optimum configuration of CA for solving various tasks of modeling dynamic processes in the future.

The book consists of eight chapters.

The first chapter is aimed at determining the scope of the use of random numbers, and it also describes the known methods for constructing PRNG. The classification of PRNG is presented and their basic properties are described.

The second chapter is devoted to the description of a brief history of development and the theory of CA construction. The main types of CA are presented. One-dimensional and two-dimensional synchronous and asynchronous CA are described.

The third chapter describes in detail the existing PRNGs based on CA. Much attention is paid to the description of the principles of constructing known PRNG based on one-dimensional and two-dimensional CA. The PRNG based on hybrid CA is considered, and also on the basis of CA with additional sources of random numbers.

The fourth chapter presents the main theoretical positions and practical implementation of PRNG based on asynchronous CA. Models of CA functioning that implement such PRNG. In addition, the versions of hardware implementation of PRNG based on asynchronous CA are presented.

In the fifth chapter are presented models, construction methods, and practical implementation of PRNG based on CA, in which not all cells realize the same local transition functions. PRNGs based on CA are also described, in which cells have different forms of neighborhoods. The basic properties of such a PRNG are described.

The sixth chapter contains a material in which methods for constructing combined PRNGs based on asynchronous CA and synchronous CA with inhomogeneous cells are set out. The basic models and structures of CA are used, which are described in the fourth and fifth chapters.

The seventh chapter gives the presentation of the use of CA with a hexagonal coating for the construction of PRNG. The PRNGs are described, which are implemented on the basis of synchronous CA and asynchronous CA, which are described in the fourth and fifth chapters. The influence of the shape of the coating and the neighborhood of the cells in the CA on the results of the operation of the PRNG are studied.

In the eighth chapter, an analysis of the quality of the described PRNGs based on CA is carried out. The technique of testing developed PRNGs using the tests ENT, NIST and graphical tests is described. The results of many experiments that describe the behavior of two-dimensional CA for different initial settings are presented.

The book is the initial author's work, which describes the study of the behavior of two-dimensional CA of various configurations and their use for constructing high quality PRNG. These studies are continuing and developing and will be published in the future in a wider format for their application.

Introduction

Hello dear readers!

I hope that this book will help all those who are interested in it, and who decided to read it. I hope that the book will help students to acquire new knowledge in Computer Science. Especially, book will help students to acquire knowledge in the field of cellular automata and in the field of information security. I very much hope that the book will help to scientific researchers to get good academic results and choose the right path for the decision of tasks they have.

This book focuses on the description of new approaches in the use of cellular automata to solve many problems. Why I chose cellular automata? Than cellular automata had attracted me? First of all, the fact that the cellular automata may give the "unpredictable" result. However, this result may be the most awaited.

To date, many problems are being solved with the help of computational tools that are implemented by finite automata. These finite automata are implemented by developers, and their behavior is predetermined. Each automaton performs an algorithm that is implemented using hardware or software.

However, there are many tasks that focus to the study of dynamic changes of the physical processes and to the behavior of the biological objects. These problems do not give a known result in advance. The solution of such problems is based on the construction of the object model. Successful implementation of the structural and functional models of the object can give the positive results in time. This approach is used for solving of the tasks, which focus to constructing artificial biological objects.

The cellular automata can help us to construct the models of many physical processes in time. They can predict us the state of the dynamic process or of a physical object in the specified future time step and with the specified external actions. For this purpose the researcher have needs of a good understanding about the organization of a physical object or process and skillfully set of its initial settings. Exactly these settings (the initial conditions) and the internal organization of a cellular automaton predetermines the behavior of the model without taking into account additional external influences. If there are external influences at each time step, the behavior of cellular automata is constantly changing its own state. However, the cellular automatons are functioning according to their internal organization.

This book examines the possibility of using cellular automata for getting it "unpredictable" states. On these states the random initial settings or the intermediate external influences are act. The possibilities of creating objects models are described. Their behavior is very difficult to predict by researcher.

Today such objects may be the pseudo random number generators that are based on the cellular automata with various forms of their construction. In order to assess their performance the set of states of a cellular automaton for a given period of operation are using. It is the set of states may be represented by a sequence of bits that indicate the status of one of the cells at each time step. On the based of this sequence are assessed the predictability of the each element of the generated sequence. If this is not possible, then is being considered that a cellular automaton randomly works.

The book presents several of a pseudorandom number generators implemented on the cellular automata. The first, second and third generators have a cells with a rectangular shape, and the fourth, fifth and sixth generators have been built on cellular automata with the hexagonal form of coating. In doing so they perform the same function of local transitions and the same methods of transmission of the active state from cell to cell. The possibilities and properties of the developed generators were studied. The emphasis on the improvement of the statistical properties of generators as well on the increasing the length of the repetition period of the generated sequences was made. Both of these parameters characterize the quality of unpredictability of the generator.

The improvement of these characteristics in the future will make it possible for us to build a model of vital processes with a long period of life. I am confident that this approach will allow the people to fight diseases based on constructed models and perhaps advance it will create better facilities, as well as will help us to find the best option among the many options offered of the solutions to the various problems.

In order to assess their behavior the known test methods were used: ENT, NIST and graphics tests. With the help of these tests, the behavior of generators is described and the new properties of cellular automata for the proposed structures were discovered.

The book presents the results of many experiments that describe the behavior of two-dimensional cellular automata. I hope these results will help many researchers who use cellular automata for their research.

I express my deep gratitude to my brother Nikolai Belan, my wife, son and nephew, as well as Ruslan Motornyuk for help and support in research.

Chapter 1
Pseudorandom Number Generators

ABSTRACT

In this chapter, the author considers existing methods and means of forming pseudo-random sequences of numbers and also are described the main characteristics of random and pseudorandom sequences of numbers. The main theoretical aspects of the construction of pseudo-random number generators are considered. Classification of pseudorandom number generators is presented. The structures and models of the most popular pseudo-random number generators are considered, the main characteristics of generators that affect the quality of the formation of pseudorandom bit sequences are described. The models of the basic mathematical generators of pseudo-random numbers are considered, and also the principles of building hardware generators are presented.

RANDOM AND PSEUDORANDOM SEQUENCES OF NUMBERS

Random sequences are widely are used in various fields. They are used in game theory, information security, in the training simulators, in the Monte Carlo methods, which numerical methods are using for the various mathematical tasks solving, and in other fields. Before the advent of computer, the random sequences was being formed by various mathematical and hardware means, invented by man. For example, the coin tossing up or the urn with balls, are

DOI: 10.4018/978-1-5225-2773-2.ch001

using and others. In the future, are compiled a table that contained a large number of random numbers.

Ideal random number sequence is being formed by human using of the various natural events and physical processes. For this purpose, people use the various methods of transformation of the analog values to digital form of number. It is believed that these analogue values are changed by randomly. Each analog value is converted into a number in the discrete intervals of time.

The source of random numbers can be a numerical value of the selected analog value at discrete time moments. For a man important is a successful search for the source of this value, which has a wide range of changes in a given interval of time. Such sources and values include the amount of noise in nonlinear electronic elements (diodes, transistors), ionizing radiation, cosmic radiation, and others.

In fact, this approach uses a conventional transformation of the analog value into its numeric equivalent. For this, researchers are being developed the special converters that consist of a primary the transducer of the physical quantity into an electrical quantity and of the electrical signal transducer into it digital equivalent.

In this approach, a sequence of random numbers $a_1, a_2, \ldots, a_i, \ldots, a_n$ is random when any of its next element can not be predicted based on analysis of the previous generated numbers.

The length of the random sequence cannot be bounded, and the range of numbers (range of values) is significantly limited. The width of the range of values depends on the generated numbers from the physical source and from an analog value digitization step.

Furthermore, the ideal random sequence can not be generated by the same source of with a certain time period.

If a random sequence of numbers has been formed by a computer means that implement the established generation algorithm, such a sequence is called a pseudo-random sequence of numbers.

A computing device that implements an algorithm generating pseudorandom numbers, a finite number of states is has. The repeat period of a pseudorandom sequence depends on a set of states, which by the chosen algorithm and by the structure of the computing device are implemented.

The computing device that generates a pseudo-random sequence of numbers, the pseudo-random number generator is called.

Three main properties are used to assess of the generated pseudo-random bit sequence.

1. The number of ones and zeros in a sequence of approximately equal and may differ only on 1.
2. Identical bit sequences should be distributed so that groups of one element are divided in half in all sequence and groups consisting of two identical elements are divided into four equal parts throughout the sequence, etc.
3. When analyzing coincidences with the selected control sequence, the coincidence number must different from the number of non-coincidences on 1 for all binary "1" of a sequence.

These properties are present within the period length of pseudorandom sequence. They characterize the unpredictability of any next element based on the elements sequence previously formed.

It should be remembered that the sequence consisting of all binary "1" may also be formed randomly.

RANDOM AND PSEUDORANDOM NUMBER GENERATORS

Random Number Generators generates in nature the random numerical sequences that are not predictable for anyone person (Sanguinetti, Martin, Zbinden, & Gisin, 2014, Tang, Wu, Wu, Deng, Chen, Fan, Zhong, & Xia, 2015). At the same time pseudorandom number generator is regarded as a source of random numbers and as a source of deterministic numbers. The structure of the pseudorandom number generator on Figure 1 is represented.

The pseudorandom number generator is an automaton with a finite set of states, which implements the specified algorithm that forming a sequence of numbers at the output (Intel Digital Random Number Generator [DRNG]; Hörmann, Leydold, & Derflinger, 2004; L'Ecuyer, 1998; L'Ecuyer, 1994;

Figure 1. The structure of the pseudorandom number generator

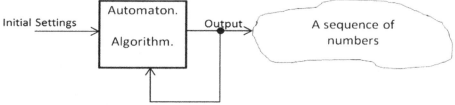

Marsaglia, 1985; Eddy, 1990; Fog, 2015; Barash, & Shchur, 2014, Tanvir, & Mahbubur, 2016).

From a user perspective the pseudorandom number generator is regarded as automaton that implements a predetermined mathematical function or structural units that have the initial states for number formation on the output at each time point. For the user, the output numbers are random, because he does not know the initial automaton settings.

At the output of pseudorandom number generator the result does not depend on external factors, and it depends on the internal organization and of the initial settings. This fact distinguishes it from the random number generator.

The pseudorandom number generator is the only source of deterministic numbers when:

- The user does not know the structure of the generator and its initial settings;
- The user knows the algorithm, but he does not know the initial settings of pseudorandom number generator;
- The user knows the initial conditions, but he doesn't know the functioning of the algorithm.

PRNG is an automaton with finite number of states and they determine the length of the repeat period of the pseudo-random sequence of numbers at its output.

All pseudorandom number generators are estimated by specialists by their main characteristics. The pseudorandom number generator has the following main characteristics.

1. The length of the repeat period of the pseudo-random sequence of numbers.
2. The High statistical properties of the generated pseudo-random sequence of numbers.
3. The speed of formation of the numbers on the output.
4. The degree of independence of numbers in the sequence from each other.
5. The range of numbers that generator generates.

The length of the repeat period of the pseudo-random sequence is characterized by a number of states and by the transitions rules between states. For example, for pseudorandom number generator based on the shift register with feedback the maximum possible period of the bit pseudorandom sequence is equal 2^L-1 (where L - the number of a register cells) (Golomb, 1967; Schneier, 1996; Lehmer, 1951; Eichenauer, Lehn, & Topuzoglu, 1988; Chugunkov, 2012; Bilan, Bilan, & Bilan, 2015; Douglas, Vanderkooy, & Vanderkooy, 1989, Babitha, Thushara, & Dechakka 2015, Sahithi, MuraliKrishna, Jyothi, Purnima, Jhansi, & Sudha, 2012). However, this period may be less. It depends on the polynomial, which determines the feedbacks in a generator.

The bit sequence statistical properties determine the distribution of "1" and "0" in the sequence. The basic postulates for the statistical evaluation of the pseudo-random sequence Solomon Golomb has formulated (Golomb, 1967). In the previous section they are described. To determine the statistical properties of the sequence a significant number of statistical tests are used (Chugunkov, 2012; National institute of standarts and technology [NIST]; Marsaglia, 1984; Gerard, 2006; Walker, 2008). These tests determine the permissible limits of the random source.

The speed of formation of the numbers is of great importance for many applications (stream ciphers, computer games, etc.). The generator hardware implementation allows increased the speed of formation of pseudo-random sequences.

The degree of independence between numbers of a random sequence is should be very high. The degree value determines influence of previously generated bits on the subsequent bits. Such a degree may be determined by the number of feedbacks in a generator.

The range of numbers is taken into account when the real decimal numbers are formed. The width of the range is determined by the maximum length of the pseudorandom sequence.

Based on the main characteristics are being selected and the necessary pseudorandom number generator are developed.

THE CLASSIFICATION OF PSEUDORANDOM NUMBER GENERATORS

A large number of pseudorandom number generator is written in modern literature. However, there is no clear classification. Basically the pseudorandom number generator are considered in point of view of their application for cryptographic transformations.

If we try to classify the pseudorandom number generator with respect to their implementation, all the generators may be implemented by the hardware and software. All the pseudorandom number generator may be described with the help of special mathematical expressions. At the same time they are being described by the different mathematical models. There are generators, which are described by the complex mathematical models that are difficult are perceived by the user. At the same time, these generators can be are clearly described as a table or as a simple electrical functional circuit. Therefore, all the existing pseudorandom number generator are being submitted by their description.

The most generalized classification divides the pseudorandom number generators by the method of mathematical description of the algorithm and hardware. The mathematical pseudorandom number generators describe the generating method of pseudorandom numbers by the mathematical model.

The hardware pseudorandom number generators are described from the perspective of use of basic electronic components and their functional characteristics. For example, pseudorandom number generators are constructed based on the shift register, the majority element, etc.

By its nature, the pseudorandom number generators generate sequence of numbers at each time step of taking into account the previously generated sequence numbers. Therefore, the pseudorandom number generator are divided into the pseudorandom number generator, which uses the feedback and pseudorandom number generators without feedback. The presence of feedbacks in the structure of the pseudorandom number generator reduces their performance. Therefore, developers are trying to reduce the amount of feedbacks.

Also the pseudorandom number generator is being divided into the individual generators and combined generators. Single generators implement the only one algorithm that forming a pseudo-random sequence of numbers. These generators create the only one indefinite numbers source.

The combined pseudorandom number generators are built using multiple single pseudorandom number generators that implement different algorithms of formation of pseudorandom numbers or they implement same algorithms, but different initial settings are having. The single generator outputs are combined by the special function (Schneier, 1996). The combined pseudorandom number generators significantly improve the properties of the generated sequence. However, their operation reliability is reduced by increasing the complexity.

According to the nature of feedbacks pseudorandom number generators are divided into generators with the linear and the nonlinear feedbacks (Golomb, 1967; Schneier, 1996; Linear Feedback Shift Registers in Virtex Devices

[LFSRVD]; Klapper, & Goresky, 1997; Lewis, & Payne, 1973). The linear feedback is characterized by a linear function on the output, and the nonlinear feedback - a nonlinear function.

All the generators are aimed at bringing them closer to the ideal properties of the source of random numbers. In practice, the based on the shift registers with linear feedback generators (LFSR) have the most popular (Sahithi, MuraliKrishna, Jyothi, Purnima, Rani, & Sudha, 2012, Babitha, Thushara, & Dechakka, 2015, David, Hoe, Comer, Cerda, Martinez, & Shirvaikar, 2012).

THE MATHEMATICAL PSEUDORANDOM NUMBER GENERATORS

The mathematical pseudorandom number generators are described by mathematical formulas and are widely described in various literature sources (Schneier, 1996; Marsaglia, 2003; Kashmar & Ismail, 2015). Mathematical generators are often called algorithmic pseudorandom number generator. They implement the algorithm on the given mathematical model. In such generators, each successive generated number functionally depends upon the previous generated numbers in sequence.

$$N_{i+1} = f\left(N_0, N_1, ..., N_{i,}\right)$$

Such pseudorandom number sources provide cycles repeated infinitely often. These cycles are called periods of repetition.

First, a linear congruential generator thing is examined (LCG), described by the following model (Schneier, 1996; Lehmer, 1951; Thomson, 1958; Eichenauer, Lehn, & Topuzoglu, 1988).

$$X_n = \left(a \cdot X_{n-1} + b\right) \bmod m.$$

This generator was proposed D. Lehmer in 1949. It allows you to generate a sequence of numbers from 0 to m-1. The period of such generator does not exceed m and depends upon the successful selection values of *a*, *b* and *m*.

Such generators are quite simple to be implemented, but they are predictable. Therefore, they are rarely used in serious applications.

Non-linear functions are used to improve the quality of functioning of the linear congruential generator. These include generators, based on quadratic and cubic functions.

$$X_{n+1} = \left(a \cdot X_n^2 + b \cdot X_k + c \right) \bmod m \, ,$$

$$X_{n+1} = \left(a \cdot X_k^2 + b \cdot X_n^2 + c \cdot X_k + d \right) \bmod m \, .$$

Combinations of such generators improve their statistical properties and increase the size of the repetition period.

Fibonacci generator has replaced congruent generators came, because the first one has better properties than the congruent generators. The most common Fibonacci generator is the generator, described by the following formula (Knuth, 1969).

$$N_k = \begin{cases} N_{k-a} - N_{k-b}, & if \quad N_{k-a} > N_{k-b} \\ N_{k-a} - N_{k-b} + 1, & if \quad N_{k-a} > N_{k-b} \end{cases} ,$$

where

N_k - real numbers in the range [0,1);
a, b - positive integers.

The generated random number sequences possess statistical properties. The period of evaluation according to the formula (Knuth, 1969).

$$T = \left(2^{\max(a,b)} - 1 \right) \cdot 2^r \, ,$$

where r - number of bits in the real number mantissa.

Numbers *a* and *b* affect the values of the numbers of generated sequences. For the success of the Fibonacci generator a lot of pairs of numbers have been picked, such as (24, 55) (37, 100) (1029, 2281).

PRNGs are also known being based on the Fibonacci sequence, described by the following models (Knuth, 1969).

$$X_{k+1} = \left(X_k + X_{k-1} \right) \bmod m \,,$$

$$X_{k+1} = \left(X_k + X_{k+1} \right) \bmod m \,.$$

The length of the generator period exceeds m, but only a few numbers match the random distribution.

Mersenne Twister

Mersenne Twister was developed in 1997 by Makoto Matsumoto and Takuji Nishimura (Matsumoto, & Nishimura, 1998; Matsumoto, & Kurita, 1992). It is based on the properties of Mersenne primes of the following form $N_n = 2^n - 1$, where n – integer. The algorithm passes stringent tests DIEHARD. The algorithm is described by the following model

$$x_{k+n} := x_{k+m} \oplus \left(x_k^u \mid x_{k+1}^l \right) A \,,$$

where

k = 0,1,2, ...; n - an integer that indicates the degree of recurrence;
m - an integer, 1 <m <n;
A - the size of the matrix W×W with elements from F2 = {0,1};
W – machine word size; | - Bitwise OR;
$\oplus$ - XOR function;
x_k^u - Senior (W-r) bits; x_{k+1}^l - Lower r bits.

The repeat sequence numbers period is 2^{19937}-1 and pseudo-random number sequence generation is implemented in 623 measurements. This corresponds to a very low correlation between successive values. In fact, the Mersenne Twister is represented by linear feedback shift register, in which the following condition is generated by shifting a word vertically and insert a new word to the end (Matsumoto, Nishimura, Hadita, & Saito 2005).

Algorithm Blum-Blum-Shub (1986)

Algorithm Blum-Blum-Shub implements mathematical source of pseudorandom numbers, proposed in 1986 by Lenore Blum, Manuel Blum, and Michael Shub (Blum, Blum, & Shub, 1986). It is based on the following mathematical model:

$$X_{k+1} = \left(X_k\right)^2 \bmod M \,,$$

where $M = p \cdot q$ - the product of two large prime numbers.

Both numbers p and q should possess the excess of 3 when divided by 4. Start number of BBS - the generator is calculated by the formula:

$$X_{k+1} = \left(X\right)^2 \bmod M \,.$$

The X number is chosen by the user and it is prime to the number M.

At each n - m step of the algorithm the number that does not exceed M is formed. To implement a pseudo-random bit sequence on each discrete time step, select one (usually younger) bit of number X_{n+1}. Sometimes one can choose parity bit equal to 0, or odd, equal to 1.

The algorithm is original because it makes possible to calculate the number of n - m discrete step without intermediate n calculations. It is enough to know the initial values that are inserted into the following formula:

$$T = \left(X_0^{2^n \bmod (p-1)(q-1)}\right) \bmod M \,.$$

The algorithm has high statistical properties and is good for cryptography. However, it possesses a low operation speed being hardware implemented. Low operation speed of BBS algorithm does not allow using it for streaming encryption.

Middle: Square Method

A simple algorithm, which was proposed by John von Neumann in 1946 (Knuth, 1969).

According to the algorithm of the previous random number is squared and averages are extracted from the result. The disadvantages of this method are the appearance of zeros in the sequence, which also lead to the appearance of zeros in the following numerical values.

In fact, all random number generators described by mathematical models are represented by the mathematical formula of the form

$$X(t+1) = f[z(t)],$$

where t - a discrete time step, and z - number.

This formula indicates the dependence between the number in the next time step and the numbers in the previous steps. The function f[] is selected so that reverse recovery of the number shall not happen. This means the impossibility of restoring sequence number restored from the resulting number.

In this case, the function must be such as to allow for a plurality of input arguments to receive the same number. This indicates that all of the input values can not predict the number of the output.

The set of input arguments can be divided into subsets so that each subset will have only one value of the function f []. This can be described by the following model. Assumed a_i^j is the value of the i-th argument of the function in the j-th set of ($i = \overline{1, k}$, $j = \overline{1, L}$), the model can be represented as follows

$$f\left(a_i^j\right) = y_j, \; \mathrm{f}\left(\mathrm{a}_i^j\right) = \mathrm{y}_j.$$

The value k for each group can be different. Usually, these functions are based on the mod M function.

THE HARDWARE PSEUDORANDOM NUMBER GENERATOR

Hardware PRNG (HPRNG) are the sources of pseudorandom numbers, described by electronic circuits (Neves & Araujo, 2014; Babitha, Thushara, & Dechakka, 2015; Schneier, 1996). HPRNG can be described by means of special mathematical expressions as well. However, it is simpler and easier to describe them by electronic circuit.

Linear Feedback Shift Register

The most thoroughly and accessibly described in the literature HPRNG, is the one based on the linear feedback shift register (Babitha, Thushara, & Dechakka,

2015; Golomb, 1967; Sahithi, MuraliKrishna, Jyothi, Purnima, Jhansi Rani, & Sudha, 2012; Schneier, 1996; Lewis & Payne, 1973). They are thoroughly studied and successfully used in cryptography in implementing streaming encryption. Shift registers with linear feedback (LFSR) comprises (Figure 2) shift register (RS_{sh}), which consists of n bits (S_0, S_1,...,S_{N-1}), switching system (SC), adders block modulo 2 (BS2).

The original bit sequences are written into the level S_i shift register. This bit sequence is represented in the RS_{sh}. The number of bits RS_{sh} determines the length of the bit sequence. At each time step the next bit of a random sequence is formed and the contents of the shift register are shifted by one bit. The contents of the leftmost digit changes. Its value is calculated by function of all the other bits RS_{sh}.

The CA defines the function, implemented by the feedback. The signals are formed on the control inputs ($input_{cont}$) with the help of which the connection of selected XOR gate of BS2 is performed.

The connecting system carries out controlled XOR items connection in BS2 block to the output of the respective bits of the shift register S_i.

There are two options in building of the connection diagrams: connection of each element by XOR switches (Figure 3, a), by passing of the respective elements by XOR switches (Figure 3, b.).

Example LFSR is shown in the Figure 4 and Table 1.

Table 1 shows an example of the formation of pseudo-random sequence of 10 time steps of the shift registers with linear feedback shift.

Figure 2. The structure of the LFSR

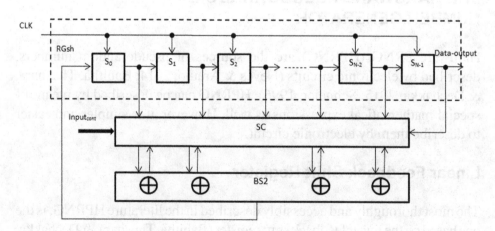

Figure 3. The functional implementation of the switching of the XOR elements in accordance with the selected polynomial

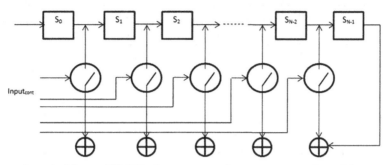

a) switching of XOR elements to the outputs register bits

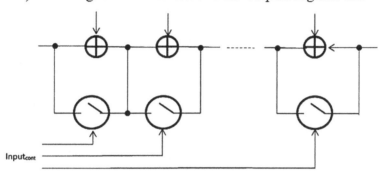

б) switching of XOR elements in accordance with the selected polynomial

Figure 4. Example of the LFSR

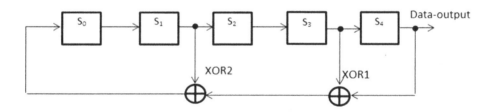

Theoretically, shift registers with linear feedback can generate a pseudo-random bit sequence with a maximum period of 2^n-1 (where n is a number of the shift registers with linear feedback bits). At the same time, a number of the shift registers with linear feedback states can pass under certain initial configurations and installations. The shift registers with linear feedback, which has passed all 2^n-1 states to the loop, is called a maximal length the

Table 1. Example of the work of generator for LFSR

Time step	S_0	S_1	S_2	S_3	S_4	XOR1	XOR2	Sequence
0	• 1	• 0	• 1	• 1	• 0	• 1	• 1	• 0
1	• 1	• 1	• 0	• 1	• 1	• 0	• 1	• 01
2	• 1	• 1	• 1	• 0	• 1	• 1	• 0	• 011
3	• 0	• 1	• 1	• 1	• 0	• 1	• 0	• 0110
4	• 0	• 0	• 1	• 1	• 1	• 0	• 0	• 01101
5	• 0	• 0	• 0	• 1	• 1	• 0	• 0	• 011011
6	• 0	• 0	• 0	• 0	• 1	• 1	• 1	• 0110111
7	• 1	• 0	• 0	• 0	• 0	• 0	• 0	• 01101110
8	• 0	• 1	• 0	• 0	• 0	• 0	• 1	• 011011100
9	• 1	• 0	• 1	• 0	• 0	• 0	• 0	• 0110111000
10	• 0	• 1	• 0	• 1	• 0	• 1	• 0	• 01101110000

shift registers with linear feedback. Maximum bit sequence formed by them is called M-sequence. Feedbacks correspond to coefficients of the characteristic polynomial,

$$b(x) = c_n x^n + c_{n-1} x^{n-1} + \ldots + c_1 x^1 + 1, \ c \in \{0,1\}.$$

If $c = 1$, the feedback is present, and 0 corresponds to the absence of communication. All operations are performed with the help of XOR function.

The output LFSR sequence is called linear recurring sequence of n-th order over GF(2) field. Maximum length of pseudorandom bit sequence is generated if the characteristic polynomial is primitive GF(2) field.

For each generated bit sequence there is the characteristical polynomial of the lowest degree. This polynomial is called the bit pattern polynomial.

The shift registers with linear feedback, which generate M sequences, are called maximum length registers.

Nonlinear Feedback Shift Register

The nonlinear feedback shift registers are more complicated to organize. The difficulty lies in the complexity of the formation of the pseudo-random sequence with good statistical properties, as well as big repetition period.

The feedback in the nonlinear feedback shift register can be implemented arbitrarily. The example of such feedback is exhibited in Figure 5.

It may give a random sequence with bad statistical properties and short repetition period. Generators on the basis of non-linear connections require a detailed and individual study and analysis.

Feedback With Carry Shift Register, FCSR

FCSR was proposed in 1994 by Mark Goresky and Andrew Klapper, independently at the same time with Gerge Marsag and Arif Zaman, Couture, and Lekuer. (Schneier, 1996; Klapper & Goresky, 1997; Klahher, 1995; Klahher & Goresky, 1994). In this generator all the bits that are displayed in the feedback are summed between each other and the contents of the transfer register. Mod2 function is implemented and the result becomes the new contents of the transfer register. FCSR structure exhibited in Figure 6.

The maximum FCSR period is equal to q-1. The number q defines branch and should be a prime number for which that 2 is a primitive root

$$q = 2q_1 + 2^2 q_2 + ...2^n q_n - 1 = \sum_{i=1}^{n} 2^i q_i \; .$$

Figure 5. The nonlinear feedback shift register

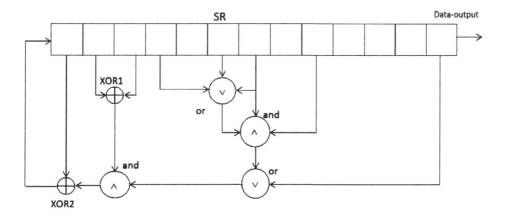

Figure 6. FCSR structure

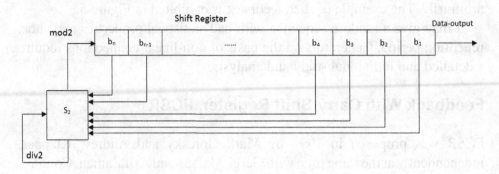

Geffe Generator

A large number of pseudorandom number generator is realized based on one or more LFSR. They are described in many different literature sources (Schneier, 1996; Geffe, 1973; Sahithi, MuraliKrishna, Jyothi, Purnima, Jhansi, & Sudha, 2012). Combinations of several shift registers with linear feedback are aimed at increasing the length of the repeat period and the improvement of the statistical properties of the bit sequence. One of these pseudorandom number generators constructed by k + 1 the shift registers with linear feedback is Geffe generator (Figure 7) (Schneier, 1996; Geffe, 1973).

The Geffen generator output is described as:

Figure 7. The Geffe generator structure

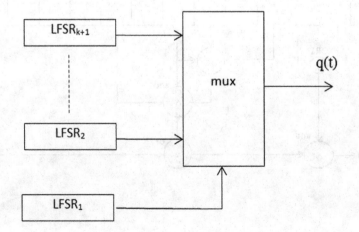

$$q_G = \left(x_1 \wedge x_2 \right) \vee \left(\overline{x_1} \wedge x_3 \right),$$

$$q_G = \begin{cases} x_2, & \text{if } x_1 \quad true \\ x_3, & \text{if } \overline{x_1} \quad false \end{cases},$$

The period of such generator is equal to $\left(2^{m_1} - 1 \right)\left(2^{m_2} - 1 \right)\left(2^{m_3} - 1 \right)$, where m_1, m_2 and m_3 – length of the first, second and third the shift registers with linear feedback respectively.

For such generator a linear complexity of the code is defined by the formula

$$L = \left(n_1 + 1 \right) n_2 + n_1 n_2 ,$$

where n_i is LFSR$_i$ length.

The period of the generator is equal to the product of all the shift registers with linear feedback, if the degrees of their primitive polynomials are mutually prime.

Geffe Generator realized on the multitude of the shift registers with linear feedback, which multiply reduces the reliability of functioning.

Threshold Generator

The threshold generator is the result of the original decision, which increases its quality in comparison with the previous generators (Schneier, 1996). It uses a large odd number of the shift registers with linear feedback (Figure 8). Used the shift register with linear feedback must be of relatively prime lengths, as well as primitive feedback polynomials.

Majority block implements a majority function. At its output the logical signal "1" is formed, if there are more than half of the "1" signals at its inputs and the logic "0" if there are more than a half of the zero signals at its inputs.

Each bit is formed in accordance to the logical expression at the output of the threshold generator (for three the shift registers with linear feedback)

$$b = \left(a_1 \wedge a_2 \right) \oplus \left(a_1 \wedge a_3 \right) \oplus \left(a_2 \wedge a_3 \right).$$

Figure 8. The structure of the threshold generator

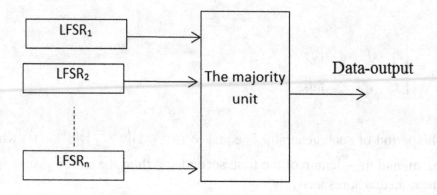

For a bigger quantity LFSR3 formula is made more complicated as well as the structure of the majority block.

Linear complexity threshold generator is bigger than of the previous ones. Value of linear complexity for three the shift registers with linear feedback represented in (Schneier, 1996) and equals

$$L = n_1 n_2 + n_1 n_3 + n_2 n_3.$$

In the same paper (Schneier, 1996) the author does not recommend to use it because it does not withstand the correlation attacks.

Stop-And-Go Generator

"Stop-and-go" generators are implemented in three the shift register with linear feedback. One controls operation of the other two generators. Three modifications of the generator are considered in Schneier (1996).

The first shift register with linear feedback can manage only one the shift register with linear feedback and two. Such control is that the first the shift register with linear feedback allows or does not allow second and third LFSRs to make the shift. In fact, the first shift register with linear feedback controls the clock frequency of the other LFSRs.

Generator Stop-and-Go, in which the first shift register with linear feedback controls the clock frequency only of the second shift register with linear feedback is called Beth-Piper (Beth & Piper, 1984). The structure of such a generator is shown in Figure 9.

Figure 9. Generator "stop-and-go" Beth-Piper

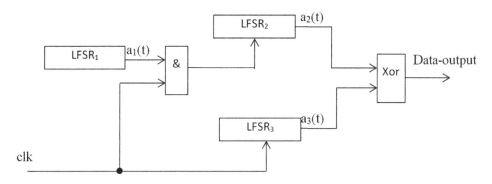

The signal from the output $LFSR_1$ goes to the clock input $LFSR_2$ only when the input CLK is present the next clock pulse, which is supplied to the clock input $LFSR_3$. When logical «1» (a_1 (t) = 1) signal is present at the $LFSR_1$ output $LFSR_2$ shifts information by one digit right.

In other cases, the information is not shifted in $LFSR_2$, $LFSR_3$ shifts information by one bit at each clock pulse reception at the CLK input.

Nobody managed to determine its linear complexity (Schneier, 1996). However, it is not resistant to the correlation attacks (Schneier, 1996; Zeng, Yang, Wei, & Rao, 1991).

The second modification of generators "stop-and-go" is an alternating generator. This generator provides content $LFSR_2$ shift if logical signal "1" is present at the $LFSR_1$ output and $LFSR_3$ shifts information if logical signal "0" is present at the $LFSR_1$ output. The diagram of this pseudorandom number generator is exhibited in Figure 10 (Schneier, 1996; Zeng, Yang, Wei, & Rao, 1991).

This generator has a long period and a big linear complexity. There were developed several generators of this type (Tretter, 1974; Vogel, 1985; Smeets, 1986).

Another modification of the generator "stop-and-go" is a generator, which consists of two LFSR. First $LFSR_1$ controls the operation of $LFSR_2$ and, conversely, $LFSR_2$ manages the information shift in $LFSR_1$. The shift to the right for $LFSR_2$ carried out when there is a transition of state from "0" to "1" at the output of the $LFSR_2$ at adjacent periods of time. Similarly $LFSR_2$ controls clock frequency $LFSR_1$ (Zeng, Eang, & Rao, 1991). Linear complexity is equal to its period.

Figure 10. Generator "stop-and-go" with the alternate control

Figure 10. Generator "stop-and-go" with the alternate control

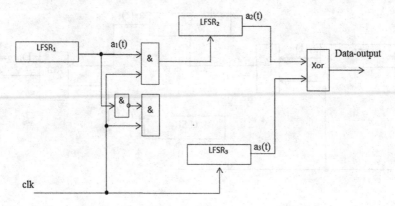

Self-Decimated Generator

Self-Decimated generators use only one shift register with linear feedback, which controls its own operation. Such generators have been proposed in two modifications. The first was proposed by Ryan Ryuppel (Schneier, 1996; Ruepel, 1987). In this modification, the control signal is the output signal from the shift register with linear feedback. Signals of logic "1" and "0" on the output of the shift register with linear feedback define a different number of steps for the further work LFSR. The circuit of such a generator is exhibited in Figure 11 (Schneier, 1996).

The second generator was proposed Biaryll Chambers and Deiter Collmann (Schneier, 1996; Chambers & Gollmann, 1988). This generator is different in the following: the control signal isn't taken from the output of LFSR, it's taken from the output of XOR-gate, which inputs are connected to the outputs of the shift register with linear feedback bits (Figure 12).

Figure 11. Self-decimated Ryuppel generator

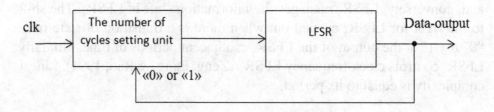

Figure 12. Self-decimated generator Gollmann and Chambers

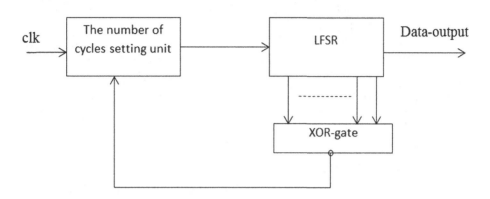

Both generators are vulnerable. However, there are improved circuits that allow toimprove their properties (Rueppel, 1992).

General Characteristics Pseudorandom Number Generator

Analysis of the literature has shown that all known hybrid pseudorandom number generator use in its composition FCSR or shift register with linear feedback to increase the statistical properties of the bit strings, length of the period and linear complexity of the code.

REFERENCES

Babitha, P. K., Thushara, T., & Dechakka, M. (2015). P. FPGA Based N - bit LFSR to generate random sequence number. *International Journal of Engineering Research and General Science*, *3*(3), 60–10.

Barash, L., Yu, & Shchur, L. N. (2014). PRAND: GPU accelerated parallel random number generation library: using most reliable algorithms and applying parallelism of modern GPUs and CPUs. *Computer Physics Communications*, *185*(4), 1343–53.

Beth, T., & Piper, F. C. (1984). The Stop-and-Go Generator. Advances in Cryptology. *Procedings of EUROCRYPT*, *84*, 88–92.

Bilan, S., Bilan, M., & Bilan, S. (2015). Novel pseudorandom sequence of numbers generator based cellular automata. *Information Technology and Security*, *3*(1), 38–50.

Blum, L., Blum, M., & Shub, M. (1986). A Simple Unpredictable Pseudo-Random Number Generator. *SIAM Journal on Computing*, *15*(2), 364–383. doi:10.1137/0215025

Chambers, W. G., & Gollmann, D. (1988). Generators for Sequences with Nesr-Maximal Linear Eqvivalence. *IKE Proceedings*, *135*, 57 - 69.

Chugunkov, E.V. (2012). *Methods and tools to evaluate the quality of pseudo-random sequence generators, focused on solving problems of information security: Textbook*. NEYAU MIFI.

David, H. K., Hoe, J. Comer, M., Cerda, J. C., Martinez, C. D., & Shirvaikar, M. V. (2012). Cellular Automata-Based Parallel Random Number Generators Using FPGAs. *International Journal of Reconfigurable Computing*, *2012*, 1-13.

Douglas, D., Vanderkooy, R., & Vanderkooy, J. (1989). Transfer-Function Measurement with Maximum-Length Sequences. *Journal of the Audio Engineering Society*, *37*(6), 419.

Eddy, W. F. (1990). Random number generators for parallel processors. *J. Comp. Applications of Mathematics*, *31*, 63–71.

Eichenauer, J., Lehn, J., & Topuzoglu, A. (1988). A nonlinear congruential pseudorandom number generator with power of two modulus. *Mathematics of Computation*, *51*(184), 757–759. doi:10.1090/S0025-5718-1988-0958641-1

Fog, A. (2015). Pseudo-Random Number Generators for Vector Processors and Multicore Processors. *Journal of Modern Applied Statistical Methods*, *14*(1), 308–334.

Geffe, R. R. (1973). How to Protect Data With Cipher That are Really Hard to Dreak. *Electronucs*, *46*(1), 99–101.

Gerard & van der Galiën. (2006). *RABENZIX Randomness Test Suite. 5.4*. Retrieved from http://members.tele2.nl/galien8/rabenzix/rabenzix.html

Golomb, S. W. (1967). *Shift register sequences*. Holden-Day.

Hörmann, W., Leydold, J., & Derflinger, G. (2004). *Automatic Nonuniform Random Veriate Generation*. New York: Springer-Verlag. doi:10.1007/978-3-662-05946-3

Intel Digital Random Number Generator (DRNG): Software Implementation Guide, Revision 1.1. (n.d.). Intel Corporation. Retrieved from https://software. intel.com/sites/default/files/m/d/4/1/d/8/441_Intel_R__DRNG_Software_ Implementation_Guide_final_Aug7.pdf

Kashmar, A. H., & Ismail, E. S. (2015). Pseudorandom number generator using rabbit cipher. *Applied Mathematical Sciences*, *9*(85-88), 4399–4412. doi:10.12988/ams.2015.5143

Klahher, A. (1995). Feedback with Carry Shift Register over Finite Field. *K.U. Leuven Workshop on Cryptographic Algorithms*. Springer – Verlag.

Klahher, A., & Goresky, M. (1994). *2-adic Shift Registers* (Technical Report N 239-93). Department of Computer Science, University of Kentucky.

Klapper, A., & Goresky, M. (1997). Feedbak shift registers, 2-adic span, and cjmdiner with memory. *Journal of Cryptology, March, 10*(2), 111 - 147.

Knuth, D. E. (1969). The Art of Computer Programming: Vol. 2. *Seminumerical Algorithms*. Reading, MA: Addison-Wesley.

L'Ecuyer, P. (1998). Random number generation. In J. Banks (Ed.), *The Handbook of Simulation* (pp. 93–137). New York: Wiley. doi:10.1002/9780470172445.ch4

LEcuyer, P. (1994). Uniform random number generation. *Annals of Operations Research*, *53*(1), 77–120. doi:10.1007/BF02136827

Lehmer, D. (1951). Mathematical methods in large-scale computing units. *Large-Scale Digital Calculating Machinery: Symp. Proc. Harvard*, 141-146.

Lewis, T., & Payne, W. (1973). Generalized feedback shift register pseudorandom number algorithms. *Journal of the ACM, 21*(3), 456–468. doi:10.1145/321765.321777

Marsaglia, G. (1984). *The Marsaglia Random Number CDROM including the Diehard Battery of Tests of Randomness.* Department of Statistics and Supercomputer Computations and Research Institute. Retrieved from http:// www.stat.fsu.edu/pub/diehard

Marsaglia, G. (1985). A current view of random number generators. In L. Billard (Ed.), Computer Science and Statistics: The Interface (pp. 3–10). Amsterdam: Elsevier.

Marsaglia, G. (2003). Random Number Generators. *Journal of Modern Applied Statistical Methods*, *2*(1), 2–13. doi:10.22237/jmasm/1051747320

Matsumoto, M., & Kurita, Y. (1992). Twisted GFSR generators. *ACM Transactions on Modeling and Computer Simulation*, *2*(3), 179–194. doi:10.1145/146382.146383

Matsumoto, M., & Nishimura, T. (1998). Mersenne twister: A 623-dimensionally equidistributed uniform pseudorandom number generator. *ACM Transactions on Modeling and Computer Simulation*, *8*(1), 3–30. doi:10.1145/272991.272995

Matsumoto, M., Nishimura, T., Hadita, M., & Saito, M. (2005). *Cryptographic Mersenne Twister and Fubuki Stream*. Block Cipher.

Neves, S., & Araujo, F. (2014). Lecture Notes in Computer Science: Vol. 8384. *Engineering Nonlinear Pseudorandom Number Generators. Parallel Processing and Applied Mathematics. PPAM 2013*.

NIST. (2010). *Computer security division. Computer security resource center*. Retrieved from http://csrc.nist.gov/groups/ST/toolkit/rng/documentation_software.html

Ruepel, R. A. (1987). Wen Shift Registers Clok Themselves. *Advances in Cryptology EUROCRYPT*, *87*, 53–64.

Rueppel, R. A. (1992). *Stream Ciphers*. In G. J. Simmons (Ed.), *Contemporary Cryptology: The Science of Information Integrity* (pp. 65–134). IEEE Press.

Sahithi, M., MuraliKrishna, B., Jyothi, M., Purnima, K., Jhansi Rani, A., & Sudha, N. N. (2012). Implementation of Random Number Generator Using LFSR for High Secured Multi Purpose Applications. *International Journal of Computer Science and Information Technologies*, *3*(1), 3287–3290.

Sanguinetti, B., Martin, A., Zbinden, H., & Gisin, N. (2014). Quantum Random Number Generation on a Mobile Phone. *Physical Review X*, *4*(031056), 1–6.

Schneier, B. (1996). Applied Cryptography: Protocols, Algorthms, and Source Code in C (2nd ed.). Wiley Computer Publishing.

Smeets, B. (1986). *A Note on Sequences generated by Clok-Controlled Shift registers. Advances in Cryptology EUROCRYPT'85* (pp. 40–42). Springer-Verlag. doi:10.1007/3-540-39805-8_5

Tang, X., Wu, Z., Wu, J., Deng, T., Chen, J., Fan, L., & Xia, G. et al. (2015). Tbits/s physical random bit generation based on mutually coupled semiconductor laser chaotic entropy source. *Optical Society of America.*, *23*(26), 33130–33141. PMID:26831980

Tanvir, A., & Md. Mahbubur, R. (2016). The Hybrid Pseudo Random Number Generator. *International Journal of Hybrid Information Technology*, *9*(7), 299–312. doi:10.14257/ijhit.2016.9.7.27

Thomson, W. (1958). A modified congruence method of generating pseudo-random numbers. *The Computer Journal*, *1*(2), 83–86. doi:10.1093/comjnl/1.2.83

Tretter, S. A. (1974). Properties of PN2 Sequences. *IEEE Transactions on Information Theory*, *IT-20*(2), 295–297. doi:10.1109/TIT.1974.1055179

Vogel, R. (1985). *On the Liner Complexity of Caseaded Sequences. In Advances in Cryptology: Proceedings oi EUROCRYPT'84* (pp. 99–109). Springer-Verlag.

Walker, J. (2008). *ENT. A Pseudorandom Number Sequence Test Program.* Retrieved from http://www.fourmilab.ch/random

Xilinx. (2007). *Linear Feedback Shift Registers in Virtex Devices.* Retrieved from http://www.xilinx.com/support/documentation/application_notes/xapp210.pdf

Zeng, K. C., Yang, C. H., Wei, L., & Rao, T. R. (1991). Pseudorandom Bit generator in Stream-Chiper Cryptography. *IEEE Computer*, *24*(2), 5–17. doi:10.1109/2.67207

Chapter 2
Fundamental of Cellular Automata Theory

ABSTRACT

In this chapter, the author reviews the main historical aspects of the development of cellular automata. The basic structures of cellular automata are described. The classification of cellular automata is considered. A definition of a one-dimensional cellular automaton is given and the basic rules for one-dimensional cellular automata are described that allow the implementation of pseudo-random number generators. One-dimensional cellular automata with shift registers with linear feedback are compared. Synchronous two-dimensional cellular automata are considered, as well as their behavior for various using local functions. An analysis of the functioning of synchronous cellular automata for the neighborhoods of von Neumann and Moore is carried out. A lot of attention is paid to asynchronous cellular automata. The necessary definitions and rules for the behavior of asynchronous cellular automata are given.

THE HISTORY OF THE DEVELOPMENT
OF CELLULAR AUTOMATA

The history of CA theories of occurrence and development are widely described in the literature (Wolfram, 1986; AUTOMATA-2008, 2008; Herrmann, & Margenstern, 2003; Wolfram, 2002; Adamatzky, 1994; Alonso-Sanz, & Margarita, 2006; Adamatzky, 2010; 10th International Conference on

DOI: 10.4018/978-1-5225-2773-2.ch002

Cellular Automata for Research and Industry [ACRI 2012]; 11th International Conference on Cellular Automata for Research and Industry [ACRI 2014]; Twelfth International Conference on Cellular Automata for Research and Industry, [ACRI 2016]). In these works, the founders of the theory of the CA is Stanislaw Ulam and John von Neumann (1940 year). The Stanislaw Ulam has recommended to use to John von Neumann a simple grid model (Pickower, 2009) for the construction of self-replicating systems problems solutions (Neumann, 1951; Kemeny. 1955).

In 1940 Norbert Wiener and Arturo Rosenblueth developed an automaton model of excitable medium (Wiener, & Rosenblueth, 1946).

Arthur Burks developed the theory of CA. John Holland used CA to adaptation and optimization solution of problems (Holland, 1966).

In 1960 Gustav A Hedlu has described many results on CA mathematical investigation (Hedlund, 1969).

In 1970, Martin Gardner published a paper in which he has described positively the "Life" game (Gardner, 1970). In the "Life" game is described the process of dying and life of a cells and their states depend on the state of life of the neighboring cells.

Stephen Wolfram has made a great contribution to the development of the CA theory. He has published papers in which was described the elementary cellular automata theory and, based on it was formed the true randomness theory (Wolfram, 1986a). Wolfram describes the set of rules that each CA cell performs. The cell goes into a state, which depends on the state of its own and the state of the neighboring cells in the previous point in time. The cell performs the function in accordance with a predetermined rule. Stephen Wolfram explores the rules and he indicates that the rule 110 may be universal. Matthew Cook has proven this statement in the year 1990. Additionally, Wolfram proposed the PRNG based on the one-dimensional CA (Wolfram, 1986b).

In 1987, Brian Silverman proposed the Turing complete cellular automaton (Dewdney, 1990).

The new continuation of the CA theory is book, which was published by Stephen Wolfram, entitled "A New Kind of Science." In this work, he examined the one-dimensional, two-dimensional and three-dimensional cellular automata. Wolfram argues that the world is discrete, and that it can be studied by CA. Due to the Wolfram theory the CAs gained immense popularity. Wolfram offered simple rules, which are still used for solving many problems.

Alonso-Sanz proposed CA with memory and the extensive analysis of their behavior and application was held (Alonso-Sanz, 2006; Alonso-Sanz, 2009; Alonso-Sanz, 2013).

Based on the obtained results Gutowitz developed a statistical analysis for classification of the Wolfram elementary cellular automata (Gutowitz, Victor, & Knight, 1987). Li and Packard have implemented these attempts (Li & Packard, 1990; Aizawa & Nishikawa, 1986; Sutner, 2009).

Adamatsky spent a good analysis of CA (Adamatzky, 1994). In later works he actively uses the theory of CA. Due to the success of CA in the solution various important tasks, the number of researchers in the CA field are increased. Every two years, a conferences are held which dedicated to the achievements of CA (ACRI) (10th International Conference on Cellular Automata for Research and Industry [ACRI 2012]; 11th International Conference on Cellular Automata for Research and Industry [ACRI 2014]; Twelfth International Conference on Cellular Automata for Research and Industry, [ACRI 2016]).The use of CA for solving of the various problems are encountered in almost all the technical focus journals.

ONE-DIMENSIONAL CELLULAR AUTOMATA

One - dimensional CA is one the cell row. Each cell performs the function on the signal value of its own state, and of the signals that determine the state of the neighborhood cells. Usually the neighborhood constitutes the two nearest cells (Wolfram, 2002; Martinez, 2013).

Currently, the one-dimensional CA is called the elementary CA (ECA). This name has become popular due to the Wolfram works. In elementary

Figure 1. The structure of the elementary cellular automata

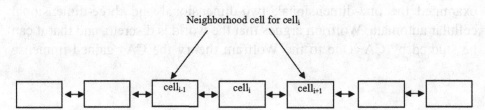

one-dimensional CA each cell can has two states: logical "1" or logical "0" states. The stricter of elementary one-dimensional CA depicted on Figure 1.

The each cell performing function

$$b_i(t) = f_i\left[b_{i-1}(t), b_i(t), b_{i+1}(t)\right],$$

where $b_i(t)$ - signal of i-th cell state at time t.

If to choose function XOR, then cell will be has 2^3 of states according to the following Table 1.

Table 1. The truth table of an elementary function transitions of the CA cells

$b_{i-1}(t)$	$b_i(t)$	$b_{i+1}(t)$	$b_i(t+1)$
• 0	• 0	• 0	• 0
• 1	• 0	• 0	• 1
• 0	• 1	• 0	• 1
• 1	• 1	• 0	• 0
• 0	• 0	• 1	• 1
• 1	• 0	• 1	• 0
• 0	• 1	• 1	• 0
• 1	• 1	• 1	• 1

Table 2. The truth table of the cellular changes state for rules 184

$b_{i-1}(t)$	$b_i(t)$	$b_{i+1}(t)$	$b_i(t+1)$
• 0	• 0	• 0	• 0
• 1	• 0	• 0	• 1
• 0	• 1	• 0	• 0
• 1	• 1	• 0	• 0
• 0	• 0	• 1	• 0
• 1	• 0	• 1	• 1
• 0	• 1	• 1	• 1
• 1	• 1	• 1	• 1

Wolfram entered $2^8 = 256$ of rules according to which each cell changes or does not change its own state. For example, for rule number 184 the cells states changing is shown in Table 2.

The elementary cellular automata application based on the fact that their state is examined at each time step. Each subsequent state is determined by an additional row of cells that have a new state in accordance with the used rule.

For example, let's take a Rule 90. It is well described in many sources of information (Wolfram, 2002). Graphically the rule 90 is represented on Figure 2.

Evolution of the elementary cellular automata changes by rule 90 in many sources is represented (Wolfram, 1983). At the same time the initial state is shown with one cell that have a logic «1» state (Figure 3).

On these figures the cells, which have a logic "1" state are arranged adjacent to cells having zero state. Example of elementary cellular automata

Figure 2. Rule 90 describing

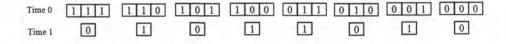

Figure 3. Evolution of the elementary cellular automata changes by rule 90 with one cell that has a logic "1" state

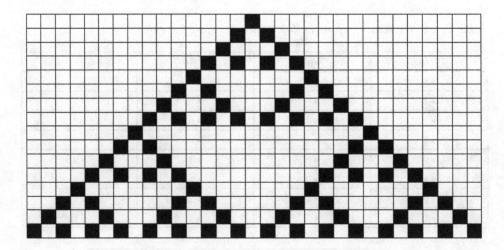

Figure 4. The elementary cellular automata evolution by rule 90 with several neighboring cells that have a logical "1" state

evolution by rule 90 with several neighboring cells that have a logical "1" state is shown on Figure 4.

The elementary rules application provides a variety of two-dimensional pictures as a result of elementary cellular automata evolution. Evolutionary elementary cellular automata representation allows describing a variety of dynamic processes. At the same time under the well-known dynamic process the researcher implementing the rules selection.

Each cell can perform function, which depends or does not depend from its own state at the previous time step. If the new state of a cell depends from its current state or from an earlier time step, then are said that CA is a CA with memory. In another case, CA is called the CA without memory.

All cells that influence the result of a function of the cell, the cell neighborhood are organizing.

Elementary cellular automata allow solving many tasks. Thanks to the successful presentation of the elementary cellular automata evolution in time and space, we can see the spatio-temporal coincidences with the various natural phenomena.

The spatio-temporal evolution of the elementary cellular automata is accessible so as and easy for understanding. This idea has inspired scientists to search for new elementary cellular automata structures for solving of the many problems in various areas of the human activity.

And yet they do not give full evidence in a many problems solving. They also have a huge disadvantage. This disadvantage is that the evolution of the one-dimensional elementary cellular automata is represented by two-dimensional array. And in order to see the desired picture we need to use a two-dimensional lattice. In addition, the two-dimensional lattice is need for elementary cellular automata with memory.

Time evolution gives us static spatial patterns of different dynamic processes. For such pictures obtaining it is difficult to predict in advance the rule and the initial state of the elementary cellular automata. Therefore, all the decisions are determined an experimental way. The rules and their combinations are selected. In fact, the natural states of the random objects are lead to the use of deterministic rules for the spatial representation of these states.

Stephen Wolfram has offered an excellent method of modeling. However, method still has several limitations that do not allow it to qualify for a universal tool for modeling.

Another contradiction, which arises in the study of this subject, is such that the spatial and temporal forms we can be obtained using an ordinary LFSR. For example, take the LFSR is shown on Figure 5.

Figure 5. Example of the LFSR

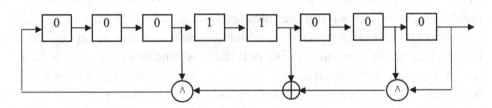

Figure 6. Space-time representation of the LFSR state that is shown on Figure 5

0	0	0	1	1	0	0	0
1	0	0	0	1	1	0	0
1	1	0	0	0	1	1	0
0	1	1	0	0	0	1	1
1	0	1	1	0	0	0	1
1	1	0	1	1	0	0	0
1	1	1	0	1	1	0	0
1	1	1	1	0	1	1	0
1	1	1	1	1	0	1	1
1	1	1	1	1	1	0	1
1	1	1	1	1	1	1	0

Figure 7. An example of two LFSR combining

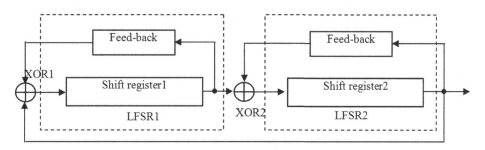

Figure 8. Spatio-temporal evolution of the states of the two LFSR, presented at the Figure 7

0	0	0	1	1	0	0	0	0	0	0	1	1	0	0	0
1	0	0	0	1	1	0	0	1	0	0	0	1	1	0	0
0	1	0	0	0	1	1	0	0	1	0	0	0	1	1	0
0	0	1	0	0	0	1	1	0	0	1	0	0	0	1	1
0	0	0	1	0	0	0	1	0	0	0	1	0	0	0	1
0	0	0	0	1	0	0	0	0	0	0	0	1	0	0	0
1	0	0	0	0	1	0	0	1	0	0	0	0	1	0	0
0	1	0	0	0	0	1	0	0	1	0	0	0	0	1	0
0	0	1	0	0	0	0	1	0	0	1	0	0	0	0	1
0	0	0	1	0	0	0	0	0	0	0	1	0	0	0	0
0	0	0	0	1	0	0	0	0	0	0	0	1	0	0	0
1	0	0	0	0	1	0	0	1	0	0	0	0	1	0	0
0	1	0	0	0	0	1	0	0	1	0	0	0	0	1	0
0	0	1	0	0	0	0	1	0	0	1	0	0	0	0	1
0	0	0	1	0	0	0	0	0	0	0	1	0	0	0	0
0	0	0	0	1	0	0	0	0	0	0	0	1	0	0	0
1	0	0	0	0	1	0	0	1	0	0	0	0	1	0	0
0	1	0	0	0	0	1	0	0	1	0	0	0	0	1	0
0	0	1	0	0	0	0	1	0	0	1	0	0	0	0	1
0	0	0	1	0	0	0	0	0	0	0	1	0	0	0	0
0	0	0	0	1	0	0	0	0	0	0	0	1	0	0	0
1	0	0	0	0	1	0	0	1	0	0	0	0	1	0	0
0	1	0	0	0	0	1	0	0	1	0	0	0	0	1	0

Evolution of the state changes of the LFSR is presented on Figure 6.

We can combine several LFSR and we will get another picture. An example of such combination is shown in Figure 7.

Each LFSR has a structure, which is presented on Figure 5. Spatio-temporal evolution of the state changes is presented on Figure 8.

Different variations with feedbacks in LFSR allow obtaining the necessary spatial and temporal pattern. In the paper (David, Hoe, Comer, Cerda, Martinez, & Shirvaikar, 2012) is shown the structure of LFSR with CAs in the selected bits register. Space-time evolution patterns for rule 90, hybrid 90/150 and rule 90/161 is shown. They are used to create LFSR based on the pseudorandom number generator.

Noteworthy is the process of obtaining such space-time evolutions in the two-dimensional area for different initial conditions, various forms of cells neighborhoods and the various rules of cells functioning.

THE SYNCHRONOUS CELLULAR AUTOMATA

Modern CA is considered as a lattice, in which the nodes are finite automatons. Each finite automaton is called a cell. If the cell can have only two states, zero or "1", automaton is called an elementary. Each cell set at any time step in the state, which depends on the state of the neighborhood cells. Cell state is determined by a local function and the function arguments are signals from the neighborhood cell outputs. In synchronous CA, all cells perform a local function at the same time that is in parallel. At that, the total picture of the states cell distribution is changed. In general, the CA changes its state.

The synchronous CA (SCA) has common properties, which are described in (Wolfram, 2002):

- The homogeneity. All cells have the same structure, external relations, and they perform the same local function.
- Discreteness of space, time and states.
- The synchronicity. All the cells perform a local function in parallel.
- Location. On the new cell state only the neighborhood cells can influence the cells, and it itself (for CA with memory).
- The local time dependence. On a limited number of previous iterations, the neighborhood cell can influence on the cell state.

Figure 9. Forms of CA spatial discretization

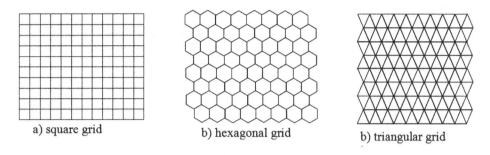

a) square grid	b) hexagonal grid	b) triangular grid

Synchronous change of CA states on the new states is called the CA evolution.

Discreteness of the CA space is determined by a lattice form. The most common form of lattices - is lattice which of squares, hexagons and triangles is composed (Figure 9).

Figure 10. Discretization by the example square, hexagonal, and triangular lattices

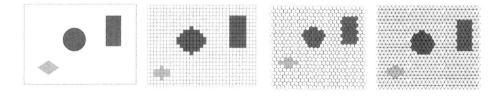

Figure 11. The von Neumann and Moore neighborhood forms

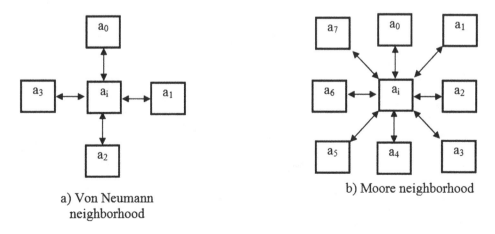

a) Von Neumann
neighborhood

b) Moore neighborhood

A cellular automaton can convert a continuous array into discrete. An example of such discretization is shown on Figure 10.

Locality of each cell is determined by the states of its neighborhood cells. For a square lattice, two types of the neighborhood are most common: von Neumann neighborhood and Moore neighborhood (Figure 11). There are different forms of the neighborhood for a square lattice. Influence of different types of the neighborhood on the edge detection is considered in the papers (Bilan, 2014; Belan, 2011).

Neighborhood forms for the hexagonal and triangular lattices are shown in Figure 12.

Figure 12. Lattices of regular triangles and hexagons

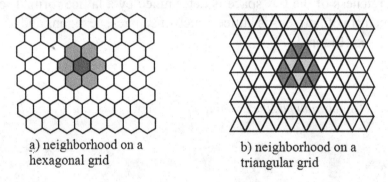

a) neighborhood on a hexagonal grid

b) neighborhood on a triangular grid

Figure 13. An example of the AND local logic function that SCA performs in during of three time iterations

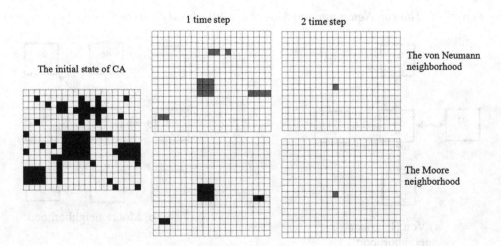

The array of regular polygons allows to obtain a maximum density of cells distribution. Other forms of lattices do not give the maximum density.

Based on homogeneous cells the synchronous cellular automata changes its state, which is formed by changing all of the cells states at each time point. All cells perform the one same function simultaneously. An example of the implementation of AND local logic function is shown on Figure 13. On Figure 13 white cells have a logic "0" state, and the dark cells are in a "1" logic state.

As we see this synchronous cellular automata can change its own state a large number of time steps. Thus, synchronous cellular automata will have a different (unequal) state. However, there are local functions, which give only one state in the first iteration step. This state remains unchanged hereinafter. One of such local logic functions is a function that implements an operation of the edge detection. This feature is considered in paper (Bilan, 2014) and it is described by model 1.

$$
b\left(t+1\right)=\begin{cases} b\left(t\right), & if \quad x_i\left(t\right)\wedge x_2\left(t\right)\wedge x_3\left(t\right)\wedge x_4\left(t\right)=0 \\ 0, & if \quad x_i\left(t\right)\wedge x_2\left(t\right)\wedge x_3\left(t\right)\wedge x_4\left(t\right)=1 \end{cases} \tag{1}
$$

where

$x_i\left(t\right), x_2\left(t\right), x_3\left(t\right), x_4\left(t\right)$ - the signals at the outputs of neighborhood cell (top, right, bottom, left) at time t;

$b\left(t\right)$ - state of a cell at time t.

For Moore neighborhood the model (1) will contain eight signals from neighborhood cells

$$
b\left(t+1\right)=\begin{cases} b\left(t\right), & if \quad x_i\left(t\right)\wedge x_2\left(t\right)\wedge ...\wedge x_8\left(t\right)=0 \\ 0, & if \quad x_i\left(t\right)\wedge x_2\left(t\right)\wedge ...\wedge x_8\left(t\right)=1 \end{cases} \tag{2}
$$

The results of the implementation of such a function are presented on Figure 14.

Figure 14. The results of the edge detection on the synchronous cellular automata for different neighborhood form

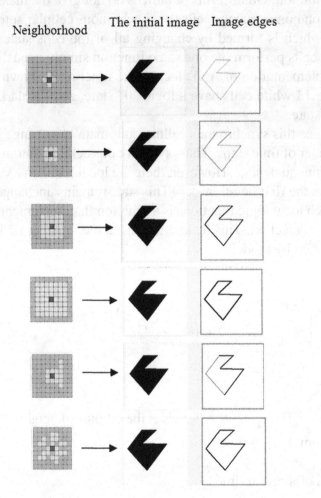

To implement the operational units, are used synchronous cellular automata and they perform a predetermined operation in a complex system.

Thus, the neighborhood form choice and the local function choice allow to create the necessary synchronous cellular automata behavior. An evolutions synchronous cellular automata variety expands the scope of their use to solve a large number of tasks.

There are also synchronous cellular automata, which consist of homogeneous and inhomogeneous cells. These SCA are called the hybrid SCA (HSCA). Cells are called a homogeneous cells, if their number is many times greater than an inhomogeneous cells. Homogeneous cells local function is different

Figure 15. Example of three HSCA iterations for a homogeneous OR function and an inhomogeneous local XOR function

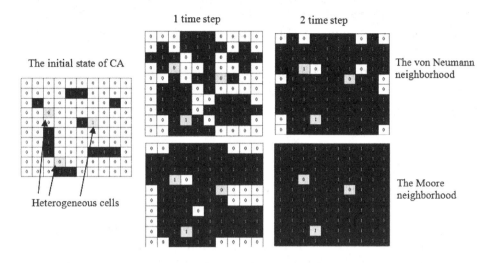

Figure 16. HSCA evolution (Figure 15) without taking into account its own cells states

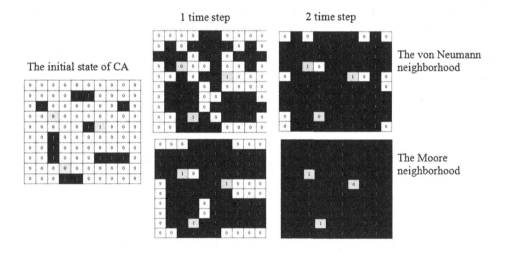

from the local inhomogeneous cells function. Inhomogeneous cells can perform the same local functions, and a various local functions. However, their number should be much less than the number of homogeneous cells.

An example of the evolution of with OR homogeneous local HSCA function and XOR inhomogeneous local function is presented on Figure 15.

For this example (Figure 15) the cells takes into account its own cell state. If we consider only the state of the neighborhood cells, the evolution of the HSCA states is represented on the Figure 16.

If the two-dimensional synchronous cellular automata to use, the user to will be difficultly to visually display the evolution on all the time steps. If we are using synchronous cellular automata with memory, there is a need for memorization synchronous cellular automata states arrays on the previous iterations. In this case, the memory capacity increases and it is complicates the synchronous cellular automata and synchronous cellular automata time operation is increased.

If we decided to use the synchronous cellular automata, and we want to get the final space-time model of a dynamic process, it is sufficient implemented by software. If synchronous cellular automata are used as a separate hardware element of the system, there is a need of accounting of all cell connections and of synchronous cellular automata itself. This significantly complicates the hardware implementation of the synchronous cellular automata.

The application synchronous cellular automata requires from developer of a good knowledge in the CA field. The researcher must good understand a synchronous cellular automata work on the several iterations of time. Usually, the developer achieves the necessary results experimentally. Man has difficulty to predict the state of the synchronous cellular automata on the following time steps of it work.

THE ASYNCHRONOUS CELLULAR AUTOMATA

The synchronous CA in the process of developing their theories does not satisfy many of the requirements that are applied to it by developers. A simultaneous change of the states of all the cells does not always gives the desired CA state. The development of the theory of CA and the increase in the number of problems that are solved using CA, has led us to the theory of asynchronous CA (ACA).

ACA is CA in which all the cells do not update its state at each time point. In the ACA the cells state depends at the next time step from the neighborhood cell states at the previous time step.

The number of asynchronous cellular automata cell depends on the asynchronous cellular automata structure and is specified by the developer. Selected the cells change their state at each time step. The cells that change their states at each selected time step is called the active cells. In asynchronous cellular automata may be are several of the active cells, as well as all asynchronous cellular automata cells may be active. From this perspective, a synchronous cellular automata is particular case of asynchronous cellular automata. The history of development and formation of ACA theory described in the papers (Fates, 2013; Fates, 2014; Sethi, Roy, & Das, 2016).

The main thing in the ACA design is rules choose, according to which cells will change its state (Schönfisch, & Roos, 1999; Fates, & Morvan, 2005; Fates, 2014). ACA is a 5- tuple $\langle L, Q, G, f, \Delta \rangle$ defined as following.

1. Q – a set of possible states of cell;
2. L - a set of possible states of the asynchronous cellular automata;
3. G – cell neighborhood that is selected for asynchronous cellular automata construction;
4. f – is the local transition rule that defined how a cell updates its state according to states located in its neighborhood.
5. Δ - is the updating method that was defines for each time t.

Obviously, the CA belongs to the class of asynchronous cellular automata in the case if the changes cell states method uses not all the CA cells at each time step. The changes cell states methods may be the following.

1. The probabilistic method. The cells with a certain probability are selected. These cells update the own state. The probability is calculated by the chosen formulas for all the selected cells. If the probability value is greater than a threshold value of probability, the cell performs the selected rule. This cell is the active cell. The probability value of each cell depends on the states of the neighborhood cells (Fates, 2013).
2. The method, based on an external control. The active cells are selected by the external control signals. For each task, a specific law of the passing of asynchronous cellular automata cells are developed. Control signals are transmitted to the control inputs of each cell. These signals set the cell to the active state, and the cell performs a local function, which changes the state of a cell itself. When there is external control, is often used the feedback with an external control.
3. The method of activating the cells based on its selection of one of the neighborhood cells. Each active cell analyzes all the states of the neighborhood cell, and it performs the local activation function. According to the results of the activation functions are selected the neighborhood cells that pass into an active state at the next time step.

4.   Temporary method. This method uses the dividing order of time on the cycles for each ACA cells or groups of cells. This means that for each cell the time interval of transition to the active state is set.

Probabilistic methods use a generation of a random number ($0<q<1$), which is compared with the probability of the process being modeled. In the ACA with a probabilistic method the local transition function is cannot be used. A set of probabilities of change of the cell state are specified. It (set) will indicate the probability of transition of the cells from one state to (in the i-th time) to another (for (i + 1)-th time step). In this case must be performed, such a condition that the state of its neighborhood cells has got a certain conditions in the i-th time step (Fates, 2013, 2014; Chou & Reggia, 1997; Agapie, 2010; Agapie, Hons, & Agapie, 2010; Agapie, Muhlenbein, & Hons, 2004; Agapie & Aus der Fuenten, 2008). Examples of a PCA functioning and of their research are considered in papers (Busic, Mairesse, & Marcovici, 2013). The probabilistic method is widely used for various processes modeling and for the many problems solving.

External control method consists in the fact that cells, which will become active at the next time step, according to the external control signals are being selected. In this case, the control can to use the state of the cells at the previous discrete time steps, and it can not to use.

In the case when asynchronous cellular automata operates by a given algorithm, the change of the active cell states is carried out. With the external control the signals mask on the asynchronous cellular automata is superimposed. This mask of 0 and 1 is composed. The 1 signal is supplied to cell activation input of a cell and also it sets the cell in an additional active state. The active cell changes its state according to the local function.

Evolution of the asynchronous cellular automata with external control without feedback is entirely dependent on the changes algorithm of the mask control signals. An example of operation such an asynchronous cellular automata is presented on the Figure 17. XOR function is a local function. The arguments of the function are the states of von Neumann neighborhood cells and own state.

As seen asynchronous cellular automata changes its state in each a discrete time step. In this case only the active cells have being functioning. In such mode, there is a sense to talk about the partial asynchronous, as there is no temporal relationship between cell states on adjacent time steps.

Figure 17. An example of an ACA external control

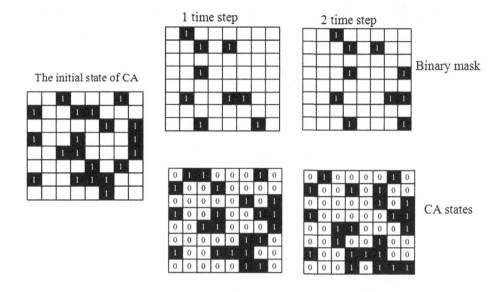

If the asynchronous cellular automata state influences on an external control on the previous discrete time interval, the control mask will change its shape according to the developed algorithm.

Let us take the example presented at the Figure 17. Let's will be use the algorithm, in which each unit in the mask will have been shifted cyclically in the row by the number of units equal to the number of cells in the corresponding asynchronous cellular automata row. For example, if in one asynchronous cellular automata row there is three cells being in state 1, then all units mask are shifted on the 3 cells to right (Figure 18).

Figure 18. Algorithm of the control mask changes

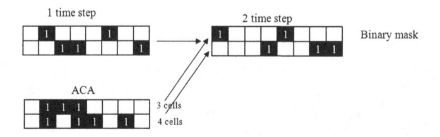

It is possible to apply other rules for the formation of the control masks. When using this method, the necessary additional control means are being introduced, which reduces the functionality asynchronous cellular automata.

Time method is based on the use of time discretization of cycles of cells transition to the active state. The cells can go into an active state according to previously set values of the duration of time steps, as well as time steps, the duration of which depends on the states of the neighborhood cell on a previous time steps.

If a constant duration of discrete time intervals are using for each cell, one group of the cells will be switched to the active state at the first time step, the second group of cells will go into an active state at the second time step, the third group - on the third time step, etc. Cells transfer into additional active states and it also changes their main information state based on the selected local function (rule).

In this method, the cells obtain additional active state by the predetermined algorithm and does not depends on the states of the cells in the previous steps. Therefore, it makes sense to talk about the local synchronicity. Example the ACA operation based on this method is shown on Figure 19. In the example shown, the cells perform XOR function from the states of cells neighborhood by the von Neumann and from own state. The cells, which have an unpaired numbering, will be set in active state on the odd time steps in each row. Cells with unpaired numbers are passing in the active state, when the even-numbered time steps are coming.

The duration time steps generation method, depending on the states of neighborhood of the cells is as follows.

Each ACA cell analyzes the neighborhood cell states and it also performs the activation function $f_{act}\left(x_1,...,x_N\right) = K$ (where N – the number of the neighborhood cells, K – the initial number of base time steps). The activation

Figure 19. Example of the asynchronous cellular automata evolution based on the temporary cells activation method, which is not dependent on a cell states at the previous time steps

Figure 20. Example asynchronous cellular automata functioning with activation of the cells on the cycle number, which is determined by the number of logic "1" cells states of the neighborhood

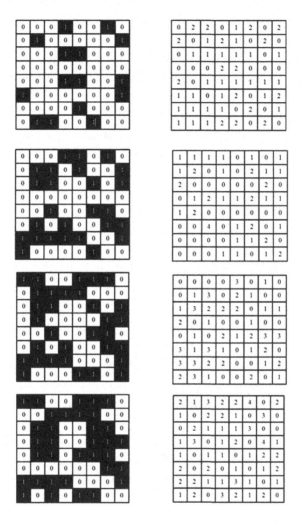

function result indicates the time step number at which cell becomes active. For example, if K = 3, the cell enters the active state on the third step of time. An example of realization of this method is presented on the Figure 20. The von Neumann neighborhood is used. The number of units in the neighborhood indicates a number of the time steps, which is used to cells switch into the active state. Each cell performs the XOR function over the local neighborhood cells states and the own state. In this example, is not considered own state of the cells while performing of the XOR function.

The obtained initial state of asynchronous cellular automata and the selected local function separates groups of active cells on each time step of. If on the current time step, the cells have the same the neighborhood cell states, cells become active on N-th discrete time step. Local functions of these cells give the same value at the current time step.

Time method is characterized by asynchronous behavior of the asynchronous cellular automata, since at each the next time step are transshipped the cells that have been identified at previous time steps.

The most common method of activation ACA cells is the neighborhood cells selection of the active cells method. On each next time step the cells become active (one or more cells), which belongs to the neighborhood cell, which was active in the previous time step (Bilan, 2014; Belan, 2011; Lee, Adachi, Peper, & Mirita, 2004; Peper, Adachi, & Lee, 2010; Manei, Roli, & Zambonelli, 2005; Boure, Fates, & Chevrier, 2012).

This method can be implemented based on the three modes:

- All the cells belong to the neighborhood and are switched to the active state at the next time step, and change their state depending on the state of it the neighborhood cells in the previous time step;
- Mode, when the active cell selects the neighborhood cell on the next time step depending on the neighborhood cell states of the active cells;
- Cell belongs to the neighborhood of the active cell and at a next time step it is switched to an active state only in the case if the local activation function of cell states of the neighborhood is 1.

The first mode is characterized by that all neighborhood cells of the active cell changes its information state on the next time step (in the additional active state is set). However, their states are different and they depend on the states of their own neighborhood cells at the previous time step.

The following model describes the cells job in the first mode.

$$b_i(t+1) = \begin{cases} b_i^{act}(t+1) = f\left[b_i^j(t)\right], & if \quad \exists b_i^{j,act}(t) = 1 \\ b_i(t), & otherwise \end{cases}$$

(3)

where

$b_i(t)$ - the information state of the cell at time t;

$b_i^j(t)$ - the state of the cells under the number j, which to the neighborhood of cell is belongs $b_i(t)$, $\left(j = \overline{1, N}\right)$;

N – the number of cells in the neighborhood of the cell $b_i(t)$;

$b_i^{act}(t+1)$ - state of cell $b_i(t)$, which has the active state at the time step t.

Active cell implements a local function f[] that can have multiple meanings. If the set values of the function is $f[] \in \{0,1\}$, the asynchronous cellular automata is a binary.

If the cell switches to the active state, it may only be active at one time step or at all following time steps. At the same time, all active cells have different states and a local function are performing f[].

In this mode, the number of active cells is increased to completely fill by the active cells the asynchronous cellular automata. The active cells set into an inactive state at each subsequent time step that in many modifications is provided. This mode is used for many tasks in different fields.

In the second mode, the process of the transmission active state to the selected neighborhood cells is implemented. The active neighborhood cell performs the local state function, as well as the additional local activation function, which determines the next active cell that belongs to the neighborhood cells. At the same time the active cell remains active or it goes into a state of calm at the next time step. In this mode, the cell requires an additional active state, and additional connections between neighborhood cells. The structure of the asynchronous cellular automata in this mode will be considered in more detail in the following sections.

If the cells are set to an active state and it depend on the states of their own neighborhoods cells, in the asynchronous cellular automata the third mode is used. The third mode is described in the papers (Belan, 2011; Belan & Belan, 2012, 2013) and it is used for efficient image processing and pattern recognition. In more detail the third mode will be considered in subsequent chapters. The last two modes effectively are used to build a pseudorandom number generator based on two-dimensional asynchronous cellular automata.

REFERENCES

ACRI. (2012). *10th International Conference on Cellular Automata for Research and Industry*. Santorini Island, Greece: ACRI.

ACRI. (2014). *11th International Conference on Cellular Automata for Research and Industry ACRI 2014, Proceedings*. Krakov Proceedings.

ACRI. (2016). *Twelfth International Conference on Cellular Automata for Research and Industry, ACRI 2016, Proceedings*. Fez, Morocco: ACRI.

Adamatzky, A. (1994). *Identification of Cellular Automata*. Taylor and Francis.

Adamatzky, A. (Ed.). (2010). *Game of Life. Cellular Automata*. Springer. doi:10.1007/978-1-84996-217-9

Agapie, A. (2010). - Simple form of the stationary distribution for 3D cellular automata in a special case. *Physica A*, *389*(13), 2495–2499. doi:10.1016/j. physa.2010.03.011

Agapie, A., & Aus der Fuenten, T. (2008). Stationary distribution for a majority viter model. *Stochastic Models*, *24*(4), 503–512. doi:10.1080/15326340802427364

Agapie, A., Hons, R., & Agapie, A. (2010). Limit behavior of the exponencial voter model. *Mathematical Social Sciences*, *59*(3), 271–281. doi:10.1016/j. mathsocsci.2009.10.005

Agapie, A., Muhlenbein, H., & Hons, R. (2004). Markov Chain Analysis for One-Dimensional Asynchronous Cellular Automata. *Methodology and Computing in Applied Probability*, *6*(2), 181–201. doi:10.1023/ B:MCAP.0000017712.55431.96

Aizawa, Y., & Nishikawa, I. (1986). *Toward the classification of the patterns generated by one-dimensional cellular automata. In Dinamical Systems and Nonlinear Oscillators* (Vol. 1, pp. 210–222). Advanced Series in Dinamical Systems.

Alonso-Sanz, R. (2009). *Cellular Automata with Memory*. Old Sity Publishing.

Alonso-Sanz, R. (2013). Cellular Automata with Memory and the Density Classification Task. *JCA*, *8*(3-4), 283–297.

Alonso-Sanz, R., & Margarita, M. (2006). Elementary Cellular Automata with Elementary Memory Rules in Cells: *The Case of Linear Rules. Journal of Cellular Automata*, *1*(1), 71–87.

AUTOMATA-2008. (2008). *Theory and Applications of Cellular Automata*. Luniver Press.

Belan, S., & Belan, N. (2012). Use of Cellular Automata to Create an Artificial System of Image Classification and Recognition. *LNCS*, *7495*, 483–493.

Belan, S., & Belan, N. (2013). Temporal-Impulse Description of Complex Image Based on Cellular Automata. In Lecture Notes in Computer Science: Vol. 7979. PaCT2013 (pp. 291-295). Springer-Verlag Berlin Heidelberg.

Belan, S. N. (2011). Specialized cellular structures for image contour analysis. *Cybernetics and Systems Analysis*, *47*(5), 695–704. doi:10.1007/s10559-011-9349-8

Bilan, S. (2014). Models and hardware implementation of methods of Pre-processing Images based on the Cellular Automata. *Advances in Image and Video Processing*, *2*(5), 76–90. doi:10.14738/aivp.25.561

Boure, O., Fates, N., & Chevrier, V. (2012). Probing robustness of cellular automata through variations of asynchronous updating, *Natural Computing*, *11*(4), 553 - 564.

Busic, A., Mairesse, J., & Marcovici, I. (2013). Probabilistic cellular automatar, invariant measures, and perfect sampling. *Advances in Applied Probability*, *45*(4), 960–980. doi:10.1017/S0001867800006728

Chou, H. H., & Reggia, J. A. (1997). Emergence of self-replicating structures in a cellular automata space. *Phisica*, *D110*(3-4), 252–276. doi:10.1016/S0167-2789(97)00132-2

David, H. K., Hoe, J. Comer, M., Cerda, J. C., Martinez, C. D., & Shirvaikar, M. V. (2012). Cellular Automata-Based Parallel Random Number Generators Using FPGAs. *International Journal of Reconfigurable Computing, 2012*, 1-13.

Fates, N. (2013). A guided tour of of asynchronous cellular automata. Cellular Automata and Discrete Complex Systems. *19th International Workshop, AUTOMATA 2013, Proceedings* (vol. 8155, pp 15-30). doi:10.1007/978-3-642-40867-0_2

Fates, N. (2014). Guided Tour of Asynchronous Cellular Automata. *JCA*, *9*(5-6), 387–416.

Fates, N., & Morvan, M. (2005). An experimental study of robustness to asynchronism for elementary cellular automata. *Complex Systems*, *16*, 1–27.

Gardner, M. (1970). Mathematical games. The fantastic combinations of John Conways new solitaire game life. *Scientific American*, *223*(4), 120–123. doi:10.1038/scientificamerican1070-120

Gutowitz, H. A., Victor, J. D., & Knight, B. W. (1987). Local structure theory for cellular automata. *Physica D. Nonlinear Phenomena*, *28*(1-2), 18–48. doi:10.1016/0167-2789(87)90120-5

Herrmann, F., & Margenstern, M. (2003). A universal cellular automaton in the hyperbolic plane. *Theoretical Computer Science*, *296*(2), 327–364. doi:10.1016/S0304-3975(02)00660-6

Holland, J. (1966). Universal Spaces: A Basis for Studies in Adaptation. *Automata Theory, 3*, 51 - 59.

Kemeny, J. G. (1955). Man viewed as a machine. *Scientific American*, *192*(4), 58–67. doi:10.1038/scientificamerican0455-58

Lee, J., Adachi, S., Peper, F., & Mirita, K. (2004). Asynchronous game of life. *Phisica D*, *194*(340), 369–384. doi:10.1016/j.physd.2004.03.007

Li, W., & Packard, N. (1990). The Structure of the Elementary Cellular Automata Rule Spase. *Complex Systems*, *4*(3), 281–297.

Manei, M., Roli, A., & Zambonelli, F. (2005). Emergence and Control of Macro Spatial Structures in Perturbed Cellular Automata, and Implication for Pervasive Computing System. *IEEE Transaction on Systems*, *35*(3), 337–348.

Martinez, G. J. (2013). A Note on Elementary Cellular Automata Classification. *JCA*, *8*(3-4), 233–259.

Neumann, J. (1951). The general and logical theory of automata. In L.A. Jefferess (ed.), *Cerobral Mechanisms in Behavior, The Hixon Symposium* (pp. 1-31). John Wiley & Sons.

Peper, F., Adachi, S., & Lee, J. (2010). Variations on the game of life. In A. Adamatzky (Ed.), *Game of Life Cellular Automata* (pp. 235–255). London: Springer. doi:10.1007/978-1-84996-217-9_13

Pickower, C. A. (2009). *The Malt book: From Pythagoras to the 57th Dimension, 250 Milestones in the History of Mathematics*. Sterling Publishing Company, Inc.

Schönfisch, B., & Roos, A. (1999). Synchronous and Asynchronous Updating in Cellular Automata. *Bio Systems*, *51*(3), 123–143. doi:10.1016/S0303-2647(99)00025-8 PMID:10530753

Sethi, B., Roy, S., & Das, S. (2016). Asynchronous cellular automata and pattern classification. *Complexity*, *21*(S1), 370–386. doi:10.1002/cplx.21749

Sutner, K. (2009). *Classification of cellular Automata*. In R. A. Meyers (Ed.), *Encyclopedia of Complexity and Systems Science* (pp. 755–768). New York: Springer –Verlag.

Wiener, N., & Rosenblueth, A. (1946). *The mathematical formulation of the problem of conduction of impulses in a network of connected excitable elements, specifically in cardiac muscle*. Arch. Inst. Cardial.

Wolfram, S. (1983). Statistical mechanics of cellular automata. *Reviews of Modern Physics*, *55*(3), 601–644. doi:10.1103/RevModPhys.55.601

Wolfram, S. (1986). *Appendix of Theory and Applications of Cellular Automata*. World Scientific.

Wolfram, S. (1986a). Random Sequence Generation by Cellular Automata. *Advances in Applied Mathematics*, *7*(2), 429–432. doi:10.1016/0196-8858(86)90028-X

Wolfram, S. (1986b). Cryptography with Cellular Automata. *Lecture Notes in Computer Science*, *218*, 429–432. doi:10.1007/3-540-39799-X_32

Wolfram, S. (2002). *A new kind of science*. Wolfram Media.

Chapter 3
Pseudorandom Number Generators Based on Cellular Automata

ABSTRACT

In this chapter, the author considers the main theoretical solutions for the creation of pseudo-random number generators based on one-dimensional cellular automata. A Wolfram generator is described on the basis of rule 30. The main characteristics of the Wolfram generator is presented. The analysis of hybrid pseudo-random number generators based on cellular automata is carried out. Models of such generators and their realization with various forms of neighborhoods are presented. Also in the chapter is presented the analysis of the basic structures and characteristics of pseudo-random number generators using additional sources of pseudo-random numbers. As such additional sources the LFSR is used.

THE GENERATORS BASED ON ONE-DIMENSIONAL CELLULAR AUTOMATA: WOLFRAM GENERATOR

In PRNG based on one-dimensional CA the elementary cellular automata is used. One of the rules is selected and the evolution of the elementary cellular automata on the basis of this rule is studied. In addition, elementary cellular automata in the initial state is set. The signals are generated at the elementary cellular automata cell outputs in each subsequent time step and their values

DOI: 10.4018/978-1-5225-2773-2.ch003

depend from the selected rule (Wolfram, 2002, 1986a, 1986b; Bhattacharjee, Paul, & Das, 2016; Cardell & Fúster-Sabater, 2016).

First PRNG based on the elementary cellular automata was proposed by S. Wolfram and he detailed studied its properties (Wolfram, 1986a, 1986b). S. Wolfram studied the many rules and selected generators, which are similar to the LFSR.

Based rule 30 generator generates a good random sequence.

$$X_i\left(t+1\right) = X_{i-1}\left(t\right) \oplus \left[X_i\left(t\right) \vee X_{i+1}\left(t\right)\right].$$

The CA evolution by rule 30 is shown on Figure 1.

The generator on the basis of this rule has been investigated in papers (Wolfram, 1986a, 1986b, 1985). In the works is defined class of the rules that are making the elementary cellular automata by similar to the LFSR. These rules use the modulo k function. Most often к=2 is used, In this case, a function is called haw the XOR function. PRNG based on elementary cellular automata was investigated for characteristics such as length of repeat period, spatial and temporal distribution characteristics of elementary cellular automata states and size of elementary cellular automata.

Pseudorandom number generator based on one-dimensional CA have been widely studied in the works (Cattel, Zang, Serra, & Muzio, 1999; Chowdhury, Nandy, & Chattopadhyay, 1994; Sipper, 1999; Bhattacharjee, Paul, & Das, 2016; Cardell & Fúster-Sabater, 2016; Sirakoulis, 2016; Spencer, 2015). Much

Figure 1. An example of the elementary cellular automata evolution based on the rule 30

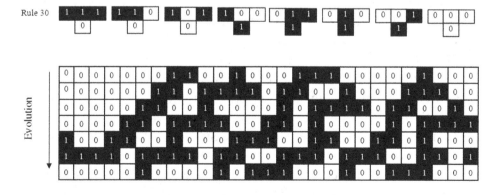

attention is paid to the study of ECA with different neighborhood structures. The structure of a neighborhood for ECE with memory is defined as

$$m - 2r + 1,$$

where r – radius of the neighborhood.

Also, the number of cells on the right (or left) of each elementary cellular automata cell is determined. For example, in paper (Abhisher, Bandyopadhyay, & Maulir, 2008) One-dimensional CA with four a neighborhood cells (4NCA) is considered. In such 4NCA r=2. 4NCA are divided into 4NCA with two right neighbors and 4NCA with two left neighbors. The structures of these neighborhoods are shown on Figure 2.

The analysis of 4 NCA rules was spent. For this the known tests were used. Variations rules and their compositions were studied. On the basis 4NCA the generators can generate a pseudo-random sequence of a high quality.

Researches of a one - dimensional CA on the basis of various structures of neighborhoods and the rules, is being continued. They give good results. However, they do not indicate the theoretical list of recommendations for obtaining the high quality pseudorandom number generator. Until now, we do not have the necessary characteristic indices for building PRNG based on the elementary cellular automata.

THE HYBRID PSEUDORANDOM NUMBER GENERATORS BASED ON CELLULAR AUTOMATA

Hybrid pseudorandom number generators (HPRNG) based on the CA use, in which the local transition function are not same for each cell (Rubio & Sanchez, 2004; Cattell & Muzio, 1996; Seredynski, Bouvry, & Zomaya, 2004; Sipper & Tomassini, 1996; Chen, Chen, Guan, & He, 2016; Sirakoulis, 2016). HPRNG uses hybrid CA (HCA). In the hybrid cellular automata the several liner local transition functions by Wolfram are used.

For hybrid cellular automata description is used the record {u,v} (where $u < v$). Symbols u and v determine the functions, which were proposed by Wolfram. For example, in paper (Rubio, & Sanchez, 2004) pairs of numbers {60, 90}, {60,150}, {90,170}, {102,150}, {150,240} were studied. For each pair, the number of rejected bit sequences was determined and also the line hybrid cellular automaton without deviation was selected.

Figure 2. The neighborhood structures with r=2

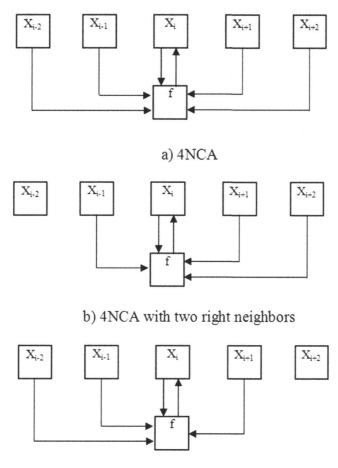

a) 4NCA

b) 4NCA with two right neighbors

b) 4NCA with two left neighbors

In papers (Cattell & Muzio, 1996; Serra, Slater, Murio, & Miller, 1990; Martin & Sole, 2008) hybrid cellular automata are considered, in which cells carry out two rule: rule 90 and rule 150. In such one-dimensional HCAs the information is presented as a binary vector $M = \left[d_0, d_1, ..., d_{N-1}\right]$.

$$d_i = \begin{cases} 0, & if \quad i-th \quad cell \quad use \quad rule \quad 90 \\ 1, & if \quad i-th \quad cell \quad use \quad rule \quad 150 \end{cases}. \qquad (1)$$

Rule 90 and 150 the following models are described

$$a_i\left(t+1\right)_{90} = a_{i-1}\left(t\right) + a_{i+1}\left(t\right)\left(\bmod 2\right),$$

$$a_i\left(t+1\right)_{150} = a_{i-1}\left(t\right) + a_i\left(t\right) + a_{i+1}\left(t\right)\left(\bmod 2\right).$$

In line HCA (LHCA) evolution can be represented as

$$C\left(t+1\right) = M \cdot C\left(t\right)\left(\bmod 2\right),$$

where

$C\left(t+1\right)$ stand for the transpose matrix $C\left(t\right)$,

M – is celled the transition matrix.

M consists of coefficients that in the selected rules are involved.

For a combination of two linear local transition function two rules are used

$$a_i\left(t+1\right)_u = \alpha_u \cdot a_{i-1}\left(t\right) + \beta_u \cdot a_i\left(t\right) + \gamma_u \cdot a_{i+1}\left(t\right)\left(\bmod 2\right),$$

$$a_i\left(t+1\right)_v = \alpha_v \cdot a_{i-1}\left(t\right) + \beta_v \cdot a_i\left(t\right) + \gamma_v \cdot a_{i+1}\left(t\right)\left(\bmod 2\right),$$

In this case

$$M = \begin{pmatrix} \beta_{\varepsilon_0} & \gamma_{\varepsilon_0} & 0 & \dots & 0 & \alpha_{\varepsilon_0} \\ \alpha_{\varepsilon_1} & \beta_{\varepsilon_1} & \gamma_{\varepsilon_1} & \dots & 0 & 0 \\ \cdot & \cdot & \cdot & \cdot & \cdot & \cdot \\ \cdot & \cdot & \cdot & \cdot & \cdot & \cdot \\ \cdot & \cdot & \cdot & \cdot & \cdot & \cdot \\ \gamma_{\varepsilon_{n-1}} & 0 & 0 & \dots & \alpha_{\varepsilon_{n-1}} & \beta_{\varepsilon_{n-1}} \end{pmatrix} \tag{2}$$

$$\varepsilon_i = \left(1 - d_i\right)u + d_iv;\ 0 < i \le n - 1.$$

Generators based on LHCA perform the following operations. The initial conditions are selected

$$C\left(t=0\right)=\left[a_0\left(t=0\right),...,a_n\left(t=0\right)\right],$$

Also the liner local transition functions are selected. LHCA evolution is formed $C\left(t=0\right),...,C\left(t+k-1\right)$. The bit sequences are estimated by the obtained evolution and the sequences based on the selected rules are formed.

In the two-dimensional LHCA also the several linear rules are used (Temir, Siap, & Arin, 2014). The 2D - hybrid cellular automata evolution is studied and the necessary rules as well as necessary cells are selected.

All the pseudorandom number generator are constructed on the basis of hybrid cellular automata are characterized by the fact that the process of their creation the researchers carried out in the experimental way. The specialists use special tests to select the best designs and combinations of rules. This approach does not set rigid limits to select the best design.

Limitations are basically a combination of rules {u, v} for the one-dimensional CA. For the two-dimensional HCA lot of restrictions was not defined. These include: the dimension of the number of cells with different rules, the cell layout with different rules and etc.

At this point in time are not given us a strict restrictions on building pseudorandom number generator based HCA.

Furthermore, hybrid cellular automata considered as CA, in which the set of cells are represented by disordered array. The neighborhood of each cell may have a different structure. Also the number of a neighborhood cells may be equal, and all the cells can perform the same function of local transitions. The number of cells in a neighborhood a neighborhood power M_N is called. Example the hybrid cellular automata with different a neighborhood structures and at the same power is presented on Figure 3.

The one of the hybrid cellular automata cells is selected for the generating a pseudo-random sequence. Signals of states of this cells form a one bit (0 or 1) at each discrete time step. An example of hybrid cellular automata evolution and of a two-dimensional pseudo-random sequence generated by hybrid cellular automata is depicted on Figure 4. The generated bit sequences displays the state of the main cell at given times on 50 time steps and they have the following meanings

$Q_{hom} = 0110111100011001101111001001111101100010101011000100;$

Figure 3. An example of the hybrid cellular automata with different forms of a neighborhood $M_N=24$

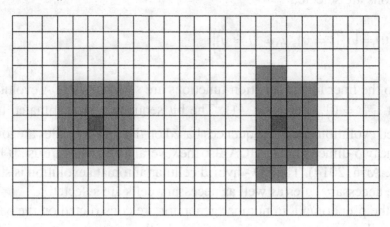

Q_{inhom} = 01101111100011001101111001001111101100010101100010;

PRNG based on hybrid cellular automata require a further study. For today is not developed recommendations, in which may be indicate: the number of inhomogeneous cells, the hybrid cellular automata size, a neighborhood structures and their powers.

THE PSEUDORANDOM NUMBER GENERATORS BASED ON CELLULAR AUTOMATA WITH ADDITIONAL SOURCE OF THE PSEUDORANDOM NUMBERS

Today, many different pseudorandom number generator based on CA is developed and is studied. Special attention was paid to the PRNG based on one - dimensional CA. It is caused by the fact that the ECA evolution allows visual assess the quality of the pseudorandom number generator work. However, has already been proved that such PRNGs form the pseudorandom bit sequences that do not meet the requirements of high statistical properties (Suhinin, 2010a, 2010b; David, Hoe, Comer, Cerda, Martinez, & Shirvaikar, 2012). They are not suitable for cryptography and their characteristics coincide with the characteristics of LFSR.

Another thing is the use of two-dimensional CA. Homogeneous 2D-CA did not give the necessary results for the implementation of high quality pseudorandom number generator. The pseudorandom number generators that

Figure 4. Space-time HCA state diagrams and pseudo-random bit sequence is formed by the one cell

are constructed on inhomogeneous CA have the better characteristics. The different types of neighborhoods and local cell function have been studied. However, they do not provide generating of the high quality pseudorandom sequences of numbers. As a rule, specialists use LFSR, since it is the most simple and understandable. LFSR itself also did not generate sequences of pseudo-random numbers with good statistical properties. However, LFSR and CA combining may give the expected result. In this situation, one of them may be the main. The main generator specifies the initial pseudo-random sequence of numbers, and another may improve its statistical properties. In such a way various modifications CA to improve the properties of LFSR are used (David, Hoe, Comer, Cerda, Martinez, & Shirvaikar, 2012; Tkachik, 2003).

In these papers is shown that CA are combined with LFSR with using XOR gates (Figure 5).

Such an organization gives good results, which is proved by DIEHARD tests (David, Hoe, Comer, Cerda, Martinez, & Shirvaikar, 2012; Tkachik, 2003). In such configurations are also carried out the experimental analysis of CA configurations, and also LFSR are selected. In fact, is used a lot of "weak" sources of random bits to improve the quality of the main source (LFSR in this case). Such pseudorandom number generator is inhomogeneous and it requires knowledge of the theory of LFSR construction and CA theory.

A second embodiment of the pseudorandom number generator is the use the LFSR as an additional source of random number. In this case, main element is the KA.

Figure 5. The combination of CA and LFSR

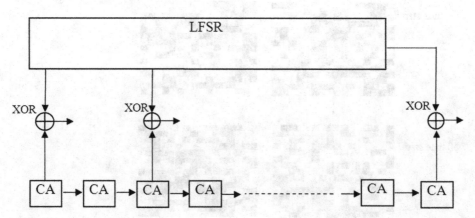

To resume normal operation of CA best of all the LFSR to use as an additional source of random numbers. LFSR generates an additional bit, which is an additional argument for the local transition function. This bit can be an additional argument only for active CA cell or for all KA cells.

For example, we use the combination of the elementary cellular automata, which operates by rule 30, and a simple LFSR on 5 bits. The sequence of operation of such a pseudorandom number generator is shown on Figure 6. The bit sequence is selected, which is formed of the 10th ECA cell and the bit sequence, which is formed at the output of LFSR. Also the total sequence using XOR function is represented.

In the present example, the additional bit does not influence the state of the active cell in the next time step. Therefore, such a pseudorandom number generator has the union of cycles. Although in the elementary cellular automata the state of the cells change influenced neighborhood cells.

Figure 6. An example of the implementation of the PRNG based on KA with additional LFSR

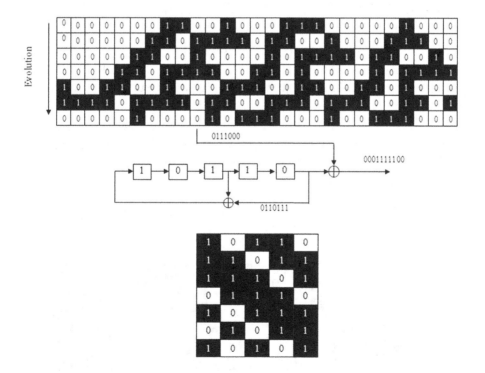

If an additional bit of LFSR affects cell state in the next time step, the sequence is less predictable. Example of the pseudorandom number generator operation when the state of the active cells depends on additional bit is shown on Figure 7.

We see a variety of paintings on the Figure 6 and Figure 7. The elementary cellular automata evolution without of the additional bit influence is different from the ECA evolution with the additional bit influence. In fact, the second elementary cellular automata operates as a hybrid elementary cellular automata. One more embodiment of the PRNG is the use of the influence of LFSR bits on all the elementary cellular automata cells (Figure 8). In such a structure, all the elementary cellular automata cells change their states according to the specified rules. Each cell ECA has a neighborhood consisting of 3 cells. The state of the third cell according to other rule is changed. It depends on the LFSR states of cells at each time step.

The generated bit sequences are different for each variant. Also the elementary cellular automata evolutions of each variant are different. PRNG based on one-dimensional KA have a certain period of repetition and its linear complexity. In fact, PRNG is realized on the basis of a combination of several LFSR. Their statistical properties are improved.

In the papers (Suhinin, 2010a, 2010b) pseudorandom number generators are implemented on the basis of two-dimensional CA with the additional LFSR. CA size is selected 37×11 of the cells (the prime numbers). To generate a pseudo-random sequence the value of the subarray size cells 32×8 are used. The signal from the LFSR output by XOR function is added to the state of the both selected CA cells. Output bits of the first and second AC are summed by XOR function. The result of this function generates a resulting pseudorandom sequence bits in a discrete time step.

Figure 7. An example of the implementation of the pseudorandom number generator based on CA, in which the cell states depend on the additional bits

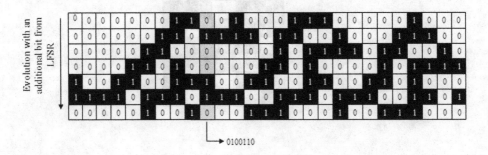

Figure 8. The pseudorandom number generator based on the elementary cellular automata and the cells depend on the states of LFSR bits

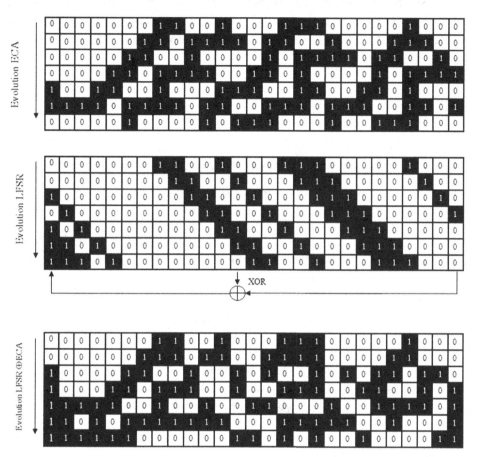

The lower limit of the period of pseudo-random sequence is determined by the structure LFSR. If on the CA state the external sources are not influenced, the period of the output sequence is determined from the ratio

$$T_S \leq 2^G,$$

where G – the sum of the two cells CA and bits of LFSR.

Generators of this type deep enough are investigated and they showed good statistical properties. Dimensions AC and subarrays have been determined experimentally. The main problem is the use of additional sources of random numbers. Afflicts by the fact that CA can not form a high-quality pseudorandom bit sequence as an independent source. However, the very structure of CA suggests otherwise. Now specialists understand and they conduct research in order to find the basic scientific foundations of pseudorandom number generator building based on CA with good statistical properties of the output sequence.

REFERENCES

Abhisher, S., Bandyopadhyay, S., & Maulir, U. (2008). Pseudorandom Pattern Generation by a 4-Neighbohood Cellular Automata Based on a Probabilistic Analyses. *Proceedings of the International MultiConference of Engineers and Computer Scientists, 2*, 19–21.

Bhattacharjee, K., Paul, D., & Das, S. (2016). Pseudorandom Pattern Generation Using 3-State Cellular Automata. In S. El Yacoubi, J. Wąs, & S. Bandini (Eds.), Lecture Notes in Computer Science: Vol. 9863. *Cellular Automata. ACRI 2016* (pp. 3–13). doi:10.1007/978-3-319-44365-2_1

Cardell, S. D., & Fúster-Sabater, A. (2016). Linear Models for the Self-Shrinking Generator Based on CA. *JCA, 11*(2-3), 195–211.

Cattel, K., Zang, S., Serra, M., & Muzio, J. C. (1999). 2-by-n hybrid cellular automata with regular configuration: Theory and application. *IEEE Transactions on Computers, 48*(3), 285–295. doi:10.1109/12.754995

Cattell, K., & Muzio, J.C. (1996). Syntesis one-dimensional linear hybrid cellular automata. *IEEE Trans. on Computer-Aided Design of Integrated Circuits and Systems, 15*(3), 325 – 335.

Chen, B., Chen, F., Guan, J., & He, Q. (2016). Glider Collisions in Hybrid Cellular Automata Rule 168 and 133. *JCA, 11*(2-3), 167–194.

Chowdhury, D. R., Nandy, S., & Chattopadhyay, S. (1994). Additive cellular automata. *Theory and Applications Journal, 1*(2), 12–15.

David, H. K., Hoe, J. Comer, M., Cerda, J. C., Martinez, C. D., & Shirvaikar, M. V. (2012). Cellular Automata-Based Parallel Random Number Generators Using FPGAs. *International Journal of Reconfigurable Computing, 2012*, 1-13.

Seredynski, F., Bouvry, P., & Zomaya, Y. (2004). Cellular automata computtions and secret rey cryptography. *Parallel Computing, 30*(5-6), 753–766. doi:10.1016/j.parco.2003.12.014

Sipper, M. (1999). The emergence of cellular computing. *Computers*, *32*(7), 18–26. doi:10.1109/2.774914

Sipper, M., & Tomassini, M. (1996). *Co evolving parallel random number generators. In Parallel Problem Solving from Nature – PPSN IV* (pp. 950–959). Berlin: Springer Verlag. doi:10.1007/3-540-61723-X_1058

Sirakoulis, G. Ch. (2016). Parallel Application of Hybrid DNA Cellular Automata for Pseudorandom Number Generation. *JCA*, *11*(1), 63–89.

Spencer, J. (2015). Pseudorandom Bit Generators from Enhanced Cellular Automata. *JCA*, *10*(3-4), 295–317.

Suhinin, B. M. (2010a). High generators of pseudorandom sequences based on cellular automata. *Applied Discrete Mathematics, 2*, 34 – 41.

Suhinin, B. M. (2010b). Development of generators of pseudorandom binary sequences based on cellular automata. *Science and education*, (9), 1–21.

Temir, F., Siap, I., & Arin, H. (2014). On Pseudo Random Bit Generators via Two-Dimentional Hybrid Cellular Automata. *Acta Physica Polonica A*, *125*(2), 534–537. doi:10.12693/APhysPolA.125.534

Tkachik, T. E. (2003). A hardware random number generator. *Lecture Notes in Computer Sciences: Vol. 2523. Proceedings of the Cryptografic Hardware and Embedded System (CHES'02)* (pp. 450 – 453). Springer.

Wolfram, S. (1985). Origins of randomness in physical system. *Physical Review Letters*, *55*(5), 449–452. doi:10.1103/PhysRevLett.55.449 PMID:10032356

Wolfram, S. (1986a). Random Sequence Generation by Cellular Automata. *Advances in Applied Mathematics*, *7*(2), 429–432. doi:10.1016/0196-8858(86)90028-X

Wolfram, S. (1986b). Cryptography with Cellular Automata. *Lecture Notes in Computer Science*, *218*, 429–432. doi:10.1007/3-540-39799-X_32

Wolfram, S. (2002). *A new kind of science*. Wolfram Media.

Chapter 4
Pseudorandom Number Generators Based on Asynchronous Cellular Automata

ABSTRACT

The fourth chapter deals with the use of asynchronous cellular automata for constructing high-quality pseudo-random number generators. A model of such a generator is proposed. Asynchronous cellular automata are constructed using the neighborhood of von Neumann and Moore. Each cell of such an asynchronous cellular state can be in two states (information and active states). There is only one active cell at each time step in an asynchronous cellular automaton. The cell performs local functions only when it is active. At each time step, the active cell transmits its active state to one of the neighborhood cells. An algorithm for the operation of a pseudo-random number generator based on an asynchronous cellular automaton is described, as well as an algorithm for working a cell. The hardware implementation of such a generator is proposed. Several variants of cell construction are considered.

DOI: 10.4018/978-1-5225-2773-2.ch004

ASYNCHRONOUS CELLULAR AUTOMATON MODEL FOR THE REALIZATION OF A RANDOM NUMBER GENERATOR

The analysis of known CA showed that the one-dimensional ECA does not implement a high-quality PRNG as a single homogeneous source of pseudo-random numbers. All ECA cells change their state for a given function of local transitions in each subsequent time step. HCA based on the one-dimensional CA also have a number of weaknesses. As mentioned earlier, one-dimensional CA may be replaced on the LFSR (Schneier, 1996; Bardell, 1990).

It is more promising to look at two-dimensional CAs. We can use a synchronous or asynchronous CA. In this section, we will look at the structure and principles of the asynchronous cellular automata functioning of with one active cell (ACA active cells may be more).

The asynchronous cellular automata with one active cell is determined as a normal two-dimensional classical CA, in which all the cells are set to perform the same function of local transition (LTF), and only one cell performs LTF and resets its state at each subsequent time step.

One cell ACA performs local transition function among all the other cells and resets its state at the current time step, is called the active cell.

Also it is called an active cell if it has an active state. Each cell asynchronous cellular automata is in the main information state. This state is determined by the state of the cell signal. For a hardware implementation asynchronous cellular automata important information state determined by the state of memory cell element (flip-flop) and by the value of the signal at its output. In addition, each asynchronous cellular automata cell may be having additional active state. In hardware implementation, is considered that a cell is located in an active state, if an additional memory element (additional trigger) have logic "1" state.

We know the possible states of asynchronous cellular automata cells. However, we do not yet know the rules of the transition asynchronous cellular automata cells in the active state. At this point in time the two variants of the transition is determined by author.

1. An active cell at the current time itself determines which neighborhood goes into the active state in a next time.
2. Each cell belonging to the neighborhood of the active cell decides to move it to an active state or not.

The first version of the transition of cells in an active state is determined by the function of transmission in active state (FTAS). Arguments of the function of transmission in active state of the active cell are the information cells states signals, which belong to the neighborhood of the active cell at the current time. In this case, the cell becomes active; if on the one of the active input the signal of logical "1" state is presented. This is the only condition for the transition cells in the active state. The cell becomes active at the next moment and does not depend on the basic information cells states of the surrounding area at the current time.

The second variant of cells transition to an active state next time step is characterized in that the cell analyzing basic information states of own neighborhood cells and cell analyzes additional active state own neighborhood cells. If one of the active cells inputs has a logical "1" signal (this means that one of the neighborhood cells is active), the cell performs the local transition function over the main information states of its neighborhood cells. If LTF give the result of the logical "1", then the cell becomes active the next time step.

The function of transmission in active state and local transition function for both the active state transmission options are selected by experimentally or analytically. Generalized structure of the cell behavior in such ACA is shown on Figure 1.

Figure 1. The behavioral ACA cell interface

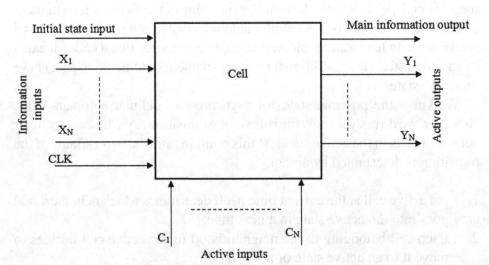

The cell has an initial setting input, N data inputs $(X_1,\ldots, X_N)$ and N of active inputs $(C_1,\ldots,C_N)$. Also, the cell contains the main data output and N active outputs $(Y_1,\ldots, Y_N)$. Such ACA cells interface allows to realize both the transfer active state modes from cell to cell. The difference is in the implementation of the internal structure of the cell for each mode.

The first active state transmission mode will consider. In this mode, the cell has N of the active outputs. We shall also be considered asynchronous cellular automata with the one active cell in each discrete time step t. The cell work in the first mode is described by following models.

$$b_{i,j}\left(t+1\right) = \begin{cases} f\left[b_{i,j}\left(t\right),b_{i,j}^1\left(t\right),\ldots,b_{i,j}^k\left(t\right)\right], & if \quad \exists C_{i,j}^l\left(t\right)=1 \;, \\ b_{i,j}\left(t\right), & in \quad othe \quad case \end{cases} \tag{1}$$

$$b_{i,j}^{act}\left(t+1\right) = \begin{cases} 1, & if \quad \exists b_{i,j}^{act,l}\left(t\right)=1 \\ 0, & in \quad othe \quad case \end{cases}, \tag{2}$$

where

$l = \overline{1,k}$;

k – the number of cells, that make up the cells neighborhood;

$b_{i,j}^{act}\left(t+1\right)$ - the active signal state of the cell with the coordinates (i, j) at time step t+1;

$b_{i,j}^{act,l}\left(t\right)$ - activity state of a cell that belongs to the neighborhood cells with the coordinates (i, j) at time step t.

If $b_{i,j}^{act}\left(t+1\right)=1$, then the cell has an active state and if $b_{i,j}^{act}\left(t+1\right)=0$, then this cell it has a passive state (not active).

Model (1) indicates that the cell performs the function $f\left[b_{i,j}\left(t\right),b_{i,j}^1\left(t\right),\ldots,b_{i,j}^k\left(t\right)\right]$, if it is in active state. Model (2) indicates that cell can pass into the active state at the next time step and this cell has one of the neighborhood cells, which have active state at the current time step. The active signal from the active cell is transmitted only to one cell of the neighborhood at the next time step.

To select the next active cell, into each cell is introduced additional transfer function of the active signal, ie, each cell must have k active signal outputs. Each such output is connected to the input active of the signal receiving of the corresponding neighborhood cell.

If we say that the A cell transmits the active signal to the B cell, then on the active output (Y_{A_B}=1) logical "1" signal is present, which comes into the active input (C_{A_B}=1) B cell. With this statement, the cell transition in an additional active state is described by the following mathematical model.

$$b_{i,j}^{act}\left(t+1\right) = \begin{cases} 1, & if \quad \exists C_{i,j}^{l}\left(t\right) = 1 \\ 0, & in \quad othe \quad case \end{cases}, \tag{3}$$

where $C_{i,j}^{l}\left(t\right)$ - signal on one of active input of the cell with the coordinates (i, j) at time t ($l = \overline{1,k}$).

This signal is enters to the 1-th active cell input with the coordinates (i, j) from one of the active outputs of the cell, which belongs to the neighborhood cells with the coordinates (i, j).

With the help of models (1) - (3) is described by the process of changing of the information cell states and the process of transformation in the additional active state. However, the process of form an active signal on one of the outputs of the active cells is not described. For this purpose, the following model is used.

$$Y_{i,j}^{l}\left(t+1\right) = \begin{cases} 1, & if \quad f^{act}\left[X_{1}\left(t\right),...,X_{k}\left(t\right),b_{i,j}\left(t\right)\right] = f\left[S_{l}\right], \\ 0, & in \quad othe \quad case \end{cases} \tag{4}$$

where S_{l} - sets of binary signals, on which $Y_{i,j}^{l}\left(t+1\right) = 1$.

The number S of sets is equal to $S = 2^{k+1}$. Wherein also $S_{l} \subset S$. Function $f^{act}\left[X_{1}\left(t\right),...,X_{k}\left(t\right),b_{i,j}\left(t\right)\right]$ is a function that has k + 1 inputs and k outputs.

In fact, this function has k of values. These values indicate the neighborhood cell, which is switching into an active state at the next time step (t+1).

Models (1) - (4) describe the state of each CA cell. According to these models, the cell can be in two states: the basic and additional states. The ground state of a cell has during the entire of the work time. It can have two basic states "0" and "1". Only one ACA cell has an additional active state. Only this cell can change its main state. In the active state, only one cell can be converted and this cell has in among of a neighborhood cells a one active cell. Function $f^{act}\left[X_1(t),...,X_k(t),b_{i,j}(t)\right]$ in model (4) the function of transmission in active state is called. This function selection is of great importance, since it determines the movement of the active cell on the asynchronous cellular automata area.

Let us consider an example of transmitting of the active state from cell to cell. For this we use FTAS is presented by Table 1. We assume that a von Neumann neighborhood and ACA with memory are used.

The main Information states of asynchronous cellular automata cells change according to local transition function, which is selected as an XOR function. The main information state of asynchronous cellular automata cells is being changed according to local transition function, which as an XOR function is selected. An example of the ACA evolution with the describing initial settings is shown on Figure 2.

In this example the numbering of the neighborhood cells is carried out according to the Figure 3.

Figure 3 graphically demonstrates an active cell movement. With this selection of local transition function and the function of transmission in active state are possible different trajectories for the active cell movement on the asynchronous cellular automata area. Also may be the cycles. Cycles are characterized by repetitions of the trajectory after a certain number of discrete time steps.

In this example, we used a fairly complex function that depends on the 5 arguments and it has 4 values. You can also begin to form a function that depends on such a number of arguments, which depends on the number of function values. For the above example the number of values of equal $4=2^2$. Hence, the developer can take a number of function arguments, which is equal to 2. We represent the function with two arguments and of four values by Table 2.

The table shows that to transmit of the active state only the two adjacent cells on top and on the right are considered. Signal $Y_i(t+1)=1$ $\left(i=\overline{1,4}\right)$

Table 1. An example FTAS

N	X_1	X_2	X_3	X_4	$b_{i,j}(t)$	$Y_1(t+1)$	$Y_2(t+1)$	$Y_3(t+1)$	$Y_4(t+1)$
32.	• 0	• 0	• 0	• 0	• 0	• 1			
33.	• 0	• 0	• 0	• 0	• 1		• 1		
34.	• 0	• 0	• 0	• 1	• 0			• 1	
35.	• 0	• 0	• 0	• 1	• 1				• 1
36.	• 0	• 0	• 1	• 0	• 0	• 1			
37.	• 0	• 0	• 1	• 0	• 1		• 1		
38.	• 0	• 0	• 1	• 1	• 0			• 1	
39.	• 0	• 0	• 1	• 1	• 1				• 1
40.	• 0	• 1	• 0	• 0	• 0	• 1			
41.	• 0	• 1	• 0	• 0	• 1		• 1		
42.	• 0	• 1	• 0	• 1	• 0			• 1	
43.	• 0	• 1	• 0	• 1	• 1				• 1
44.	• 0	• 1	• 1	• 0	• 0	• 1			
45.	• 0	• 1	• 1	• 0	• 1		• 1		
46.	• 0	• 1	• 1	• 1	• 0			• 1	
47.	• 0	• 1	• 1	• 1	• 1				• 1
48.	• 1	• 0	• 0	• 0	• 0	• 1			
49.	• 1	• 0	• 0	• 0	• 1		• 1		
50.	• 1	• 0	• 0	• 1	• 0			• 1	
51.	• 1	• 0	• 0	• 1	• 1				• 1
52.	• 1	• 0	• 1	• 0	• 0	• 1			
53.	• 1	• 0	• 1	• 0	• 1		• 1		
54.	• 1	• 0	• 1	• 1	• 0			• 1	
55.	• 1	• 0	• 1	• 1	• 1				• 1
56.	• 1	• 1	• 0	• 0	• 0	• 1			
57.	• 1	• 1	• 0	• 0	• 1		• 1		
58.	• 1	• 1	• 0	• 1	• 0			• 1	
59.	• 1	• 1	• 0	• 1	• 1				• 1
60.	• 1	• 1	• 1	• 0	• 0	• 1			
61.	• 1	• 1	• 1	• 0	• 1		• 1		
62.	• 1	• 1	• 1	• 1	• 0			• 1	
63.	• 1	• 1	• 1	• 1	• 1				• 1

Figure 2. An example of the ACA evolution with one active cell

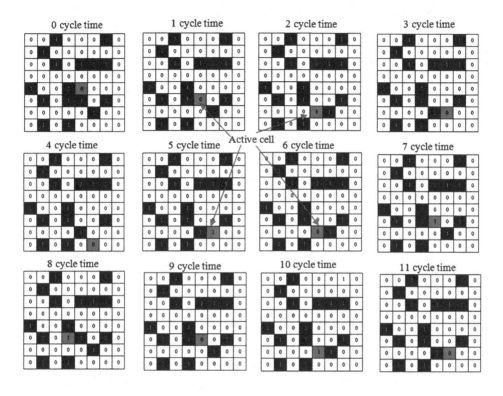

Figure 3. The numbering of the neighborhood cells

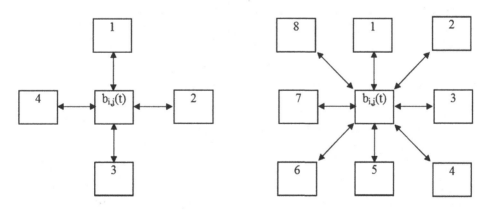

a) Numeration for Newman neighborhood   b) Numeration for Moor neighborhood

Table 2. The encoding table of the signal transitions to adjacent cells of the neighborhood.

set N	$X_1(t)$	$X_2(t)$	$Y_1(t+1)$	$Y_2(t+1)$	$Y_3(t+1)$	$Y_4(t+1)$
• 0	• 0	• 0	• 1	• 1	• 0	• 0
• 1	• 0	• 1	• 0	• 1	• 0	• 0
• 2	• 1	• 0	• 0	• 0	• 1	• 0
• 3	• 1	• 1	• 0	• 0	• 0	• 1

indicates that the cell with a number i becomes active at time step (t+1). This cell at (t + 1) discrete time step will perform the LTF.

An example of the functioning of the asynchronous cellular automata is presented on Figure 4. At the zero time step the initial state of ACA cells are formed. State of the cell at time (t + 1) is formed by the following formula

$$
Q_{i,j}(t+1) = \\
b_{i,j}(t) \oplus X_1(t) \oplus X_2(t) \oplus X_3(t) \oplus X_4(t) \tag{5}
$$

On the Figure 4 the initial setting ACA in the 0-th time step is shown. On the first time step the control cell is selected that is highlighted in the center of the cells intersection that belong to the neighborhood of the control cells. Right of the asynchronous cellular automata a formula that calculates the state of the active cell is indicated. The neighborhood of the cell code is also shown. This code indicates the number of the neighborhood of cells, which sets to an active state.

Moore's neighborhood is a classic neighborhood cell that has more degrees of freedom. Encoding Moore neighborhood cells is shown on Figure 3b. This coding is used when selecting the next active cells which belong to the neighborhood. In addition the choice of the next active cells need not necessarily depend on the number of binary combination sorting. For example, the choice of cells to which the active signal is transmitted, may be performed by determining the number of logical "1". These binary units (logical "1s") and their location determine the state of the neighborhood cells.

The order of transfer of the active signal to a neighboring cell is carried out according to the rule of the oldest binary unit. This indicates that the transfer is made to the neighborhood cell, which is at logic "1" and the cell has the biggest number among of a neighborhood cells numbering. For example, if

Figure 4. CA operation example for LTF from Table 2.

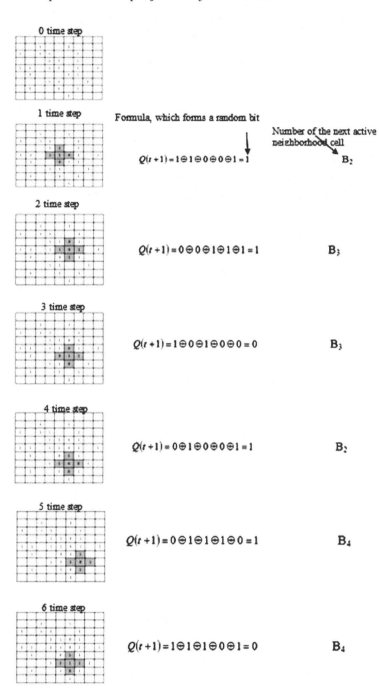

Table 3. Example of the neighborhood cell coding

Number of the neighborhood cells	• 1	• 2	• 3	• 4	• 5	• 6	• 7	• 8
The neighborhood cell state	• 1	• 0	• 1	• 1	• 0	• 1	• 0	• 0

the neighborhood cells have a state by Table 3, the active signal is transmitted to the neighborhood cell with number at the next time step.

Example of asynchronous cellular automata operation based on Moore's neighborhood with the choice of the older logical "1" in the neighborhood is shown on Figure 5.

In this example, the outer cells of rows and columns between themselves a neighborhood are organized. This can be seen on Figure 5. on 8, 11 and 14 time steps. This case shows that the control cell with a neighborhood moves on the ACA area according to the function, given the appropriate logical expressions (6).

$$
\begin{cases}
Y_1 = X_1 \wedge \overline{X_2} \wedge \overline{X_3} \wedge \overline{X_4} \wedge \overline{X_5} \wedge \overline{X_6} \wedge \overline{X_7} \wedge \overline{X_8} \\
Y_2 = X_2 \wedge \overline{X_3} \wedge \overline{X_4} \wedge \overline{X_5} \wedge \overline{X_6} \wedge \overline{X_7} \wedge \overline{X_8} \\
Y_3 = X_3 \wedge \overline{X_4} \wedge \overline{X_5} \wedge \overline{X_6} \wedge \overline{X_7} \wedge \overline{X_8} \\
Y_4 = X_4 \wedge \overline{X_5} \wedge \overline{X_6} \wedge \overline{X_7} \wedge \overline{X_8} \\
Y_5 = X_5 \wedge \overline{X_6} \wedge \overline{X_7} \wedge \overline{X_8} \\
Y_6 = X_6 \wedge \overline{X_7} \wedge \overline{X_8} \\
Y_7 = X_7 \wedge \overline{X_8} \\
Y_8 = X_8 \vee \overline{X_1} \wedge \overline{X_2} \wedge \overline{X_3} \wedge \overline{X_4} \wedge \overline{X_5} \wedge \overline{X_6} \wedge \overline{X_7} \wedge \overline{X_8}
\end{cases}
\tag{6}
$$

As mentioned above, it has a value choice of local transition function and the function of transmission in active state, and also the neighborhood structure plays the role. The shape of the trajectory of movement of the active signal depends on these basic initial settings. In such asynchronous cellular automata an adverse events is the existence of cycles. Cycle of path in the asynchronous cellular automata is called the path of movement of active signal

Figure 5. An example of the asynchronous cellular automata on the basis of Moore neighborhood is organized

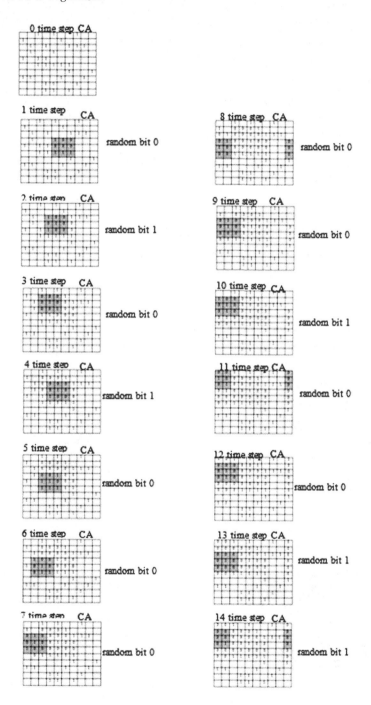

that periodically is repeated. Cycles may be a different time durations and cycles may also have various forms. Also of great importance is the initial state of the asynchronous cellular automata and the initial choice of the active cell. Example of the cycle at one time step is represented on Figure 6. Here asynchronous cellular automata cells perform the function of transmission in active state according to Table 2.

The function of transmission in active state used, according to which the active signal is transmitted to the neighborhood cell, which is in the state of the logic "1" and has the biggest number in the numbering of cells in neighborhood among neighborhood cells with the logical "1" state. In the simulation, the asynchronous cellular automata with such the function of transmission in active state the cycles may also appear. As a local transition function, the XOR function is used. An example of the cycle's appearance for such an implementation of the function of transmission in active state and local transition function is presented on Figure 7. The von Neumann neighborhood is used.

Figure 6. Examples of asynchronous cellular automata cell conditions that give temporary cycles in one time step

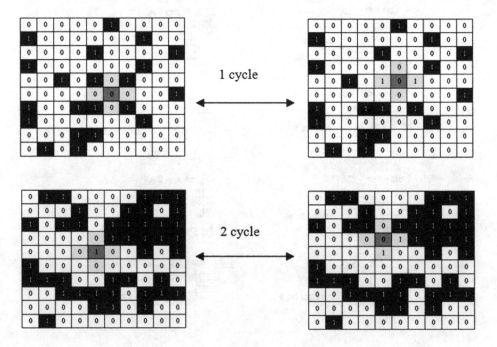

Figure 7. Examples of asynchronous cellular automata state, which give the cycles when implementing of the second method

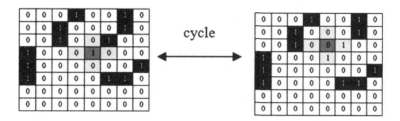

In the second method, the disadvantage is that the control cell will never pass into the cell, which has a zero state. In this case, all the asynchronous cellular automata cells will be set in the zero state in the long time of functioning.

The first method differs from the second in that in the active state can pass the cell that is at logic "1" or "0". A combination of both methods in time allows to reduce the probability of occurrence closed cycles. Especially important is the definition of algorithm of a method search. However, studies have shown that in this embodiment there are cycles. Example of the obtained cycle when operating asynchronous cellular automata with using the two methods is presented on Figure 8.

The methods use a one active cell in each discrete time step. Each additional active cell introduces an additional uncertainty of the asynchronous cellular automata states. Such asynchronous cellular automata with one or more active cells has been successfully used in the construction of high-quality pseudorandom number generator.

ASYNCHRONOUS CELLULAR AUTOMATON MODEL BASED ON THE CELLS WITH ONE ACTIVE OUTPUT

In the previous section, we have considered ACA in which each cell has been set up on certain signaling function activation and the function of transmission in active state. Each cell, which had an active state, determines the active cell in the next time step. Each cell has such a number of active outputs Y_N how many cells creates a neighborhood. Each of its active outputs is connected to one of the active inputs chosen neighborhood cells. In this case, into the next time point the cell passes into the active state when on a one of its active inputs there is a logical "1" signal. All cells of such asynchronous cellular automata perform two functions being in active state.

Figure 8. Examples of the obtained cycles in asynchronous cellular automata when changing of the active signal transmission methods in time

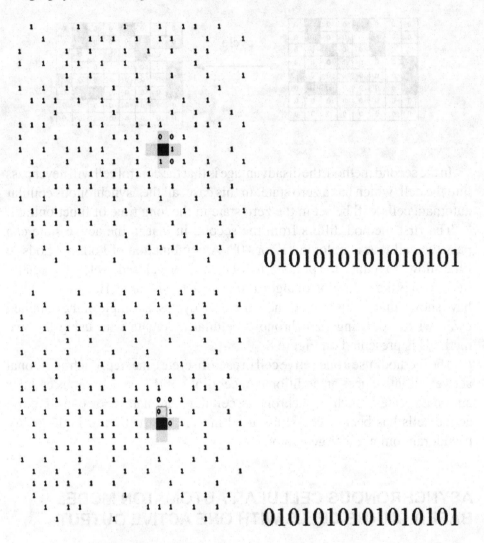

1. Function of cell install in the information state, if a cell is active.
2. The formation active signal function on one of the active outputs.

In this section, we consider other types of asynchronous cellular automata. In such asynchronous cellular automata a cells can switch to the active state under the following conditions:

- There is a signal of a logical "1" on a one of its active inputs;
- The cell is set in a certain main information state S_{cell};
- A neighborhood cell state of the control cells.

Selected main information state is determined by its own state, and by the state of its neighborhood cells. Cell, which switched to the active state may change its state and perform local transition function, and not change its state.

The active cell, which does not change its main information state, is transponder of the active signal. Such a cell is selected for transmitting the active signal and it must have specific properties. According to previously defined properties are selected the asynchronous cellular automata cells to spread active signal. The direction of propagation of the active signal is determined by its LTF of the neighbor's cells.

Cell structure of asynchronous cellular automata implemented by the second embodiment is shown on Figure 9.

This cell contains one active output, unlike the first variant. The signal from this output is transmitted to the active inputs of the neighborhood cells.

ACA cell by the second variant can be represented by the following model.

Figure 9. Graphical representation of asynchronous cellular automata cells by the second variant is implemented

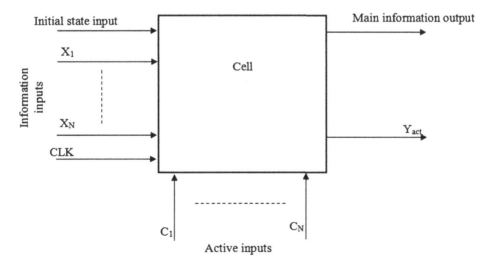

$$b_{i,j}(t+1) = \begin{cases} f\left[X_1(t),...,X_N(t)\right], & if \quad \bigvee_{l=1}^{N} C_l = 1 \\ b_{i,j}(t), & in \quad othe \quad case \end{cases}, \tag{7}$$

where

$X_i(t)$ - signal on the i-th cell information input with the coordinates (i, j) at time t $\left(l = \overline{1,N}\right)$;

C_l - signals on the l-th active cell input.

The model describes the main information state and its change at any given time step. The cell performs the function $f\left[X_1(t),...,X_N(t)\right]$ and switches to the active state, if on one of its active inputs is present the logic "1" signal $C_l = 1$. Active cells do not perform FTAS that indicates the next active cell. From of the active cell output a signal comes to active inputs of all neighborhood cells at the same time. Cells of neighborhoods that have a certain state take an active signal and are switched to the active state. Thus, the cell can be described by the performed functions tuple.

$$\left\langle f\left(X_1,...,X_N\right), f^{act}\left(X_1,...,X_N\right), N \right\rangle.$$

The model shows that the cell is described by the main information state, by an additional active state and by a neighborhood.

The switching of cell into the additional active state is described by the following model

$$b_{i,j}^{act}(t+1) =$$

$$\begin{cases} 1, & if \quad \exists C_{i,j}^l(t) = 1 \quad and \quad f_{i,j}^{act}\left[X_1(t),...,X_N(t)\right] = 1, \\ 0, & in \quad othe \quad case \end{cases} \tag{7}$$

where $C_{i,j}^l(t)$ - signal on one active inputs of the cell with the coordinates (i, j) at time t;

$f_{i,j}^{act}\left[X_1\left(t\right),...,X_N\left(t\right)\right]$ - function that characterizing the cells transition to the active state.

The model indicates when the cell can be in the additional active state. To switch cells into additional active state must calculate the value of the activation function $f_{i,j}^{act}\left[X_1\left(t\right),...,X_N\left(t\right)\right]$. If $f_{i,j}^{act}\left[X_1\left(t\right),...,X_N\left(t\right)\right]=1$ at time t, it is ready to go into the additional active state, in the case where $C_{i,j}^l\left(t\right)=1$.

Let us consider a few examples of the implementation of the asynchronous cellular automata with active cells. The first example characterizes only the process of transfer of additional active state from cell to cell of the asynchronous cellular automata. The ground state of the active cell does not change. We use the following activation function that is described by Table 4. The von Neumann neighborhood is used. Also we take into account that $\bigvee_{l=1}^{N}C_l=1$.

Activation function is described by Table 4 assumes the value a logical "1" if the number of neighborhood cells of the active cell, having an active logic

Table 4. The truth table for the function of activation

N	$X_1(t)$	$X_2(t)$	$X_3(t)$	$X_4(t)$	$f^{act}(t+1)$
16.	• 0	• 0	• 0	• 0	• 0
17.	• 0	• 0	• 0	• 1	• 0
18.	• 0	• 0	• 1	• 0	• 0
19.	• 0	• 0	• 1	• 1	• 1
20.	• 0	• 1	• 0	• 0	• 0
21.	• 0	• 1	• 0	• 1	• 1
22.	• 0	• 1	• 1	• 0	• 1
23.	• 0	• 1	• 1	• 1	• 1
24.	• 1	• 0	• 0	• 0	• 0
25.	• 1	• 0	• 0	• 1	• 1
26.	• 1	• 0	• 1	• 0	• 1
27.	• 1	• 0	• 1	• 1	• 1
28.	• 1	• 1	• 0	• 0	• 1
29.	• 1	• 1	• 0	• 1	• 1
30.	• 1	• 1	• 1	• 0	• 1
31.	• 1	• 1	• 1	• 1	• 1

"1" state is more than or equal to 2. Example of the asynchronous cellular automata evolution for such an activation function is shown on Figure 10.

In the present example, we can see that not all the cells can are switched to the active state. In addition, not all of cells that have more than two neighboring cells with the state of logical "1" is transferred into the active state. The reason for this situation is that none of its neighboring cells can not be active in the process of asynchronous cellular automata evolution. Still another feature of this asynchronous cellular automata is that the cell converts to the additional active state and it remain in this state throughout the operation time asynchronous cellular automata. Also, with each subsequent time steps the number of active cells increases. The process of propagation of active cells in time ends, if among active cell neighbors not cells, in which the activation function equal 1.

The second asynchronous cellular automata configuration is asynchronous cellular automata, wherein the active cells are switched from the active state to the passive state at the next discrete time step. At each time step in the active state can switch those cells that are at the previous time step are in the passive state. In addition, the model must be performed (7). The asynchronous cellular automata evolution for our example on the basis of the second configuration is shown on Figure 11.

We can see that from the seventh time step, the cycle begins. This means that the change of ACA states is performed from 5 and 6 time steps. In this

Figure 10. Example of the asynchronous cellular automata evolution to activate function represented by Table 4

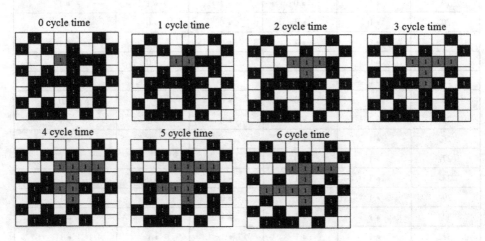

Figure 11. Example of the asynchronous cellular automata evolution based on the second configuration

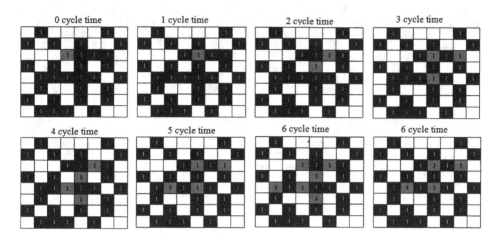

case, we can use the asynchronous cellular automata to implement of the periodic function of the asynchronous cellular automata states.

In this mode, the behavior of the cell is described by the following model.

$$
b_{i,j}^{act}(t+1) =
\begin{cases}
1, & if \quad \exists C_{i,j}^{l}(t) = 1 \quad and \quad f_{i,j}^{act}\left[X_1(t),...,X_N(t)\right] = 1 \\
0, & if \quad \bigvee_{l=1}^{N} C_{i,j}^{l} = 0 \quad or \quad f_{i,j}^{act}\left[X_1(t),...,X_N(t)\right] = 0 \quad or \quad b_{i,j}^{act}(t) = 1
\end{cases}
.
$$

$$(8)$$

In model (8) the active state of the cells at the previous time step t is indicates.

The third configuration implements asynchronous cellular automata properties that provide a mode where the cell can not switch into an active state at the next time step, if it had an active state at a previous time step. This configuration allows the wave propagation of the active state from the initial active cell. However, such an asynchronous cellular automaton operates as long as the last possible cell does not go into an active state. For the proposed initial, an asynchronous cellular automaton state the evolution will have the form shown on Figure 12.

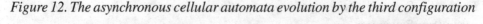

Figure 12. The asynchronous cellular automata evolution by the third configuration

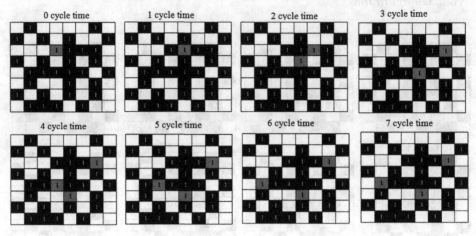

The third asynchronous cellular automata configuration is characterized by the presence of active cells set. This asynchronous cellular automata does not reproduce the cycles and repetitions of asynchronous cellular automata states. At the end of the asynchronous cellular automata work the outside active cells remains. The location of outside active cells depends on the initial state of the asynchronous cellular automata and on the active cells.

The fourth configuration implements asynchronous cellular automata, in which there is only one active cell at each time point. The cell of this asynchronous cellular automata is described by the model.

$$
b_{i,j}^{act}\left(t+1\right)=
\begin{cases}
1, & if \quad \exists C_{i,j}^{l}\left(t\right)=1 \quad and \quad f_{i,j}^{act,l}\left[b_{i,j}^{1,l}\left(t\right),b_{i,j}^{2,l}\left(t\right),...,b_{i,j}^{N,l}\left(t\right)\right]=1 \\
0, & if \quad \bigvee_{l=1}^{N} C_{i,j}^{l}=0 \quad or \quad or \quad b_{i,j}^{act}\left(t\right)=1
\end{cases}
\tag{9}
$$

where

$b_{i,j}^{1,l}\left(t\right)$ - state of the cell, which belongs to the neighborhood with the number 1 of the cell, which was active in the previous time step t;

$f_{i,j}^{act,l}\left[b_{i,j}^{1,l}\left(t\right),b_{i,j}^{2,l}\left(t\right),...,b_{i,j}^{N,l}\left(t\right)\right]$ - the function of transmission in active state of cells with number l, which belongs to the neighborhood of the active cell in the previous moment of time t and this cell has the coordinates (i, j).

In fact, every cell performs the function of transmission in active state of signals of the state cells that make up the neighborhood of the active cell in the previous time step. At the same time, this cell is included into this neighborhood. The model shows that only a single neighborhood cell of the active cell will pass into the active state at the next time t+1. In this mode, the cells have the most complex hardware implementation compared to the previous modes.

The main characteristic is that the function of transmission in active state implemented on the basis of the cell numbering priority in the neighborhood. This priority is given by the states of this neighborhood cells. The one cell, which has the biggest priority, becomes active in the next time step. For example, such a function may indicate a cell with a biggest number in the neighborhood among of neighborhood cells, which have a logic "1" state. An example of such a priority for the Moore neighborhood is presented on Figure 13.

For our example, we choose the function of transmission in active state that selects the neighborhood cell with the biggest number among neighborhood

Figure 13. An example of the transmission of the active state by priority

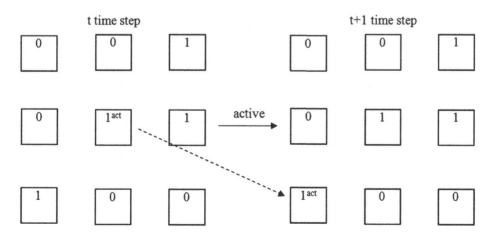

Figure 14. The asynchronous cellular automata evolution with the fourth configuration of the active signal transmission

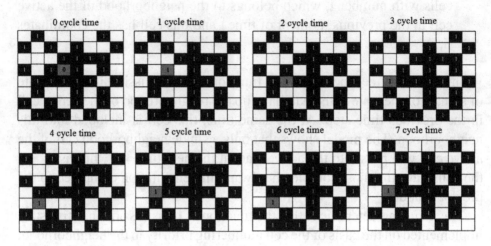

cells with a state of logical "1". The asynchronous cellular automata evolution is presented on Figure 14.

The asynchronous cellular automata evolution indicates that an active signal may move only among cells that have a logic "1" state. In addition, asynchronous cellular automata with the fourth configuration can generate cycles and repeats of the movement paths of active signal. The trajectory of movement of the active signal depends on the initial installations of asynchronous cellular automata and on the FTAS choice.

The considered asynchronous cellular automata are very limited. The reason for this is that the asynchronous cellular automata cells do not change their main information state and do not perform local transition function. Further we will consider asynchronous cellular automata, in which cells change their main state.

Let us consider the possible combinations of asynchronous cellular automata with different modes of transmission of the active state. These modes are described above.

The first mode of the asynchronous cellular automata operation increases the number of active cells with each subsequent time step. If the cell is switched to an active state at time t, at the following discrete time steps this cell remains in the active state. The following model describes the main informational state of cells in this mode.

$$b_{i,j}(t+1) =$$

$$\begin{cases} f\left[X_1(t),...,X_N(t),b_{i,j}(t)\right], & if \quad \exists C_{i,j}^l = 1 \quad and \quad b_{i,j}^{act}(t) = 0 \quad and \quad f_{i,j}^{act}\left[X_1(t),...,X_N(t)\right] = 1 \\ b_{i,j}(t), & in \quad othe \quad case \end{cases}$$

$$(10)$$

Example of the evolution of the asynchronous cellular automata, in which each cell performs the XOR function as local transition function is shown on Figure 15.

Active signal propagates through the cells similarly as shown in the example on Figure 10. Since the state of active cells varies according to the local transition function, the propagation of the active cells may be different. On the Figure 15 an active signal transmission process ends at 5 time step.

The second cell activation mode is characterized in that an active cell transmits an active signal to the adjacent cell at the next time step, and itself in a passive state is set. The model (10) describes the main informational state of cells in this mode. Example of the asynchronous cellular automata evolution for the second mode is presented on Figure 16. Local transition function is the same as for the previous example.

Figure 15. The asynchronous cellular automata evolution during the first transmission mode active state and the local transition function that implement a XOR function

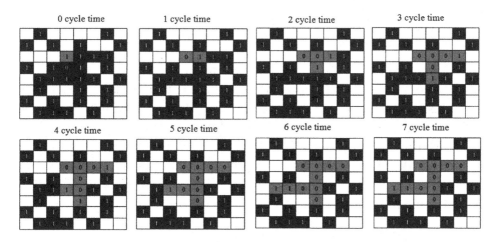

Figure 16. The asynchronous cellular automata evolution during the second transmission mode active state and the LTF that implement a XOR function

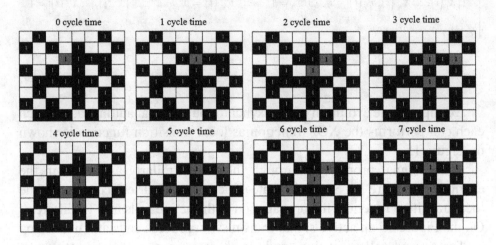

Repetition of states also begins with of the sixth time step. However, one cell has changed its state under the influence of local transition function.

The third active state transmission mode describes the main informational state by the following model.

$$
b_{i,j}(t+1) =
\begin{cases}
f\left[X_1(t),...,X_N(t)\right], & if \quad \exists C_{i,j}^l = 1 \quad and \quad f_{i,j}^{act}\left[X_1(t),...,X_N(t)\right] = 1 \\
b_{i,j}(t), & if \quad \bigvee_t b_{i,j}^{act}(t) = 1
\end{cases}
$$

$$(11)$$

The model says that if the cell at some point in time is less than $(t + 1)$ is active, it does not perform local transition function and its main information state does not change. The example of the local transition function computing and the asynchronous cellular automata evolution for our settings is presented on Figure 17.

The fourth mode of the asynchronous cellular automata operation is provided by the main informational state of the cell, which is described by the following model.

Figure 17. The asynchronous cellular automata evolution and the local transition function are being calculated by the active cells in the third mode

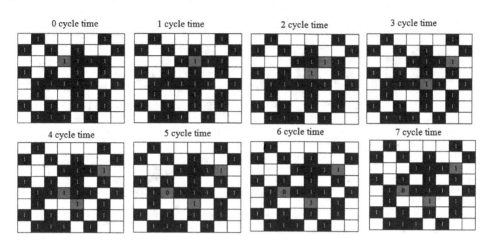

$$b_{i,j}(t+1) =$$

$$\begin{cases} f\big[X_1(t),...,X_N(t)\big], & if \quad \exists C_{i,j}^l = 1 \quad and \quad f_{i,j}^{act,l}\big[b_{i,j}^{1,l}(t),...,b_{i,j}^{N,l}(t)\big] = 1 \\ b_{i,j}(t), & if \quad b_{i,j}^{act}(t) = 1 \quad or \quad f_{i,j}^{act,l}\big[b_{i,j}^{1,l}(t),...,b_{i,j}^{N,l}(t)\big] = 0 \quad or \quad \bigvee_l C_{i,j}^l = 0 \end{cases}$$

$$(12)$$

In formula there is a strict condition that the cell performs the local transition function at time (t + 1) if it was active at the moment of time t.

As described in the example in Figure 15 a change in the main informational states is presented in Figure 18.

The last mode implements the asynchronous cellular automata with one active cell. The active cell can transmit active states in different directions. The trajectory of movement of active signal can be unpredictable, as active cells change their main information asynchronous cellular automata state during its functioning. For this reason, asynchronous cellular automata operation time and motion trajectory length of the active signal may be significantly is increased.

The analysis of all the possible modes allows us to confidently claim that ACA that works in the fourth mode is most suitable for creating pseudorandom number generator.

Figure 18. Changing the main information states of active cells on the basis of an example shown on Figure 15

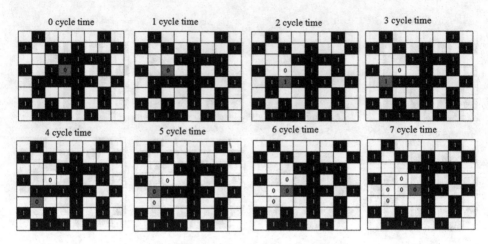

THE PSEUDORANDOM NUMBER GENERATORS MODELS BASED ON ASYNCHRONOUS CELLULAR AUTOMATA

Different CA configurations are used to construct a pseudorandom number generator. These include both SCA and the asynchronous cellular automata. As was shown above that pseudorandom number generator based on existing CA is vulnerable. If all cells change their state at each time step according to the local transition function, it is possible to determine this local function. In this regard, the most effective is the use of asynchronous cellular automata, in which not all cells change their main informational state at each time step. In this section, we use the asynchronous cellular automata with one active cell, which is described in detail above.

Let us consider the pseudorandom number generator, which is implemented on the asynchronous cellular automata with one active cell. The pseudorandom number generators of this type is the asynchronous cellular automata with one active cell at each time step of its work. Bits of the pseudorandom bit sequence are formed from active cells outputs at each discrete time step. In fact, the asynchronous cellular automata structure is a structure of the pseudorandom number generator. It is only necessary to use additional means of switching, which realize the connection of the information output of the active cell to the pseudorandom number generator output at each time step. The general structure of this pseudorandom number generator is presented on Figure 19.

Figure 19. The general pseudorandom number generator structure based on the CA

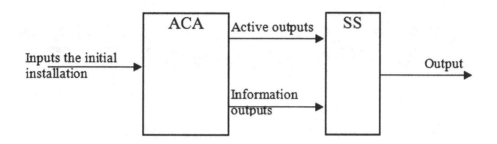

The pseudorandom number generator is made up of asynchronous cellular automata and the switching system (SS). SS output is the output of the pseudorandom number generator. SS has two groups of inputs. The first group of inputs is connected to the information outputs Q of asynchronous cellular automata cells. The second group of SS inputs connected to the active outputs Y of cells. The inputs of the second group run by connecting the inputs of the first group to the output of pseudorandom number generator. The signals at the inputs of the second group give such a command to the SS, what a one of the inputs of the first group is need to connect to the SS output. The first group number of inputs equal to the dimension of ACA or the number of ACA cells. Also, the number of inputs of the second group is equal to the number of asynchronous cellular automata cells.

All the pseudorandom number generators cells perform the local transition function and the function of transmission in active state. However, the modeling of this pseudorandom number generator has shown that sooner or later in asynchronous cellular automata the cycles and repetitions of certain transitions are formed. It does not at the output of a pseudorandom sequence. In order to eliminate such cycles an additional bit are used. This additional bit from one of the asynchronous cellular automata cells is selected.

The additional bits using improves the quality pseudorandom number generator. However, it complicates algorithm of its work, and hardware implementation. Additional bit is selected from cells, which at each time step by a certain algorithm are being selected. The simplest algorithm consists in a sequence of a cells enumeration in each row. An example of such enumeration is presented on Figure 20.

There are various variants of the formation of an additional bit on its own ACA structure. For example, an additional bit can be calculated from the states of the neighborhood cells. This greatly simplifies the hardware and

Figure 20. An example of the formation of an additional bit

software implementation of the pseudorandom number generator. We can choose state signal from any a neighborhood cells, namely, this signal will participate in the performance of local transition function as two arguments. However, this variant does not always produce the desired result. A convenient option is the value of the additional bit is calculated by the additional functions $f_{add}\left[X_1(t),...,X_N(t)\right]$. For example, we can set the function of the following form

$$f_{add}\left[X_1(t),...,X_N(t)\right] = \left(X_1 \wedge \overline{X_2} \wedge X_3\right) \vee \left(\overline{X_1} \wedge \overline{X_3} \wedge X_4\right).$$

The asynchronous cellular automata based on the von Neumann neighborhood is organized. Then the value will be formed within each cell. In this case, the additional hardware of the asynchronous cellular automata will not develop. This function is performed by the cell itself. The value of this function forms the active cell. This approach leaves the asynchronous cellular automata as a core element PRNG.

The next model forms informational state of a cell based on the Moore's neighborhood

$$b_{i,j}(t+1) = C_1(t) \oplus C_2(t) \oplus ... \oplus C_8(t) \oplus b_{add}(t) \oplus b_{i,j}(t),$$

where $b_{add}(t)$ - state of the cell, the value of which an additional bit generates.

For the initial installation of the generator, the following actions are performed.

1. The asynchronous cellular automata structure and its geometric covering are selected.

2.   The cell structure of the neighborhood is selected.
3.   The asynchronous cellular automata coverage map is selected.
4.   The coordinates of the initial active asynchronous cellular automata cell is assigned.
5.   The local transition function and the function of transmission in active state are assigned.
6.   A method of a bit forming of an additional sequence is selected.

Geometric covering displays a geometric shape of the cells. This takes into account the fill ability and density of the cell location in the asynchronous cellular automata. Previously we mentioned about the most widespread shapes, which are a rectangle, a hexagon and a triangular shapes. The asynchronous cellular automata structure is determined by the structure the neighborhood and by the main functions of the cell, as well as by the problems that are solved with the help of asynchronous cellular automata.

The coverage map determines the distribution of logic "1" and "0" on the asynchronous cellular automata area. This distribution makes it possible to select the cells that must be set to a logic "1" state and the cells that must be set to logical "0" state.

A PRNG itself is created through 1, 2, 5 and 6 actions. After the implementation of these actions, the 3 and 4 actions are selected.

Initial installation of the pseudorandom number generator is formed by selecting a card of the asynchronous cellular automata coating and by the coordinates of the initial active cell.

If we change structure of the neighborhood, the pseudorandom number generator structure changes, as the relationships structure change between cells, as well as the internal structure of the cell itself changing. If we change the LTF and FTAS, the internal structure of the cell is changed. This situation also leads to a change in the structure of the PRNG. The forming additional bits method changing causes a change in an additional processing circuit or of the internal cell structure.

Let consider the most efficient generators, based on the described asynchronous cellular automata. These generators are different from each other by the method of the additional bits forming.

In each generator is used FTAS, which consist as follows (Bilan, Bilan, & Bilan, 2015; Bilan, Bilan, Motornyuk, Bilan, & Bilan, 2016; Bilan, Bilan, & Bilan, 2015). On the odd time step of generator operation the active cell transmits the active state to the cell of it's the neighborhood, which has a biggest number among the cells of the neighborhood that are in a state of a logical "1". At the not odd time step, the neighborhood cell of the active cell is selected, and it has the biggest number of numbering among other the neighborhood cells that are in the zero state. Graphically, this process is presented on Figure 21.

The following model describes such FTAS for a neighborhood cells under l number

$$b_{i,j}^{act,l}(t+1) =$$

$$\begin{cases} 1, & if \ \exists C_{i,j}^l(t) = 1 \ and \ (t+1)\bmod 2 = 1 \ and \ f_{i,j}^{act,l}(t) = \overline{b_{i,j}^l(t)} \vee b_{i,j}^{l+1}(t) \vee ... \vee b_{i,j}^N(t) = 1 \\ 1, & if \ \exists C_{i,j}^l(t) = 1 \ and \ (t+1)\bmod 2 = 0 \ and \ f_{i,j}^{act,l}(t) = \overline{b_{i,j}^l(t)} \vee b_{i,j}^{l+1}(t) \vee ... \vee b_{i,j}^N(t) = 0 \\ 0, & in \ other \ case \end{cases}$$

$$(13)$$

The model (13) consists of three rows, two of which indicate an additional active logic "1" state.

For the first generator the additional bits are selected as follows.

The ACA states are remembered at the zero time step. Then sequential reading of signals of the cells states in each row from left to right is performed.

Figure 21. Example of the neighborhood cells numbering and the active transmission process for the described FTAS

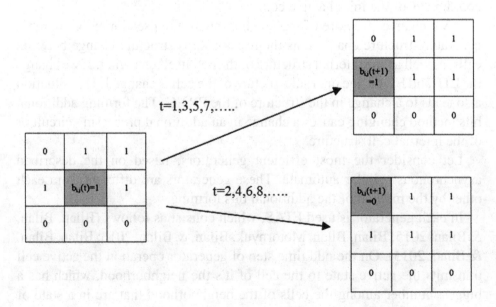

This process is shown on Figure 20. The reading is carried out with help R×L time step (where R×L – the ACA size value). After R×L time steps the current state of the ACA on the R×L time step are remembered. From this next asynchronous cellular automata state, the process of formation of additional bit is repeated. Such stored state is called the binary slice of the asynchronous cellular automata states. The next ACA slice are obtained on the 2(R×L) time step.

The PRNG based on asynchronous cellular automata operates in according to the following method.

1. The map of the asynchronous cellular automata states is recorded.
2. In the asynchronous cellular automata the initial cell for the beginning of the spread of the active signal are selected.
3. The local transition function as a XOR function on the values of state signals of the neighborhood cells, on the own condition and on the value of the additional bit at each time step are performed.
4. The value of the resulting bit at the generator output is generated.
5. The active signal of one of the neighborhood cells by an assigned local function is transferred.

The initial active cell can be selected randomly. The formed by a pseudo-random sequence structure depends on the initial settings. At the data output of the cell, which is active in the current time, the generated bits at each time step are being retrieved. The example of operation of the first generator is shown on Figure 22.

This generator has a disadvantage, which is that the generator needs the additional hardware and software expenses to implement of the memorization of the bit ACA slices. Such circumstances lead to a decrease of the speed.

To simplify generator and to improvement its quality allows another way of the additional bits generation. Additional bits are read from the current state asynchronous cellular automata cells. At the same time the enumeration of cells similar to the first generator. In the second generator the intermediate storage of the binary asynchronous cellular automata slices through a assigned number of time steps is not used. Cells function in a similar way. At the same time the active cell and the cell, which forms an additional bits may coincide. An example of the functioning of such a pseudorandom number generator is presented on the Figure 23.

Comments can determine the value of intermediate bits and the bits of the result at each time step. On Figure 23 can see how the active signal is

Figure 22. The example of operation of the first generator

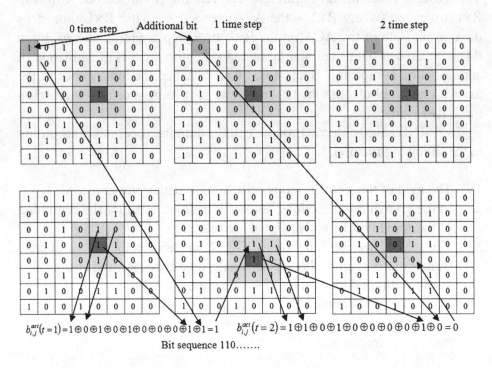

$$b_{i,j}^{act}(t=1)=1\oplus0\oplus1\oplus0\oplus1\oplus0\oplus0\oplus0\oplus1\oplus1=1 \qquad b_{i,j}^{act}(t=2)=1\oplus1\oplus0\oplus1\oplus0\oplus0\oplus0\oplus0\oplus1\oplus0=0$$

Bit sequence 110.......

Figure 23. An example of the functioning of the pseudorandom number generator with the internal asynchronous cellular automata scanning

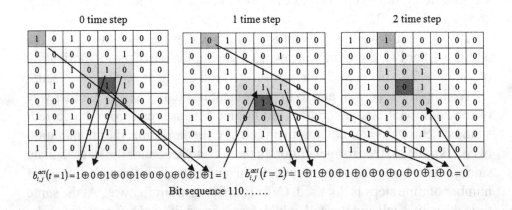

$$b_{i,j}^{act}(t=1)=1\oplus0\oplus1\oplus0\oplus1\oplus0\oplus0\oplus0\oplus1\oplus1=1 \qquad b_{i,j}^{act}(t=2)=1\oplus1\oplus0\oplus1\oplus0\oplus0\oplus0\oplus0\oplus1\oplus0=0$$

Bit sequence 110.......

transmitted from cell to cell and how the state of each active cell is changed. In the proposed generators have not feedback, and performance is determined by performing a simple LTF and by the time that it takes to transfer of the active signal from cell to cell.

THE STRUCTURE OF ASYNCHRONOUS CELLULAR AUTOMATA FOR IMPLEMENTATION THE PSEUDORANDOM NUMBER GENERATOR

The generalized PRNG structure based the asynchronous cellular automata is presented on Figure 19 (Bilan, Bilan, Motornyuk, Bilan, & Bilan, 2016; Bilan, Bilan, & Bilan, 2015). It includes two main units: the asynchronous cellular automata implement unit and switching system SS. The SS performs connection of the main informational outputs of the active cell to the output of the generator. The first unit is asynchronous cellular automata. The asynchronous cellular automata creates indeterminacy. Earlier, we looked at two variants of pseudorandom number generator building. In this section we will look at their detailed structure.

The structure of the first pseudorandom number generator is shown on Figure 24.

Figure 24. The structure of the first pseudorandom number generator

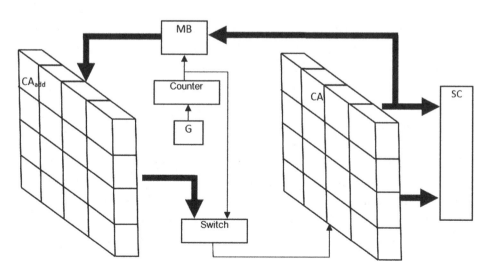

The PRNG consists of two cellular automata: the main and additional (CA_{add}). In the CA_{add} is stored initial CA state, which is being recorded into the memory buffer (MB). This state is stored during the $D \times L$ time steps (where $D \times L$ – the size of the two-dimensional CA). CA operates according to the method described in the previous section for the first pseudorandom number generator.

Counter (Counter) counts the number of pulses at the generator output (G). When its content is equal to $D \times L$, the current state of the CA is recorded in MB CA_{add}. At each time period G operation the switch (Switch) connects own output to one of its inputs. The switch inputs are electrically connected to the respective outputs of cells of the CA_{add}. In fact, the Switch implements a forming method of the additional bits. The switching system provides a generator output connection to the informational output of the active cells at the current time step.

We see that the main element of the PRNG is an asynchronous cellular automaton. In this respect, there is need to develop an electrical circuit of the one cell. The cell should performing the selected LTF and the function of transmission in active state. In addition, the cell must perform all the operations at certain time steps. For the implementation of the first pseudorandom number generator the cell of should have the following interface (Figure 25). The asynchronous cellular automata are implemented on the basis of the Moore neighborhood.

Among all cell inputs the additional inputs are appeared C'_i. These inputs are connected to the outputs of the active state $(Output_{act})$ of all cells of the neighborhood cells. Also the inputs of the setting of the information state are be there $(input_{inf\_st})$ and the inputs of settings in the additional active state $(input_{act\_st})$, the reset inputs $(reset_{inf}, reset_{act})$ and a clock input (CLK).

Inputs C'_1 are converted the cell to an inactive state after the active signal transmission by this cell to another adjacent cell. The setting inputs and reset inputs for initial cell units are designed.

According to Figure 25, the graph-scheme of the algorithm of operation of the cell ACA on Figure 26 is presented.

In Figure 26, the basic information state of the cell is denoted as B(t), and the active state is designated as A(t). The counter state is indicated as Count.

At the initial time, the cell is set to the basic information state of logical "1" or "0" (B(t)="1" or "0"). Also, the cell can be set to the active (A(t) = 1) or inactive (A(t) = 0) state. The time step counter is set to zero (Count:=0).

Figure 25. A graphical representation of asynchronous cellular automaton cells for the implementation of the first pseudorandom number generator

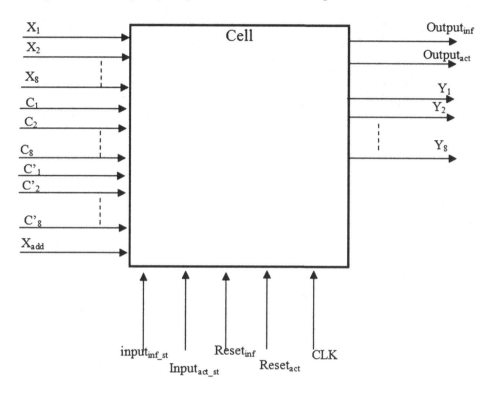

After the initial settings, the active state of the cell is checked. If the cell has an active state (A (t) = 1), then the local function of the cell state is performed according to formula

$$f_{inf}(t) = X_1 \oplus X_2 \oplus ... \oplus X_8 \oplus X_{cell} \oplus X_{add},$$

where X_i – signal at the i-th information input of the cell;

X_{cell} – signal value of own state of cell;
X_{add} – the additional bit value.

The time step number is checked. For this, the remainder of the divide of the contents of the counter of time step is determined in according to the function (Count)mod2 $\neq$ 0. If the remainder of dividing by 2 is zero {(Count)

Figure 26. The graph-scheme of the algorithm of operation of the ACA cell presented in Figure 25

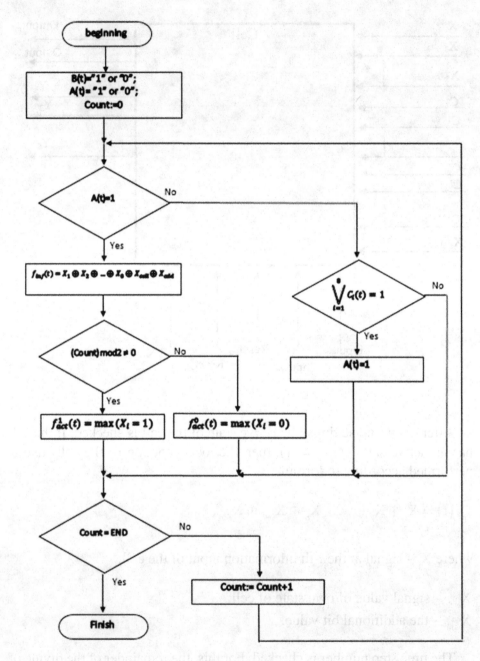

mod2 = 0}, then the function of local transitions is performed at an even time step { $f^0_{act}(t) = \max(X_i = 0)$ } according to Figure 21. If the remainder of dividing by 2 is equal to one {(Count)mod2 = 1}, then the function of local transitions is performed at an odd time step { $f^1_{act}(t) = \max(X_i = 1)$ } according to Figure 21. The contents of the counter are checked and if the counter code is equal to the final value (Count = END), Then the work of the cell ends. If the number of time steps is insufficient (Count $\neq$ END), then its contents is increased by one (Count:= Count + 1).

If the cell is not active (A (t) = 0), then the presence of the signal of logical "1" on one of the active inputs ($C_i(t)$) of the cell is checked. If a logical "1" signal is present on one of the active inputs { $\bigvee_{i=1}^{8} C_i(t) = 1$ }, then the cell becomes active (A(t)=1). Further, the contents of the counter are checked and the cell continues to function according to the algorithm presented.

The functional circuit of the ACA cell for implementation of the first pseudorandom number generator is presented on Figure 27.

There are non-standard blocks that implement LTF and the function of transmission in active state in the functional circuit of the cell. The cell consists of two flip-flops: a base and additional, as well as the counting trigger, which controls by the implementation the function of transmission in active state unit. Triggers are controlled by the leading front of the CLK signal. The main trigger T_{inf} is equipped with enable input, which is connected to the direct output of the T_{add}. Also T_{add} controls the implementation FTAS block (CC_{TASF}).

The ideal timing diagram of a cell operation are shown on Figure 28.

Timing diagrams are shown for the two modes of the cells operation:

- The initial setting mode;
- The current work cell mode.

The second mode arbitrarily was selected. The ideal timing diagrams do not take into account the delay of real circuits.

A second generator has more simple structure (Bilan, Bilan, & Bilan, 2015; Bilan, Bilan, Motornyuk, Bilan, & Bilan, 2016). Difficulties make up the organization of switching systems for generating additional bits and of the bits of the output sequence. The structure of the second PRNG is shown on Figure 29.

In this generator, most complex is scheme of formation additional bit and the cell outputs connections, which form additional bits to the inputs of the

Figure 27. The functional circuit of the asynchronous cellular automaton cell for implementation of the first pseudorandom number generator

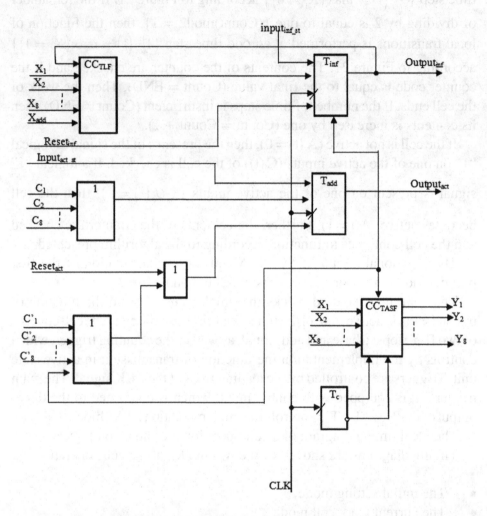

active cell. To implement this, in the circuit a complex switching system, which sets the law of formation of additional bits is used.

The complexity of the switching system is the large number of inputs, which are more than 2 times of the amount of CA cells. The active cell outputs are control inputs of the switching systems, and main information outputs ACA cells are information inputs, which are connected to one output by signals on the control inputs.

The switching circuit that generates additional bits is shown on Figure 30.

Figure 28. The ideal timing diagram of the asynchronous cellular automaton cell operation

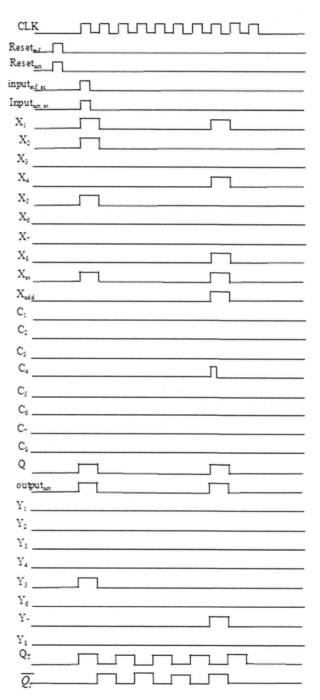

Figure 29. The second generator structural circuit

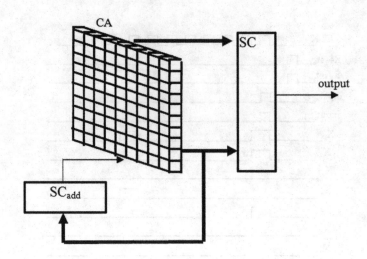

Figure 30. The functional circuit of the switching system

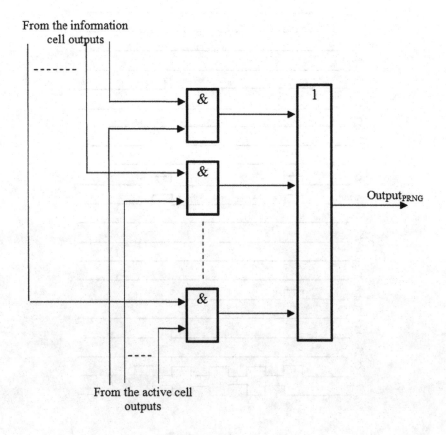

Figure 31. The functional circuit of the switching circuit

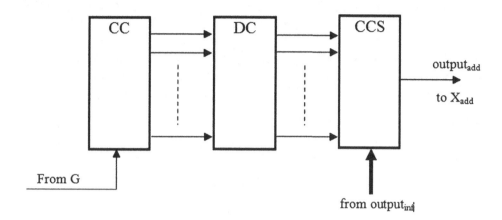

The switching circuit is not complex. However, a large number of AND gates and a multi-input OR gates the switching system has.

An additional switching circuit has a more complex structure (SC_{add}) for the formation and distribution of additional bits. The scheme consists of a control counter (CC), the decoder (DC) and a combinational circuit (CCS). The functional circuit CA_{add} is shown in Figure 31.

CC and DC are used to control by connection of the information inputs to the output of the CCS. The CCS has the structure as the SC (Figure 30).

A second generator has better dynamic of a changes state, since the active cell can change its state several times until such time as it will form an additional bit. Furthermore, the duration of the period of the pseudorandom sequence increases.

REFERENCES

Bardell, P. H. (1990). Analysis of Cellular Automata Used as Pseudorandom Pattern Generator. *Proceedings of 1990 International Test Conference*, 762-768.

Bilan, S., Bilan, M., & Bilan, S. (2015). Application of Methods of Organization of Cellular Automata to Implement Devices of Forming Pseudorandom Sequences, Information Technology & Computer Science. *11th Annual International Conference on Information Technology & Computer Science*, 17-18.

Bilan, S., Bilan, M., & Bilan, S. (2015). Novel pseudorandom sequence of numbers generator based cellular automata. *Information Technology and Security*, *3*(1), 38–50.

Bilan, S., Bilan, M., Motornyuk, R., Bilan, A., & Bilan, S. (2016). Research and Analysis of the Pseudorandom Number Generators Implemented on Cellular Automata. *WSEAS Transactions on Systems*, *15*, 275–281.

Schneier, B. (1996). Applied Cryptography: Protocols, Algorithms, and Source Code in C (2nd ed.). Wiley Computer Publishing, John Wiley & Sons, Inc.

Chapter 5

The Pseudorandom Number Generators Based on Cellular Automata With Inhomogeneous Cells

ABSTRACT

The fifth chapter deals with the use of hybrid cellular automata for constructing high-quality pseudo-random number generators. A hybrid cellular automaton consists of homogeneous cells and a small number of inhomogeneous cells. Inhomogeneous cells perform a local function that differs from local functions that homogeneous cells realize. The location of inhomogeneous cells and the main cell is chosen in advance. The output of the main cell is the output of a pseudo-random number generator. A hardware implementation of a pseudo-random number generator based on hybrid cellular automata is described. The local function that an inhomogeneous cell realizes is the majority function. The principles of constructing a pseudo-random number generator based on cellular automata with inhomogeneous neighborhoods are described. In such cellular automata, inhomogeneous cells have a neighborhood whose shape differs from that of neighborhoods of homogeneous cells.

DOI: 10.4018/978-1-5225-2773-2.ch005

THE METHOD AND MODELS OF PSEUDORANDOM NUMBER GENERATION BASED ON CELLULAR AUTOMATA WITH INHOMOGENEOUS CELLS

Generators considered above have a number of the structural disadvantages. These generators require the constant additional operations, which for the additional bits of formation are intended. In addition, generators use complex switching circuit for constant connection of the generator output to the output of the active ACA cells. Both generators have a large number of connections, which reduces the reliability of operation.

To eliminate these drawbacks and of increasing of the period of repeating pseudo-random sequence in the work the pseudorandom number generator that contains cellular automata with homogeneous and inhomogeneous cells, is investigated.

The homogeneous cells are called all cellular automata cells, which the same local transition function perform. Inhomogeneous cells are called cells, which perform a different function than local transition function of the homogeneous cells. At the same time an inhomogeneous cells is much less of the homogeneous cells. Such cellular automata else are called as hybrid cellular automata (HCA).

The locations of the cells, as well as their number are an important moment for the initial settings.

Such a pseudorandom number generator consists of one cellular automata. For the operation of the generator is initially being made the advanced settings.

1. The size of cellular automata is being selected.
2. The number of inhomogeneous cells are being selected and their location are being created.
3. The local transition function for homogeneous and inhomogeneous cells are being selected.
4. The cell, whose output is the output of the generator, is being selected.

After the initial settings, a generator starts to generate a pseudo-random bit sequence at the output of the selected cells. At each time step, the homogeneous cells perform local transition function for homogeneous cells and inhomogeneous cells will perform the local transition function for inhomogeneous cells.

In this situation, all homogeneous cells will equally change its state according to the homogeneous local transition function. Only inhomogeneous cells will be changing its state by another law. Homogeneous cell of the cell neighborhood will be change its state under the influence of inhomogeneous cells that constantly makes the changes to state of the cellular automata. In this case, the inhomogeneous cells in the neighborhood of homogeneous cells change their state not as the rest the homogeneous cells of the neighborhood.

Traditional classical cellular automata without inhomogeneous cells lead to short cycles or to the installation of the cellular automata cells in the state of logical "1" or "0". This situation is shown on Figure 15 (Chapter 2).

This example shows that important is the choice of a local transition functions for homogeneous and inhomogeneous cells. Also good effect gives an increase in the number of the inhomogeneous cells.

However, the hybrid cellular automata as a separate element with simple local transition function can not be used as pseudorandom number generator. To solve this problem allows the constant comparison of the hybrid cellular automata current state with the states obtained at the previous time steps. This approach dramatically increases the spent time on the forming each bit of the pseudo-random sequence. The work of such pseudorandom number generator can be represented by the following model.

$$
B_{HCA}(t+1) =
$$
$$
\begin{cases}
\left\{ b_{i,j}(t+1), h_{i,j}(t+1) \right\}, & if \quad \forall B_{CA}(\tau < t+1) \neq B_{CA}(t) \\
\left\{ b'_{i,j}(t+1), h'_{i,j}(t+1) \right\}, & if \quad \exists B_{CA}(\tau < t+1) = B_{CA}(t+1)
\end{cases}
\qquad (1)
$$

where

$B_{CA}(t+1)$ - the cellular automata state at time t+1;

$B_{CA}(\tau < t+1)$ - the cellular automata state in previous times step before time
t inclusively $\left(\tau = \overline{0, t} \right)$;

$b_{i,j}(t+1)$, $b'_{i,j}(t+1)$ - the set of the homogeneous cell states at time t+1;

$h_{i,j}(t+1)$, $h'_{i,j}(t+1)$ - the set of the inhomogeneous cell states at time t+1.

The set $b_{i,j}(t+1)$ different from a set $b'_{i,j}(t+1)$ by location of the homogeneous cells. This location is differs by the amount of inhomogeneous cells. This means that the cells that were inhomogeneous, are being became a homogeneous. At the same time, the selected homogeneous cells become inhomogeneous. The number of transformed homogeneous cells is equal to the number of the inhomogeneous cells.

The model (1) is simplified. However, it available describes the generator behavior. Consider the example of the operation of the generator for the homogeneous AND function and an inhomogeneous OR function. For this a inhomogeneous cell is selected (Figure 1).

The above example shows that these functions lead to the installation of the cellular automata cells into a logical "0" state. In state logical "1" can lead the use of two inhomogeneous cells using the OR function for homogeneous cells and AND functions for inhomogeneous cells. This choice of functions leads to cellular automata field filling by the states logical "1" (Figure 2).

Let us take the 5 inhomogeneous cells with the same cellular automata dimension (Figure 3). The homogeneous OR function and the inhomogeneous AND function is used.

Figure 1. An example of pseudorandom number generator operation with an inhomogeneous cell

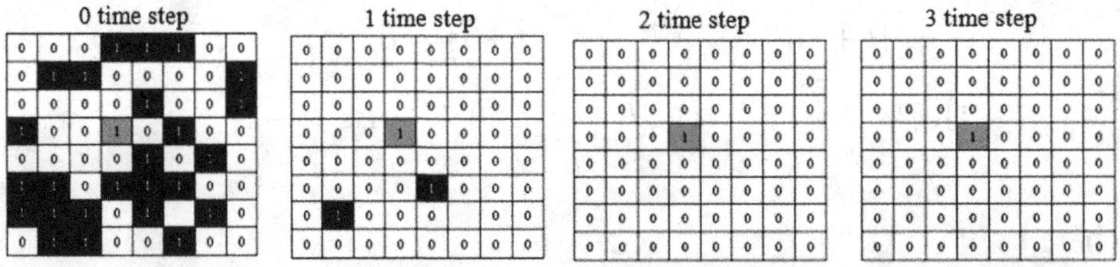

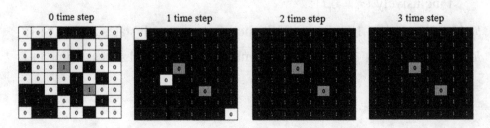

Figure 2. An example of the pseudorandom number generator operation with two inhomogeneous cells

Figure 3. An example of the pseudorandom number generator operation with five inhomogeneous cells

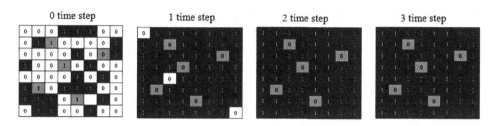

From all three examples (Figure 1, Figure 2, Figure 3) we see that on the second and third time steps cellular automata states are coincide. From this it follows that, according to the method, the inhomogeneous cells change their location. After the third time step already other cells perform an inhomogeneous function, and those that were inhomogeneous cells begin to perform a homogeneous local function. However, these examples clearly demonstrate that at the fourth and fifth time steps also cellular automata states are coincide.

This situation confirms the need for careful selection of the local transition function. We see that it is not necessary to use the local transition functions, which implement a dominant influence on the state of the cell. The dominant effect of a local transition function is determined that the presence of one state in the neighborhood of the cell translates to the same state of active cell. For example, if the local transition function is realized on the basis of the logic OR function, then the cell switches into logic "1" state, if there is a neighborhood cell, which has a logic "1" state.

Cellular automata evolution analysis allows to conclude that the local transition function should give a result that depends on the ratio of the number of cells that are at logic "1" or "0". The most suitable local transition function for the construction of pseudorandom number generator based on the hybrid cellular automata is XOR function and the majority function.

Consider the example of the construction of a pseudorandom number generator in which homogeneous cells perform XOR function and inhomogeneous cells perform the majority function. The majority function takes the value, which is greater among all values. If the number of neighborhood cells which have a logic "1" state is greater than the number of neighborhood cells, which have a logic "0" state, the control cell switches into a logic "1" state.

For example, we choose a von Neumann neighborhood and one an inhomogeneous cell. This generator has a size 8×8 and its operation is shown in Figure 4. The cellular automata with memory is used.

The generator behavior at the first time steps does not give a qualitative pseudorandom bit sequence. However, there are no of the coincidences of the cellular automata states with previous states at each time step. Coincidences are begun at the seventh time step with zero time step. From this moment an inhomogeneous cell changes its location. Such an organization gives the following bit sequence 001000100.

Let's introduce two inhomogeneous cells and let's investigate the behavior of the generator (Figure 5). Choosing the same initial installations, as in the previous example.

The inhomogeneous cell number increase improves the quality of the formed bit sequence. At the 14th time step cellular automata state coincides with the cellular automata states on the tenth time step. This is the first coincidence of the cellular automata states. The bit sequence formed in this example has the form 001010101010101. As can be seen, it has good statistical properties. However, the coincidence require additional time expenses.

Consider the influence of neighborhood form on the generator operation quality. For this we take the same initial state of the HCA and Moore's neighborhood is being applied. Example of a generator operation with one an inhomogeneous cell based on the Moore neighborhood is shown on Figure 6.

Figure 4. An example of the pseudorandom number generator operation based on hybrid cellular automata with one an inhomogeneous cell and with a cellular automata size 8×8. The homogeneous cells perform XOR function, and an inhomogeneous cell performs a majority function

Figure 5. An example of the behavior of a pseudorandom number generator with two inhomogeneous cells

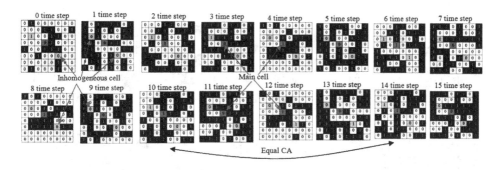

Figure 6. Example of a generator behavior with one an inhomogeneous cell based on the Moore neighborhood

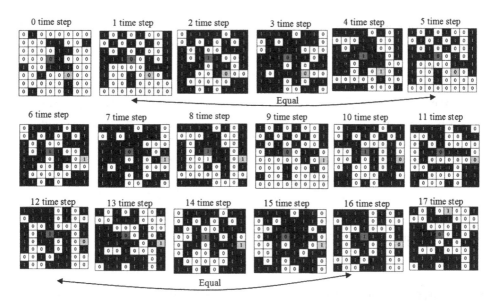

The Moore neighborhood using improves the properties of the generated sequence and the coincidence occurs at 5th time step with the HCA state at the first time step, as well as the coincidence takes place through the next 11th time steps with HCA state on the 12th time step. The formed bit sequence during 20 time steps has the following form 00101010101010101010. The use of two inhomogeneous cells gives us a picture of the behavior of the generator, which is shown on Figure 7.

Figure 7. The behavior of the generator built on the basis of cellular automata with the Moore neighborhood and two inhomogeneous cells

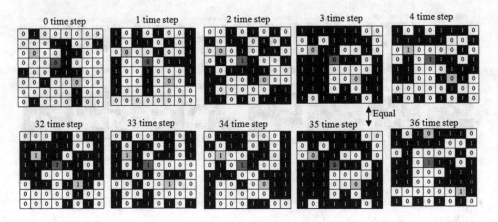

Generator based on cellular automata with two inhomogeneous cells also does not give stable operation. There are coincidences on the 35th time step. After that, all thirty five state arrays of the cellular automata are removed. Inhomogeneous cells change their location. The CAs states are beginning to remember from a 36th time step. A new count of the cellular automata arrays is began and the comparison is carried out again. The binary sequence has the following form: 00101001100110011011000110001111110. Inhomogeneous cells states at each time step is displayed in pairs: 00 00 00 01 11 10 10 01 11 10 10 00 10 11 10 11 11 11 10 10 11 10 11 00 00 10 11 10 01 01 00 11 11 01 00 11

An increase in the size of cellular automata of the generator allows to improve the quality of work and the number of inhomogeneous cell is increased.

HARDWARE IMPLEMENTATION OF PSEUDORANDOM NUMBER GENERATORS BASED ON CELLULAR AUTOMATA WITH INHOMOGENEOUS CELLS

The pseudorandom number generator based hybrid cellular automata with heterogeneous cells have a simpler structure than the previously described pseudorandom number generator. Moreover cells may also be in a one of two states. Besides, the pseudorandom number generator requires a large volume of memory. The structure of such a pseudorandom number generator is shown on Figure 8.

Figure 8. The structure of the pseudorandom number generator with inhomogeneous cells

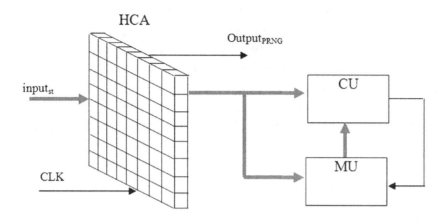

The pseudorandom number generator contains the hybrid cellular automata, the comparison unit (CU) and a memory unit (MU). At the initial time the hybrid cellular automata in the initial state is set. The states of the homogeneous and inhomogeneous cells are assigned. A local transition function is selected. The size of the hybrid cellular automata and the number inhomogeneous cells are being selected. The main cell, which on the output form a pseudo-random sequence are being selected.

After the initial settings the pseudorandom number generator begins to operate. At each discrete time step the hybrid cellular automata changes its state. The homogeneous cell implement a local transition function for homogeneous cells and inhomogeneous cells perform local transition function for inhomogeneous cells. Each state of the hybrid cellular automata in MU at each time step are recorded. All recorded states in MU are compared with the current state of the hybrid cellular automata formed at this time step. Comparison is carried out in CU and if the current state does not coincide with any of the previous states of HCA, the code of the current status is written in the MU. If the code of the current state of the hybrid cellular automata coincides with one of the previously recorded hybrid cellular automata code, the MU is cleared.

If on the current time step was coincidence, the inhomogeneous cells change their location in the hybrid cellular automata area. The coincidence of the current state of HCA tells us about what repetition HCA states is being began, and consequently a bit sequence is repeated.

To avoid repetition, inhomogeneous cells change its own coordinates in the field of HCA. This situation allows to avoid of another cycle of the bit sequence. After resetting MU at the next time step is being began the memorizing hybrid cellular automata states at subsequent time steps. Also, each successive state of the hybrid cellular automata is compared with all the stored states of the hybrid cellular automata, which with the new coordinates of the inhomogeneous cells are obtained.

To increase the length of the period of formation of a pseudorandom sequence is important choice of changes algorithm of the coordinate's inhomogeneous cell.

The realization of a pseudorandom number generator on the based hybrid cellular automata requires the construction of cells that can perform two functions. The cell can also perform only one of two a local transition function at each time step.

The cell can be represented by the following structure (Figure 9).

The hybrid cellular automata cell contains the flip-flop (T), the commutator (C) and two functional units (FU1, FU2). The first functional unit FU1 perform a local transition function for homogeneous cells and the second FU2 calculates a local transition function for an inhomogeneous cell. The

Figure 9. Block-diagram of HCA cells

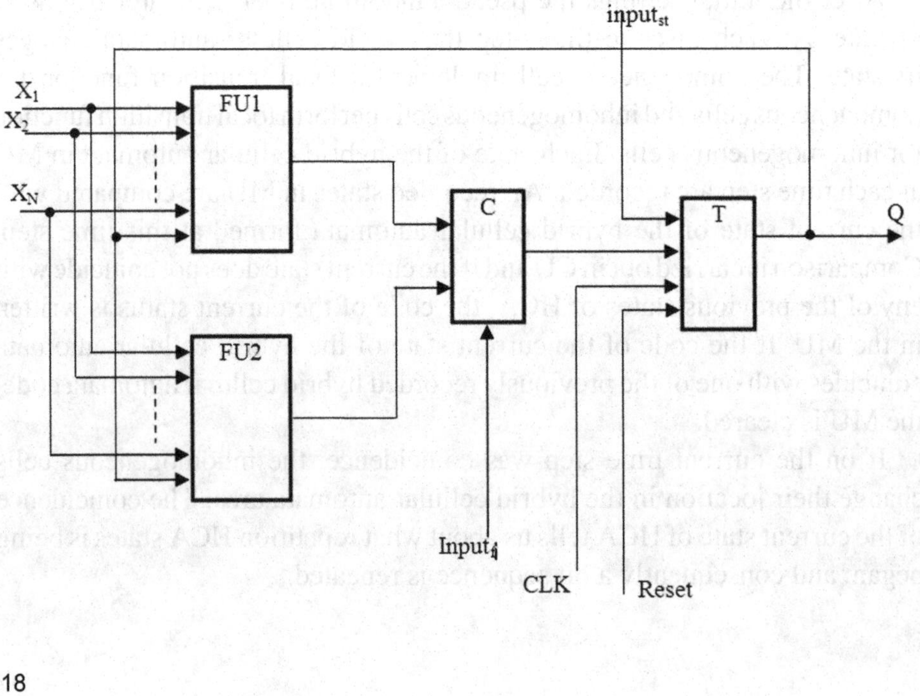

commutator connects to the own output of one of their outputs of FU1 and FU2. The signal from the switch output controls the flip-flop state by the every arriving pulse to the CLK input. The switch operation is controlled by a signal on its control input (input$_f$). For automata with memory the flip-flop output Q is connected to one of the inputs FU1 and FU2.

Thus, a cellular automata cell interface has the form is shown on Figure 10.

In accordance with Figure 10, the block diagram of the algorithm for the operation of the CA cell with an inhomogeneous cell on Figure 11 is presented.

All the notations on the block-diagram of the algorithm (Figure 11) are similar to the notations that in Figure 26 in chapter 4 are shown. This algorithm describes the majority function, which is represented by the formula

$$f_2\left(t\right) = Majority\left(X_1, X_2,..., X_8, X_{cell}\right)$$

The majority function forms one value from N + 1 arguments. The values of the arguments are chosen from the binary set {0, 1}. The result of the majority function is "0" if at the inputs the number of logical "0" signals are greater than the logical "1" signals and vice versa.

At the initial time step, the cell is set to the ground state and the mode of homogeneous work of the homogeneous cell (Gt) = 0) or an inhomogeneous cell are chosen (G(t)=1).

If the cell is running in a inhomogeneous cell mode, at each time step it implements the majority function [$f_2\left(t\right) = Majority\left(X_1, X_2,..., X_8, X_{cell}\right)$], and if the cell works in the homogeneous cell mode, then it realizes the function of addition by modulo 2 over the signals of the states of the neighborhood cells and the eigenstate. The number of time steps is set in advance.

Figure 10. Graphical representation of a one hybrid cellular automata cells interface

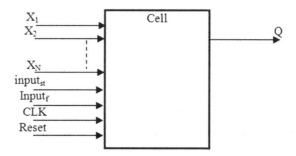

Figure 11. The block-diagram of the algorithm of the CA cell with an inhomogeneous cell, presented in Figure 10

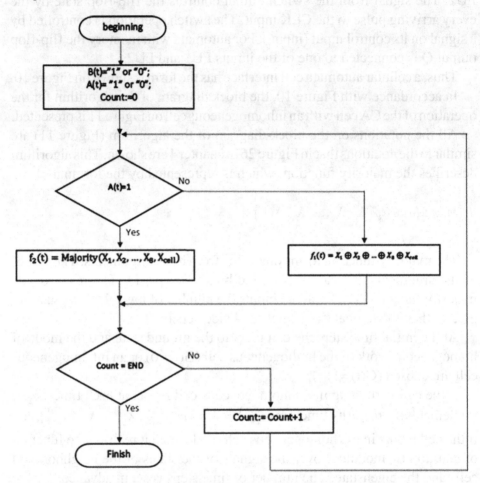

The main difficulty in the implementation of the pseudorandom number generator is to implement way to change of a location coordinates of the inhomogeneous cell. There are two options to choose of coordinates. The first method uses less electrical connections, which are arranged vertically and horizontally. The selection of cells is carried out at the intersection of the vertical and horizontal conductors. The second method uses the presence of so many connections, which corresponds to the number of the cellular automata cells.

Coordinates can be calculated by using a mathematical function. The value of the time step number may be an argument of this function. For example, for the fifth time step, the next coordinates will have values (X+5, Y+5). Another example may be a calculation of the generated number of zeros and ones. If the number of zeros is equal to 5, and the number of ones is 7, the following coordinates will have the values (X+5, Y+7).

Inhomogeneous cells become homogeneous at the next time step after the coincidence of a hybrid cellular automata states. Each inhomogeneous cell makes a constant change into the cellular automata states. The greater the inhomogeneous cells, the greater the uncertainty is introduced into the work of cellular automata. At the same time inhomogeneous cell can perform the several different local transition functions. This process requires additional researches and today is little studied.

PSEUDORANDOM NUMBER GENERATORS BASED ON CELLULAR AUTOMATA WITH INHOMOGENEOUS NEIGHBORHOODS

Earlier we used the hybrid cellular automata, which used the same neighborhood, but a different local transition function. Different local transition function in cells of one cellular automata and are created as the hybrid cellular automata. If in the cellular automata structure among all the cells there are cells whose state depends on the cells that constitute the neighborhood of another form, this cellular automata is also called a hybrid cellular automata.

Number neighborhood cell of the homogeneous and inhomogeneous cells may be equal or may vary. At the same time the neighborhoods forms is also different. If the hybrid cellular automata cells have different forms of neighborhoods and an equal number of cells, then we say that these cells are equipotent neighborhood. The cells may also perform one or different the local transition function.

The model, which describes the work of the one hybrid cellular automata cell, has the following form.

$$
b_{i,j}(t+1) = \begin{cases} f_{\text{hom}}\left[x_1(t), x_2(t), ..., x_N(t)\right], & if \quad C_F(t) = 0 \\ f_{in\,\text{hom}}\left[x_1'(t), x_2'(t), ..., x_K'(t)\right], & if \quad C_F(t) = 1 \\ b_{i,j}(t), & in \quad othe \quad case \end{cases} \tag{2}
$$

where

N – the number of neighborhood cells for a homogeneous cell;
K – the amount of neighborhood cells for an inhomogeneous cell;
$C_F(t)$ - cell behavior control signal at time t;
$x_l(t)$ - signal at the l-th input of the homogeneous cell that comes from the neighborhood cells output under number l $\left(l = \overline{1, N}\right)$;
$x_d'(t)$ - signal at the d-th input of the inhomogeneous cell which come from the output of a neighborhood cell under the number d $\left(d = \overline{1, N}\right)$.

The numbering of neighborhood cells for different types of neighborhood is different. Numbering an example for the von Neumann neighborhood and the Moore neighborhood are presented on Figure 12. In this example, a neighborhood are of different power (amount of the neighborhood cells), but may implement the same functions with a different number of the arguments

For von Neumann neighborhood N=4 (or K=4), and for Moor neighborhood N=8 (or K=8). Example of the pseudorandom number generator implementation with two or one inhomogeneous cells is presented on Figure 13.

The example shows that the increase of the inhomogeneous cells extends the period of the formed sequence. The greatest number of coincidences gives the cellular automata with low power neighborhoods. An interesting property is the use of cellular automata with various forms of neighborhoods, which

Figure 12. An example of a numbering of the neighborhood cells for homogeneous and inhomogeneous cells

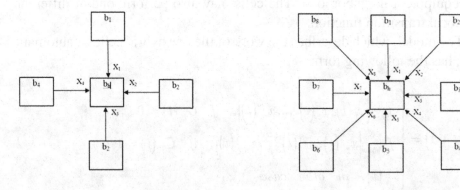

a) for Neyman neighborhood   a) for Moor neighborhood

Figure 13. An example of a pseudorandom number generator operation for one or two inhomogeneous cells. Homogeneous cells have von Neumann neighborhood and inhomogeneous cells - Moore's neighborhood

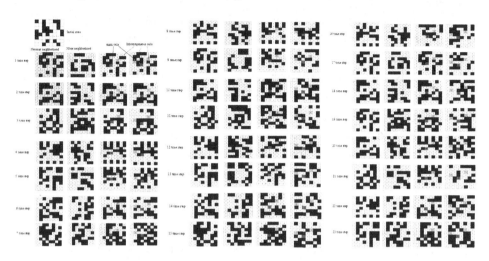

give the same length and the beginning of the cycles due to the introduction cells in of one of the cellular automata with neighborhoods of the other cellular automata. In our example, this behavior is given a homogeneous cellular automata, in which all cells have the Moore neighborhood and inhomogeneous cellular automata with von Neumann neighborhood. At the same time inhomogeneous cellular automata has an inhomogeneous cell with Moore's neighborhood. Of great importance is also the location of the inhomogeneous cells.

From Figure 12 shows that the 2nd and 3rd cellular automata have the same cycles that begin from the 1 and 17 time steps. However, the states of the two cellular automata are different from each other. The use of two inhomogeneous cells at the above example does not allow cycles. This allows us to conclude that the increase of the number of inhomogeneous cell increase the length of the period, as well as improves the properties of the bit sequence. In the example we used the same initial settings and different amounts of the inhomogeneous cells. This difference consist in the location of the second inhomogeneous cell in the second pseudorandom number generator.

The generated sequences have the following form

$Q_1 = 000011100000111100000111;$

$Q_2 = 0000011010000111100010001.$

In the first sequence is observed a cycle of the five zeros and 3 units. In the second sequence, the cycle is not observed. Introduction inhomogeneous cells in the initial time steps influences on the cell state in the own neighborhoods. With each time step inhomogeneous cell influences on the cells, which are located at a distance greater than one cell than the current time step. Therefore, we are seeing a big change, which differ from the homogeneous CA with the same structure.

In the above example, the homogeneous local transition function is used. However, there may be used inhomogeneous local transition function together with inhomogeneous neighborhoods. Thus, can be used various combinations of inhomogeneous cells. Inhomogeneous cells can combine inhomogeneous local transition function and inhomogeneous neighborhoods in the same cell, and may only have inhomogeneous local transition function and only inhomogeneous neighborhood. An example of using such combinations and cellular automata evolution is presented on Figure 14.

The results showed that the inhomogeneous cells influence to the main homogeneous cell occurs through the number of time steps equal to the lower number of cells between the main cell and the nearest inhomogeneous cell. At the same time on the first steps time the different from the state of homogeneous cellular automata is observed in neighboring cells inhomogeneous cells.

On Figure 14 in the left column is shown homogeneous cellular automata with Von Neumann neighborhood and XOR function. The second column shows the evolution of the HCA with inhomogeneous cells. Inhomogeneous cell state depends on the Moore neighborhood cells. The third column indicates hybrid cellular automata with inhomogeneous cells that implement local transition function as a majority function on the basis of the von Neumann neighborhood. In the fourth column is shown the evolution of the hybrid cellular automata with two inhomogeneous cells. The upper inhomogeneous cell differs the using of majority function, and the bottom inhomogeneous cell differs the using of the Moore neighborhood. Inhomogeneous cells have the same coordinates for each variant PRNG.

For our example, significant differences in the area of main cells begin from the sixth time step, as between the top inhomogeneous cell and the main cell is located 5 homogeneous cells. At the output of each PRNG are formed the following bit sequence

Figure 14. An example of the influence of inhomogeneous cells with different combinations of the inhomogeneous local transition function and of the inhomogeneous neighborhoods

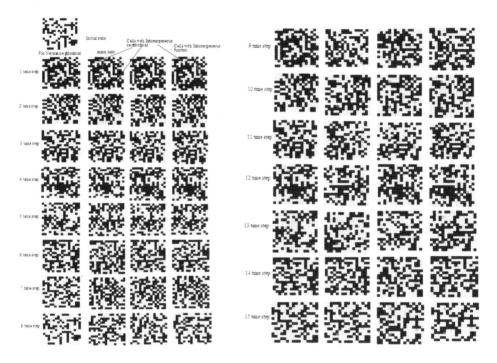

$Q_1 = 001010101000001,$

$Q_2 = 001010000101101,$

$Q_3 = 001010101000001.$

The generated sequences do not have the large groups of ones and zeros. The statistical properties of these generators with various inhomogeneous cells are investigated by various tests. The results of these studies are shown in the following chapters.

The cell of the hybrid cellular automata, which comprises an inhomogeneous cells with inhomogeneous neighborhood is shown on Figure 15. On the data inputs of the function block (FU) are connected the outputs of the nearest neighborhood cells with a radius r=1. For a rectangular coverage such cells is eight. These cells make up the Moore neighborhood.

Figure 15. Functional scheme of the hybrid cellular automata cell with an inhomogeneous neighborhoods and with a radius r=1

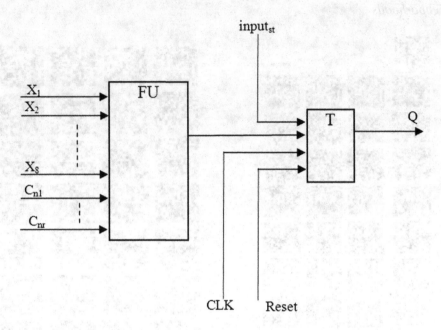

Signals that are arrive at the control inputs control the operation of the FU ($C_{n1},...,C_{nr}$). Control inputs given combination of data inputs (x_1, ..., x_8) that implement selected LTF for an inhomogeneous or homogeneous cells. The difficulty lies in the technical implementation of FU.

Chapter 6
Pseudorandom Number Generators Based on Asynchronous Cellular Automata and Cellular Automata With Inhomogeneous Cells

ABSTRACT

The sixth chapter deals with the construction of pseudo-random number generators based on a combination of two cellular automata, which were considered in the previous chapters. The generator is constructed based on two cellular automata. The first cellular automaton controls the location of the active cell on the second cellular automaton, which realizes the local state function for each cell. The active cell on the second cellular automaton is the main cell and from its output bits of the bit sequence are formed at the output of the generator. As the first cellular automaton, an asynchronous cellular automaton is used in this chapter, and a synchronous cellular automaton is used as the second cellular automaton. In this case, the active cell of the second cellular automaton realizes another local function at each time step and is inhomogeneous. The algorithm for the work of a cell of a combined cellular automaton for implementing a generator and its hardware implementation are presented.

DOI: 10.4018/978-1-5225-2773-2.ch006

MODELS AND ALGORITHMS OF PSEUDORANDOM NUMBER GENERATOR OPERATION

We have considered the possibility of building a pseudorandom number generator based on a cellular automata. In fact, this cellular automata is a key element of the pseudorandom number generator and also determines its behavior. The changes its state is carried out by the internal organization of the cellular automata. However, the interaction of a several cellular automata is curious. Until now, are not shown and the various options to influence the behavior of one cellular automata by other CA are not considered.

How CAs can influence each other's behavior?

1. The CA can change the state of all the cells.
2. CA may change the state of the selected cell at each time step.
3. CA can modify the structure of the neighborhood of one or all of the cells.
4. CA can modify the local transfer function of one of CA cells, or all of the CA cells.
5. CA can change the location of the main cells or of the inhomogeneous cells.

Thus, the above influence the cellular automata on cellular automata will be begin from dividing them onto controlled cellular automata (cellular automata, which receives control signals) and the control cellular automata (the cellular automata, which generates control signals).

Let us consider the influence of ACA on the HCA. Both of those cellular automata in the previous sections are considered. The first ACA operates as an asynchronous cellular automata. It has only one active cell changes its state at each time step of the ACA work. The second HCA function as a classic cellular automata with inhomogeneous cells.

The outputs of the each ACA cell to the control inputs of the respective HCA cells are connected. The ACA output signals change the behavior of the corresponding HCA cell. The simplest example of the PRNG controlling based on the HCA is a change in the location of the major HCA cell. The main HCA cell generates a sequence of bits at each time step. The first ACA influences on the coordinates of the main HCA cells by changing of the coordinates location of the active ACA cell. This allows to enter the additional uncertainty in the distribution of elements in the output sequence.

In this case, the active cell may be an inhomogeneous cell, and we can remove the constant comparison of current the HCA states with HCA state arrays, which at the previous time steps are formed. This increases the performance of the generator.

The behavior of the HCA cells can be described by the same model that in the previous sections is proposed. All the HCA cells change their state, but only one active cell generates the next bit sequence at the output at any given time step. At the same time, the active cell changes its location in each subsequent time step. An example of the operation of such cellular automata is shown on the Figure 1.

From the figure, we see that each subsequent bit of the formed sequence is calculated by the formula.

$$
Q\left(t+1\right) = \\
f_{i,j}\left[x_{i,j}^1\left(t\right), x_{i,j}^2\left(t\right), ..., x_{i,j}^N\left(t\right), x_{i,j}^0\left(t\right), C_{i,j}^{act,l}\left(t\right)\right].
\tag{1}
$$

This model shows that the output bit at time step t depends on the value of the active cell output signal with the coordinates (i, j), and on the signal at one of the active inputs $C_{i,j}^{act,l}\left(t\right)$ of this cell. If $\forall C_{i,j}^{act,l}\left(t\right) = 1$, the cell with the coordinates (i, j) becomes into the active state and the data output of this cell to the output of the pseudorandom number generator is connected at time step t. The situation of the connection of the information output of the active cell to the output of the pseudorandom number generator is shown on the Figure 2.

However, unlike the previous the pseudorandom number generator in this pseudorandom number generator all the cellular automata cells change their state at each time point. In addition, the active cell performs the same function as the other non-active cells.

Figure 1. An example of the functioning of a complex cellular automata

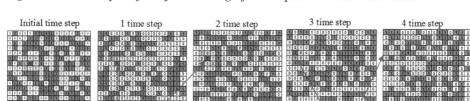

129

Figure 2. The graphical representation of the cells connection situation to the output of the pseudorandom number generator

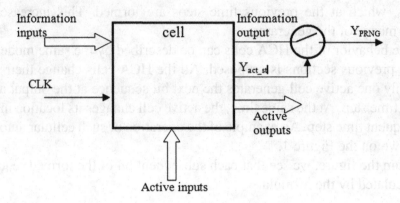

In order to make more the uncertainty in the pseudorandom number generator operation the active cell must perform as a majority LTF function or other a suitable function. This the pseudorandom number generator implements the function of the synchronous cellular automata, and to form a bit at the pseudorandom number generator output the asynchronous cellular automata operation principle is used. Examples of such the pseudorandom number generator operation are shown in Figure 3 and Figure 4.

For the first example (Figure 3) 000100110 bit sequence was formed, and for the second example (Figure 4) the following bit sequence was formed 0001......

From these examples, it is seen that the active cell can change its state in accordance with the LTF of all the cells or according to a function of the majority of cells. This approach will give a various bit sequences at the output of the pseudorandom number generator. In a first embodiment, SCA can quickly enter in a repeatable cycle, and in the second case, the SC can always change your condition during several time steps. However, in the second case the pseudorandom number generator can enter in a repeatable cycle. In fact, such the pseudorandom number generator is being built on the hybrid SC with a one an inhomogeneous cell that changes its the location at each time step.

The introduction of additional stationary inhomogeneous cells reduces the possibility of appearing of a repeated cycle. In practice, this cycle is very long and the probability of coincidence of the arrays of the states, at some the point in time is very small. This is due to the fact that one of the cells (the

Figure 3. An example of the pseudorandom number generator implemented on the SCA with asynchronous principle of generating an output bit without majority changing of the active state of the cell

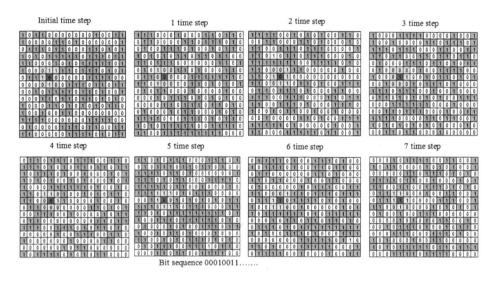

Figure 4. An example of the pseudorandom number generator implemented on the SCA with asynchronous principle of generating an output bit with majority changing of the active state of the cell

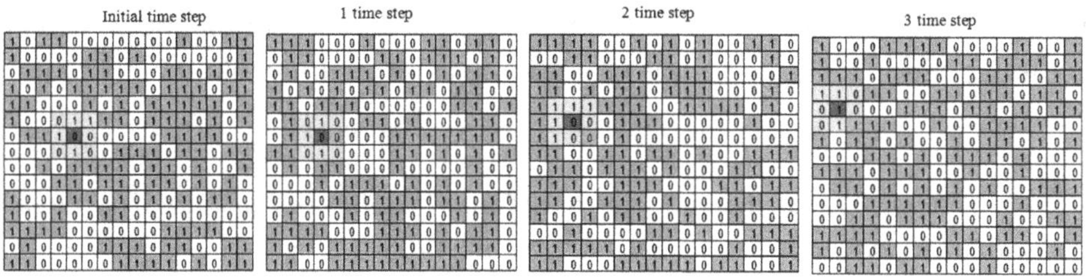

active cell) "moves" along the cellular automata field. But this coincidence of arrays is only possible under the certain initial cellular automata settings. Although in this is the set of the equal sequences. However, these bit sequences are different locations in the total generated sequence. This does not indicate on a repetition cycle.

It is very difficult theoretically to calculate the end of the cycle of the bit sequence and the beginning of the new repeat cycle since the location of separate cells in cellular automata field is changing. This change occurs during the operation of the pseudorandom number generator. A more reasonable approach is the construction of the pseudorandom number generator model and to choose the best variant on the basis of research.

Variants of the complex pseudorandom number generator that are implemented by the different cellular automata may be many. For example, the state of an inhomogeneity can be continuously is passed from cell to cell, and the active cell may be stationary. All these variants have not yet been investigated and we are not aware of their operation in practice. Although such the pseudorandom number generator constructed on the basis of the combined cellular automata show us good prospects for their research. They increase the number of possible states and, consequently, they increase the life period of the pseudorandom number generator.

HARDWARE IMPLEMENTATION OF PSEUDORANDOM NUMBER GENERATOR BASED ON THE COMBINED CELLULAR AUTOMATA

Hardware implementation of pseudorandom number generator based on the combined cellular automata may be represented by two the embodiments. The first embodiment on the using of two separate CA is based (Figure 5).

In this structure two cellular automata are used. One the cellular automata has an asynchronous operation principle, and the second cellular automata is a cellular automata as hybrid or synchronous. The outputs of all cells of the

Figure 5. The general structure of the pseudorandom number generator based on two cellular automata with the different organizations

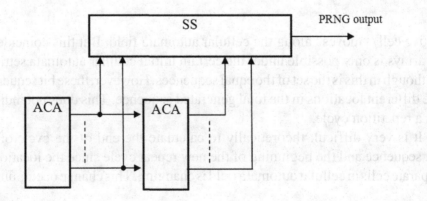

first and second cellular automata are connected to respective inputs of the switching system (SS). The output of the pseudorandom number generator is output SS. The outputs of one of the cellular automata are control. They control the connection of the selected synchronous cellular automata cell output to the output of the pseudorandom number generator at the selected time step. As control cellular automata, we can choose the asynchronous cellular automata, since it has only one cell as active at each discrete time step. From the output of this active cell a logic '1' signal comes in on one of the control inputs of the switching system. According to this one of the synchronous cellular automata cell output connected to the pseudorandom number generator output via SS. It is also A situation is possible when the state of the active asynchronous cellular automata cell is an additional argument for a local transition function of the synchronous cellular automata cells, which has the same coordinates. In this case, all synchronous cellular automata cells perform local transition function from the neighborhood cells signals, and one cell performs the local transition function from neighborhood cells signals and from asynchronous cellular automata active cells signal in the selected time step. The function of this cell has more than one argument local transition function of the remaining cells. The same cell transmits a signal to the output of the pseudorandom number generator. In this case, the output value of the next element of the bit sequence is determined by the function

$$b_{i,j}\left(t+1\right) = f\left[b_{i,j}^1\left(t\right), b_{i,j}^2\left(t\right), ..., b_{i,j}^l\left(t\right), b_{i,j}^{ACA}\left(t\right)\right]. \tag{2}$$

This function can typically be XOR function. Here $b_{i,j}^{ACA}\left(t\right)$ has a signal value on the output of the active cell with the coordinates (i, j) of the control asynchronous cellular automata.

Based on the first embodiment the division by two cellular automata is performed. However, it would be easier to combine in a single cell the function of such cellular automata.

The second variant is based on the union of two cellular automata in one. In this case, the implementation is carried out in the same cell. The graphical picture of the cell interface of the second embodiment is presented on Figure 6.

The graph-scheme of the algorithm of functioning of the cell of the combined CA on Figure 7 is presented.

As in the previous algorithms, the initial settings of the information and active states are carried out, and the counter of the time steps is set to zero

Figure 6. The cell interface by the second embodiment

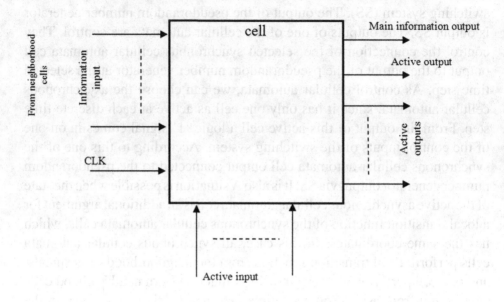

(Chapter 4's Figure 26 and Chapter 5's Figure 11). The condition of the active state ($A(t) = 1$) of the cell is checked and if the cell has an active state, it realizes the following local function

$$f\left[\begin{array}{l} x_{i,j}^1(t), x_{i,j}^2(t), ..., x_{i,j}^N(t), b_{i,j}^0(t), f_{i,j}^{act} \\ \left[x_{i,j}^1(t), x_{i,j}^2(t), ..., x_{i,j}^N(t), b_{i,j}^0(t)\right] \end{array}\right].$$

In addition, a condition is checked that determines the number of the time step (even or odd). According to this condition, the local transition functions on the odd [$f_{act}^1(t) = \max\left(X_i = 1\right)$] or on an even [$f_{act}^0(t) = \max\left(X_i = 0\right)$] time steps.

If the cell is not active ($A(t) = 0$), then the following local function is performed

$$f\left[x_{i,j}^1(t), x_{i,j}^2(t), ..., x_{i,j}^N(t), b_{i,j}^0(t)\right],$$

and then the signals at the active cell inputs ($C_{i,j}$) are analyzed. If at one of the active inputs has a logical "1" signal, the cell goes into the active state ($A(t)=1$).

Figure 7. Graph-scheme of the algorithm of functioning of a cell of a combined CA

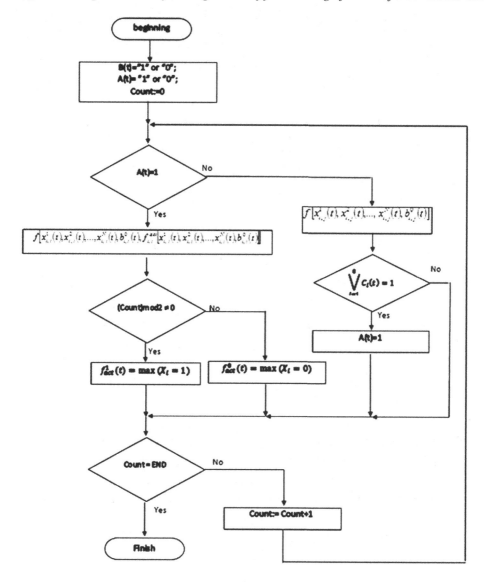

With each next time step, the cell functions according to the described algorithm.

As we can see cell interface is different from the previously reviewed embodiments. However, the cell has a different internal structure, which differs significantly from the previously reviewed structure. The internal structure of cells, we can be divided into the several functional parts (Figure 8).

135

Figure 8. The functional circuit of the internal structure of the cell

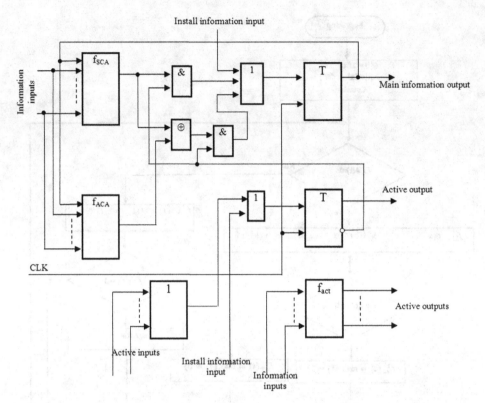

The first part is the informational. It implements two local transition functions and sets the information state of a cell at each time step.

The second part implements an asynchronous operational principle of the combined cellular automata. The second part also implements the formation and the transmission of the active signal at each subsequent time step, if it were active for the current time step. In fact, the active part may be similar to the previously reviewed cellular structures of the asynchronous cellular automata.

The information part is somewhat different from other realizations. It consists of a combinational circuit that implements the local transition function for the synchronous cellular automata, and of the combinational circuit that implements the local transition function for the asynchronous cellular automata. If the cell is not active, only the implementation of the local transition function circuit for synchronous cellular automata operates. If a cell is active, both circuits are functioning, and the generalized XOR function is realized, which sets the information state to information flip-flop

T. The active cell also generates a signal of logical "1" on one of the active outputs to the next time step.

Thus, the combined cellular automata cells work can be described by the following mathematical model

$$b_{i,j}(t+1) =$$

$$\begin{cases} f\left[x_{i,j}^1(t), x_{i,j}^2(t), \dots, x_{i,j}^N(t), b_{i,j}^0(t)\right], & if \quad \forall C_{i,j}^l = 0 \\ f\left[x_{i,j}^1(t), x_{i,j}^2(t), \dots, x_{i,j}^N(t), b_{i,j}^0(t), f_{i,j}^{act}\left[x_{i,j}^1(t), x_{i,j}^2(t), \dots, x_{i,j}^N(t), b_{i,j}^0(t)\right]\right] & if \quad \forall C_{i,j}^l = 1 \\ b_{i,j}(t), & in \quad othe \quad case \end{cases}$$

$$(3)$$

where

$b_{i,j}^0(t)$ - state of the cell with the coordinates (i, j) at time t;

$f\left[x_{i,j}^1(t), x_{i,j}^2(t), \dots, x_{i,j}^N(t), b_{i,j}^0(t)\right]$ - the local transition function, which is performed by the cell with the coordinates (i, j) not being in an active state;

$f_{i,j}^{act}\left[x_{i,j}^1(t), x_{i,j}^2(t), \dots, x_{i,j}^N(t), b_{i,j}^0(t)\right]$ - function, which also is being performed by the cell and it is in an active state;

$f\begin{bmatrix} x_{i,j}^1(t), x_{i,j}^2(t), \dots, x_{i,j}^N(t), b_{i,j}^0(t), f_{i,j}^{act} \\ \left[x_{i,j}^1(t), x_{i,j}^2(t), \dots, x_{i,j}^N(t), b_{i,j}^0(t)\right] \end{bmatrix}$ - the generalization local transition

function, which is being performed by the cell, being in active state;

$C_{i,j}^l$ - value at l-th active input of the cell.

Consider the example of the cell work. For this purpose we assume that local transition functions inactive cells and active cells is XOR function, as well as a generalized local function is also a XOR function. We will use the Moore neighborhood (N = 8), and we will take the following states of the neighborhood cells.

$X^1(t)=0$; $X^2(t)=1$; $X^3(t)=0$; $X^4(t)=0$; $X^5(t)=1$; $X^6(t)=1$; $X^7(t)=1$; $X^8(t)=1$.
State of the cells at time t $X^0(t)=1$.
Then the function f[]=$0\oplus1\oplus0\oplus0\oplus1\oplus1\oplus1\oplus1=1$.
f^{act}[]=$0\oplus0\oplus1\oplus0\oplus0\oplus1\oplus1\oplus1\oplus1=1$.
f^c[]=$1\oplus1=0$.

Thus, in accordance with our example at time t the pseudorandom number generator generates bits whose value is 0.

We see that the state of the active cell depends on a three local functions. These functions may be different. Software implementation is time consuming, and hardware implementation drastically reduces the spent time.

The combined pseudorandom number generator has a great prospect not only for the construction of the pseudorandom number generator, but also to describe the interaction of several dynamic processes with the help of a homogeneous environment.

Chapter 7

Pseudorandom Number Generators Based on Cellular Automata With the Hexagonal Coverage

ABSTRACT

The seventh chapter describes approaches to constructing pseudo-random number generators based on cellular automata with a hexagonal coating. Several variants of cellular automata with hexagonal coating are considered. Asynchronous cellular automata with hexagonal coating are used. To simulate such cellular automata with software, a hexagonal coating was formed using an orthogonal coating. At the same time, all odd lines shifted to the cell floor to the right or to the left. The neighborhood of each cell contains six neighboring cells that have one common side with one cell of neighborhood. The chapter considers the behavior of cellular automata for different sizes and different initial settings. The behavior of cellular automata with various local functions is described, as well as the behavior of the cellular automaton with an additional bit inverting the state of the cell in each time step of functioning.

DOI: 10.4018/978-1-5225-2773-2.ch007

THE PRINCIPLES OF ORGANIZATION OF THE PSEUDORANDOM NUMBER GENERATOR BASED ON THE CELLULAR AUTOMATA WITH A HEXAGONAL COVERAGE

Earlier we looked at the different types of coatings of the CA area and various geometric shapes of the cells. The most popular of the cell geometric shapes are the triangular, rectangular and hexagonal shapes. They give complete coverage of the CA area. Accordingly, various lattices are used, in sites of which are located the CA cells. In addition, cellular automata with different geometric shapes of the cells organizes the various forms of neighborhoods.

At the moment, little attention are paying the specialists the combination of cells with a variety of geometric shapes in one cellular automata. Especially no sense to use different geometric forms of the cells for the implementation of elementary cellular automata. The combination of cells with a variety of geometric shapes is used for the realization of a two-dimensional cellular automata. At the same time the cells forms are adjusted so that the geometric coverage was complete with the maximum density.

A number of advantages have hexagonal shape of the cells (Belan & Motornyuk, 2013; Nicoladie, 2014; Bilan, Motornyuk, & Bilan, 2014; Konstantinos, 2011; Avolio, Ambrosio, Gregorio, Rongo, & Spataro, 2001; Avolio, Di Gregorio, Mantovani, Pasuto, Rongo, Silvano, & Spataro, 1999; Basurto, Leon, Martinez, & Seck-Tuoh-Mora, 2013). The hexagonal coating reduces the influence of the ladder effect, and also gives good results in solving many problems.

A neighborhood of the cells that have a common side with the adjacent cell, is the set of main the cells (Figure 1).

The hexagonal coating provides unambiguous coating. Each cell has only six nearest neighbors. For the simulation of the hexagonal coating on area, divided into rectangular cells, it necessary to shift all the even lines right to the half of the cage (Figure 2).

Cellular automata with a hexagonal covering (HCCA) has a different evolution compared to cellular automata with a rectangular covering (Figure 3).

The edge cells are not change own states at every time step of an evolution for CA with hexagonal and triangular coverings. However, their condition has been influenced to the state of the neighboring cells. All the neighborhood for each of the coating are consisted of the nearest cells which have a common side with the control cell.

Figure 1. The cells of the main neighborhood with a hexagonal covering

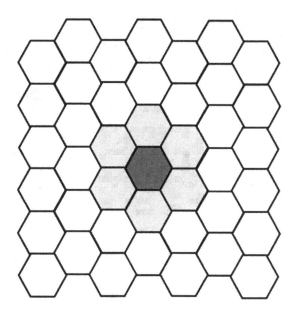

Figure 2. The modeling of the hexagonal covering with a rectangular segmentation of cellular automata area

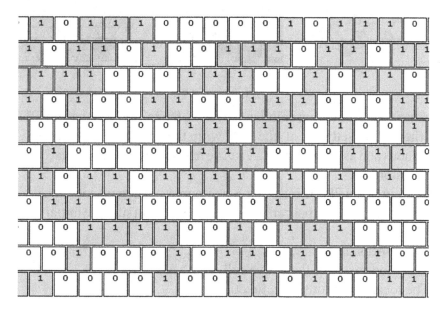

Figure 3. The CA evolution with different forms of a coverage

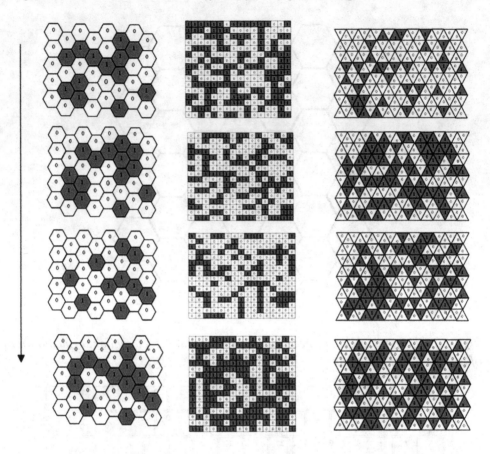

For hexagonal covering cellular automata, the initial settings are different from the initial settings of the CA with the orthogonal covering. The synchronous and asynchronous CA can be realized by the hexagonal covering cellular automata.

Modeling of the PRNG based on synchronous hexagonal covering cellular automata with a fixed output cell was taken into account such the initial settings.

1. The dimension of CA.
2. The coordinates of the active cell.
3. The local conditions cells function.
4. The initial distribution of the cell states.

For asynchronous CA are also given a local transitions function of the active cells to one of the neighborhood cells. In the asynchronous CA the cells can be in two states, and perform two local functions.

One function calculates the state of the cell, and the other function determines the active cell in the next time.

The dimension of the CA in the software model is specified by the number of rows and by the number of cells in each row. Similarly, the coordinates of the active cell are being specified.

It is important successfully select a local function for the normal operation of pseudorandom number generator. If we unsuccessfully to select the function of the local states of the active cells and the local transition function for the active cells, the CA can repeat their state, which is unacceptable for a pseudorandom number generator.

For many applications the initial state of the cells can be specified by the user or randomly.

The pseudorandom number generator based on synchronous CA that uses XOR function does not allow to achieve high quality of the generated pseudorandom bit sequence. An example of the results of such a pseudorandom number generator is presented on Figure 4. The sequence of numbers have been formed by 8 bits and has bad statistical properties.

The pseudorandom number generator construction based on ACA with a hexagonal mosaic and one active cell allows to obtain pseudo-random bit

Figure 4. The results of the pseudorandom number generator operation based on synchronous hexagonal covering cellular automata with local XOR function

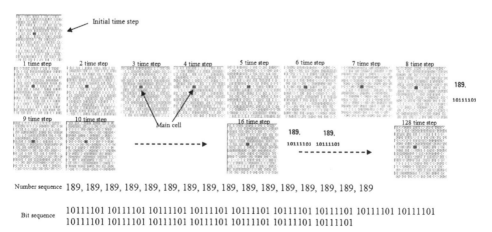

Number sequence 189, 189, 189, 189, 189, 189, 189, 189, 189, 189, 189, 189, 189, 189, 189, 189

Bit sequence 10111101 10111101 10111101 10111101 10111101 10111101 10111101 10111101 10111101
10111101 10111101 10111101 10111101 10111101 10111101 10111101

sequence with good statistical properties. At each new time step, an active cell becomes one of the six neighboring cells of the active cell on a previous time step (Figure 5).

When choosing a local function is necessary to determine equal probability of direction of motion of the active cells of the six directions. Each new direction is determined by the LTF and the states of the neighborhood cells. A result of analyzing of the "movement" of the active cell have been defined a few local functions, which are performed on paired and unpaired time steps.

LTF is implemented so that the older cell is selected (the numbering of cells is shown on Figure 6) from a larger number of states (more logical "0" or "1") in the neighborhood of the active cell. In unpaired time step is selected a neighborhood cell that has a biggest numbering among cells that are in a state of logical "1". In the even-numbered time step - older cells from the cells with a logic "0".

In addition, for reliable operation of pseudorandom number generator, the result output from the active cell have been formed with the additional bits. The value of those bit is read from the output of one of the CA cells. The cell, which forms an additional bits at each time step, is being chosen by a

Figure 5. Example of a cell states on two adjacent time steps

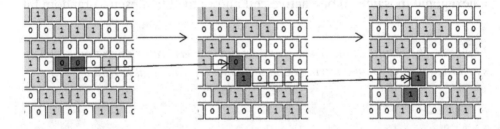

Figure 6. The encoding of the neighborhood cells with a hexagonal coverage

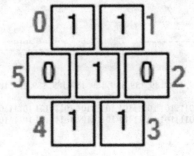

given law. In the simplest case, the additional cells are selected as a result of the linear scan of a CA (Figure 7). At the same time, the reading of the state from the selected additional CA cells can occur in two modes: direct mode (no change of state) and the state of cells in the inverting mode during the formation of additional bits.

From the above example it is seen that up to a certain time step a sequence of numbers is repeated. This step is determined at the time when the state of the active cells differ in both embodiments or is different the cell states, which form an additional bit. For the first and second embodiment in our example the following sequences are formed:

For the first variant:

129, 224, 14, 12, 212, 241, 17, 29, 8, 165, 33, 220, 82, 170, 162, 90, 45, 81, 196, 6, 37, 106, 48, 94, 12, 14, 92, 124, 49, 217, 112, 241, 96, 138,   35.

For the second variant:

129, 224, 14, 12, 212, 241, 17, 29, 8, 165, 33, 220, 82, 170, 162, 90, 62, 142, 8, 38, 125, 116, 94, 123, 18, 90, 31, 125, 90, 205, 254, 113, 117, 220,

73.

Each number is represented by the eight bit binary code. The generated bit sequence is divided into groups of eight bits. Each group represents a decimal number of the sequence. After the number 90 (16 on the numbering number) are generated other bit sequences.

If we will not separate the cycles on the even-number and uneven and if to select in the neighborhood of at each iteration step only logical "0" or only a logical "1", the result leads to filling of cells states of opposite values (Figure 8).

Experiment showed that such local transition function implementing the movement of active states in the majority of the left - down. In addition, these directions provide a pseudo-random sequence with good statistical properties.

The pseudorandom number generator based on the homogeneous CA with fixed main cell does not generate pseudo-random sequence. An example of the pseudorandom number generator operation based on the homogeneous CA with local XOR function is presented on Figure 9.

The examples show that the sequences are not pseudorandom. The generated sequences as decimal numbers are presented. The each decimal number is

Figure 7. The PRNG state with using additional bits

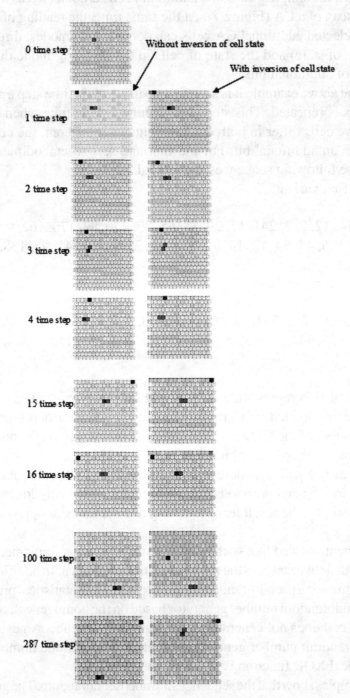

Figure 8. An example of the PRNG operation at a choice of only one state of log. "1" a) and log. "0" b)

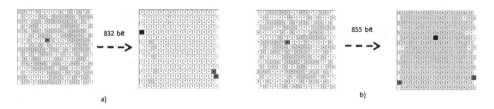

Figure 9. Examples of the pseudorandom number generator operation based on the homogeneous CA

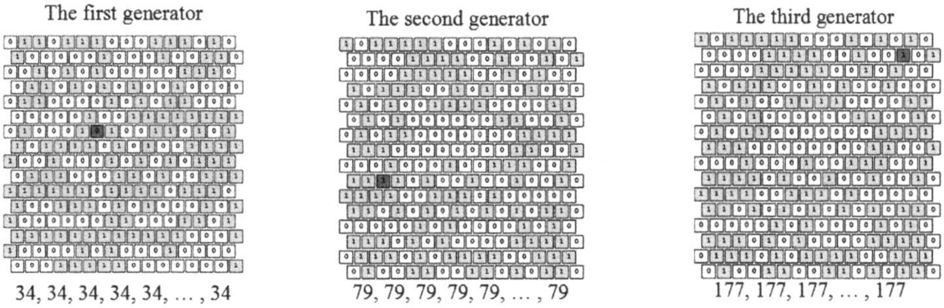

The first generator	The second generator	The third generator
34, 34, 34, 34, 34, ... , 34	79, 79, 79, 79, 79, ... , 79	177, 177, 177, ... , 177

represented by the eight-bit code. We see the different repeatable numbers for the main cells coordinates that from each other are differed.

Other distribution has a pseudorandom number generator with a local search function of a neighborhood cell with maximal number and with state of a logical "1" or a logical "0" (Figure 10).

In such the pseudorandom number generator active signal moves only in cells with a specified state. If is searched a neighborhood cell with the state of the logical "1", the active signal moves only in cells that have a logic "1" state. If the active cell becomes into a logical "0" state, then it will never be active. Over time the number of cells with a logic "1" state is reduced, and all the cells switching into a logical "0" state. A similar process occurs when choosing neighborhood cells, which have the state of the logical "0". In this case all the PRNG cells pass into the logical "1" state.

The results showed that to obtain high-quality pseudorandom bit sequence is necessary to periodically select cells with different states.

The use a local function that selects the cell neighborhood with the biggest number among a larger number of cells in a state of logical "1" or

Figure 10. Example of the pseudorandom number generator operation with search of maximal neighborhood cell that has the state of the logic "1" and "0"

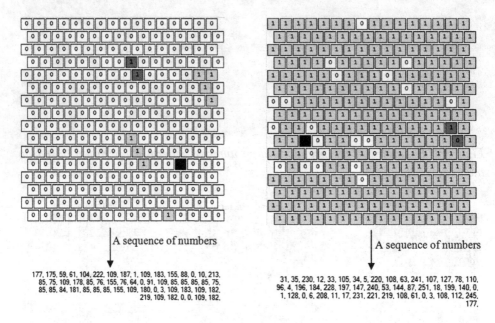

A sequence of numbers

177, 175, 59, 61, 104, 222, 109, 187, 1, 109, 183, 155, 88, 0, 10, 213,
85, 75, 109, 178, 85, 76, 155, 76, 64, 0, 91, 109, 85, 85, 85, 85, 75,
85, 85, 84, 181, 85, 85, 85, 155, 109, 180, 0, 3, 109, 183, 109, 182,
219, 109, 182, 0, 0, 109, 182.

A sequence of numbers

31, 35, 230, 12, 33, 105, 34, 5, 220, 108, 63, 241, 107, 127, 78, 110,
96, 4, 196, 184, 228, 197, 147, 240, 53, 144, 87, 251, 18, 199, 140, 0,
1, 128, 0, 6, 208, 11, 17, 231, 221, 219, 108, 61, 0, 3, 108, 112, 245,
177.

"0", the quality of the pseudorandom number generator allows to improve. For example, if of the cell neighborhood which have a logic "1" state is more than neighborhood cells having a logic "0" state, the is selected neighborhood cell, which is in the state of logical "1", and its number in the neighborhood is biggest among the other neighborhood cells in state of a logical "1". An example of the pseudorandom number generator operation with a local function is presented on Figure 11.

The example shows good statistical properties of the pseudorandom sequence.

Furthermore, the problem of the considered local functions that give predictable bit sequence can be solved. For this purpose, the cells that form an additional bit in each time step, additional functions are being specified. These functions implement actions aimed at eliminating the negative effects of a local active cell function.

For the considered local functions (Figure 10 and Figure 11) is used function to invert the state of the cell, which forms an additional bits in each time step. The results of this approach are shown on Figure 12.

We see that special influence on the final search function of the oldest neighborhood cells from the majority, this approach does not provide.

148

Figure 11. An example of operation the PRNG with the local search function of older of the most part

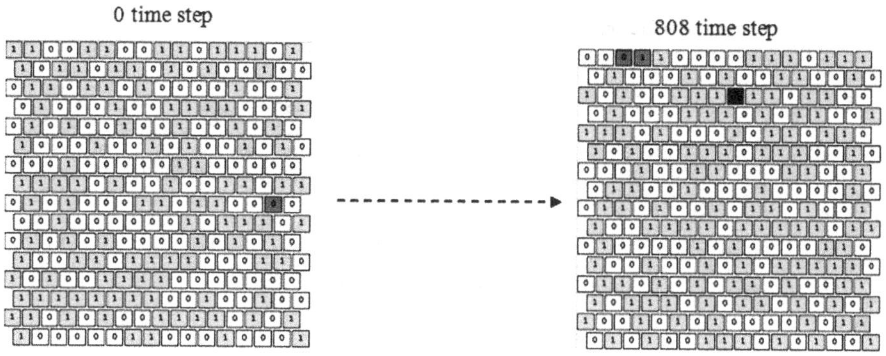

0 time step

808 time step

A sequence of numbers

51, 248, 150, 74, 35, 205, 198, 110, 71, 84, 205, 68, 112, 105, 96, 155, 245, 23, 39, 192, 139, 224, 86, 24, 182, 111, 4, 207, 205, 71, 71, 28, 104, 208, 176, 7, 181, 178, 0, 219, 193, 206, 130, 12, 101, 177, 167, 30, 246, 174, 192, 89, 62, 88, 4, 226, 199, 37, 56, 198, 198, 225, 195, 58, 21, 29, 108, 78, 13, 230, 143, 122, 121, 238, 32, 70, 53, 119, 68, 187, 105, 223, 88, 157, 18, 104, 37, 33, 51, 251, 215, 40, 42, 0, 75, 213, 191, 112, 221, 254

However, at the local elder cell search function of the states of logical "0" and "1", this approach supports a number of cells from the opposite states in a balanced state.

This approach clearly shows us that it is possible to use any local function to the active cell. To do this, the designer needs to study well the problems that arise when using a local function, and he must select a local function for the cell, which forms an additional bits. Basically, additional local function implements a recovery operation of the balance of the number of cells, between cells that have a state of logical "1" and "0".

DEVELOPMENT OF THE PSEUDORANDOM NUMBER GENERATOR BASED ON CELLULAR AUTOMATA WITH INHOMOGENEOUS CELLS AND WITH A HEXAGONAL COVERAGE

The PRNG based on the CA with a hexagonal coverage is easy implemented as the CA with inhomogeneous cells. An example of the CA software model with a hexagonal coverage is presented on Figure 13.

Figure 12. An example of the PRNG operation when the cells that form the an additional bit invert its state at each time step

Search neighborhood cells from the majority

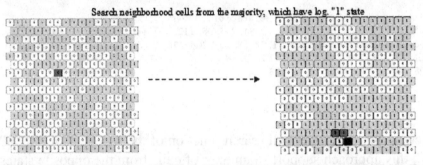

127, 110, 199, 7, 204, 184, 74, 200, 162, 0, 129, 166, 79, 234, 85, 74, 158, 170, 175, 33, 231, 4, 193, 44, 6, 99, 56, 161, 31, 244, 222, 206, 42, 49, 204, 190, 137, 216, 195, 102, 99, 21, 107, 224, 192, 42, 47, 19, 23, 18, 185, 0, 154, 133, 62, 46, 229, 127, 230, 83, 13, 45, 88, 34, 90, 137, 22, 145, 74, 234, 0, 20, 225, 170, 5, 35, 5, 85, 216, 138, 78, 96, 197, 202, 173, 119, 77, 98, 176, 119, 144, 99, 21, 134, 54, 66, 195, 11, 182, 241, 177, 182, 24, 217, 70, 121, 191, 190, 215, 162, 1, 184, 249, 9, 168, 108, 160, 77, 98, 4, 132, 200, 71, 22, 232, 162,

Search neighborhood cells from the majority, which have log. "1" state

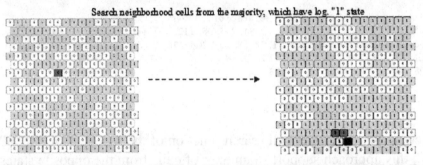

224, 190, 100, 237, 175, 84, 26, 114, 240, 180, 13, 105, 81, 190, 183, 172, 216, 189, 169, 125, 152, 198, 70, 82, 253, 3, 124, 21, 70, 46, 193, 204, 192, 130, 149, 145, 94, 181, 227, 1, 9, 169, 140, 5, 56, 50, 254, 212, 132, 31, 89, 95, 173, 107, 13, 125, 54, 4, 111, 104, 225, 96, 251, 183, 235, 100, 23, 234, 219, 106, 111, 60, 232, 114, 143, 222, 13, 184, 200, 154, 173, 31, 69, 63, 69, 141, 93, 43, 58, 237, 70, 115, 72, 246, 161, 111, 212, 145, 8, 119, 77, 115, 245, 150, 14, 238, 24, 64, 39, 94, 196, 67, 242, 84, 10, 8, 181, 95, 36, 237, 208, 1, 197, 85

Search neighborhood cells from the majority, which have log. "0" state

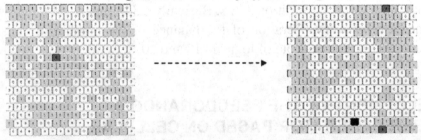

226, 12, 192, 28, 29, 78, 207, 208, 116, 247, 101, 219, 28, 18, 79, 16, 171, 126, 92, 159, 9, 193, 67, 221, 30, 177, 227, 5, 208, 33, 254, 173, 206, 133, 114, 7, 224, 248, 213, 175, 57, 0, 73, 192, 85, 71, 181, 157, 111, 122, 192, 7, 68, 250, 53, 202, 60, 139, 18, 253, 38, 114, 3, 186, 150, 102, 88, 8, 173, 67, 122, 23, 173, 25, 23, 14, 230, 237, 183, 187, 54, 177, 188, 166, 233, 233, 236, 199, 132, 36, 86, 70, 142, 225, 97, 98, 123, 214, 124, 184, 0, 39, 232, 171, 128, 31, 64, 31, 32, 190, 92, 196, 190, 241, 40, 40, 195, 210, 216, 203, 27, 21, 190, 208,

Figure 13. An example of a homogeneous CA with a hexagonal coating

This example clearly shows the disadvantages that appear due to the incorrect initial generator sets. In the illustrated example is used one cell, which is set in logical "1" state. The same cell is the main cell. At the main cell output the output bits of the output bit sequence are generated. In the represented example, the output sequence consists of ones bits. At the same time the pseudorandom number generator does not contain the inhomogeneous cells.

As a result, there is need to find of optimal solution for forming the initial settings. Must select following initial settings.

1. The number of cells that are in logical state "1" and "0", and the location of these cells.
2. Location of the main cells.
3. The number of inhomogeneous cells, as well as their location on the CA field.
4. The LTF for the homogeneous and inhomogeneous cells.

On Figure 14 is presented an example, where is shown the ACA evolution with a hexagonal coated with one cell that is in a state of the "1" and with different numbers of inhomogeneous cells.

The homogeneous cell performs the XOR function by the cellular automata with memory. Inhomogeneous cell perform the function

$$\left(X_1 \wedge \overline{X_2}\right) \vee \left(X_3 \wedge \overline{X_4}\right) \vee \left(X_5 \wedge \overline{X_6}\right).$$

The evolution of CA with one, two, three and four inhomogeneous cells are presented. Initially, the cells have the same states for all variants. During the evolution with each time step the CA cell states for each embodiment are different. Also the formed bit sequence will be different. For the present example the bit sequence will have the following form for each variant.

$Q_0 = 11111111111111111111....$

Figure 14. An example of the ACA evolution with an initial cell that is in a state of the "1" and with different numbers of inhomogeneous cells

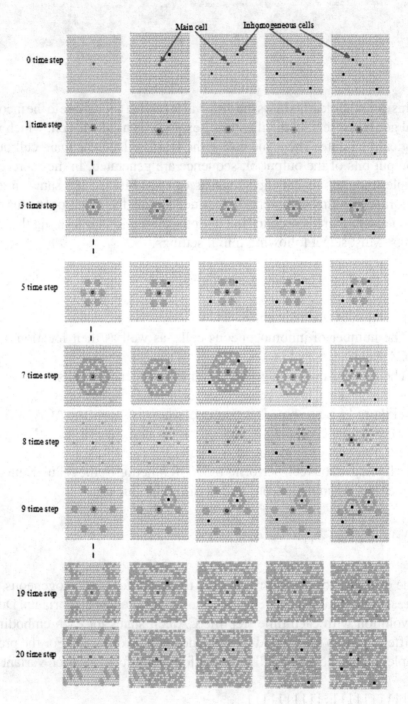

$Q_1 = 111111111111001001111\ldots..$

$Q_2 = 111111111111001001111\ldots..$

$Q_3 = 111111111111001001111\ldots..$

$Q_4 = 111111111111001001111\ldots..$

The example shows an inefficient choice of the initial generator states due to the presence of a long idle running period of the generator. The idle running is determined by the number of time step during which the inhomogeneous cells do not influence on the main cell state.

Selection of the initial cell amount, which have a logical "1" state, it's important for the quality of the forming of the bit sequence. We know that one initial cell with the state of logical "1" does not give a pseudo-random sequence at the output.

Let us consider examples of a large number of initial cells in a state of logical "1". We will also use cells that have a logical "1" states and are near (Figure 15) and cells, which across the field one by one are distributed (Figure 16).

These paintings show us that the increase in cell number that have a logical "1" state in the initial state improves the statistical distribution of ones and zeros in the generated bit sequence.

Figure 15. The pseudorandom number generator evolution with different numbers of initial cells with the state of logical "1" and are near

153

Figure 16. The pseudorandom number generator evolution with a different number of initial cells which have a logic "1" state and distributed across the cellular automata field one by one

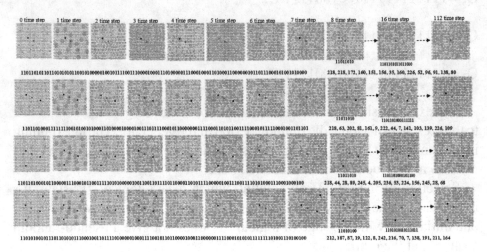

Analysis of the obtained paintings of the hexagonal covering cellular automata evolution and generated bit sequences and sequence numbers allow us to conclude that the time at the start of change (bit number, which is different from the bit sequence are generated by pseudorandom number generator based on hexagonal covering cellular automata with homogeneous cells) corresponds to the bit sequence (T_1+1). The value of T_1 equal to the number of cells between the main and heterogeneous cells.

Thus, the minimum number of time steps (bits of the sequence) that is spent for the start of changing of the bit sequence is formed by the classical hexagonal covering cellular automata without heterogeneous cells. In the classical hexagonal covering cellular automata the local transition function and the type of neighborhood coincide with the LTF and the type of neighborhood of the investigated HGCA.

However, on this time step the changes may occur at later time steps. It all depends on the initial installations of the HGCCA.

We make such comparisons, because we believe that the bit sequence, which was formed by the classic hexagonal covering cellular automata, has weak statistical properties. This sequence can be predicted because the classical hexagonal covering cellular automata can be described as LFSR. The pseudorandom number generator based on the classical hexagonal covering cellular automata has a length of the bit sequence period of is less than the

Figure 17. The diagram on the influence of inhomogeneous cell on the formed bit sequence

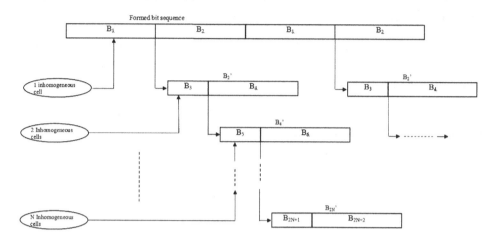

HGCCA. The introduction of inhomogeneous cells in hexagonal covering cellular automata converts it into HGCCA class, which increases uncertainty as well as is increased the length of period of the generated bit sequence. The process of influence of inhomogeneous cells on the formed bit sequence is represented on the diagram Figure 17.

In the diagram, each subsequent inhomogeneous cell is determined by the distance (number of cells) between the inhomogeneous cell and the main cell. Each additional inhomogeneous cell using introduces additional pseudo uncertainty that increases the length of the repetition period of the pseudorandom bit sequence.

The proposed pseudorandom number generator model operates as the pseudorandom number generator based on HCA with the orthogonal coverage. The pseudorandom number generator based on HCA with the orthogonal coated in the previous sections is discussed. The efficiency of such the pseudorandom number generator in the following sections will be discussed.

REFERENCES

Avolio, M. V., Ambrosio, D., Di Gregorio, S., Rongo, R., & Spataro, W. (2001). Simulating Landslides of Different Complexity with Hexagonal Cellular Automata. *Annual Conference of the International Association for Mathematical Geology: IAMG 2001.*

Avolio, M. V., Di Gregorio, S., Mantovani, F., Pasuto, A., Rongo, R., Silvano, S., & Spataro, W. (1999). Hexagonal cellular automaton simulation of the 1992 Tessina landslide. *Proceedings of IAMG 99*, 1, 291 - 297.

Basurto, R., Leon, P. A., Martinez, G. J., & Seck-Tuoh-Mora, J. C. (2013). Logic Gates and Complex Dynamics in a Hexagonal Cellular Automaton: The Spiral Rule. *JCA*, 8(1-2), 53–71.

Belan, S. N., & Motornyuk, R. L. (2013). Extraction of characteristic features of images with the help of the radon transform and its hardware implementation in terms of cellular automata. *Cybernetics and Systems Analysis*, 49(1), 7–14. doi:10.1007/s10559-013-9479-2

Bilan, S., Motornyuk, R., & Bilan, S. (2014). Method of Hardware Selection of Characteristic Features Based on Radon Transformation and not Sensitive to Rotation, Shifting and Scale of the Input Images. *Advances in Image and Video Processing*, 2(4), 12–23. doi:10.14738/aivp.24.392

Konstantinos, B. B. (2011). Hexagonal is Circular Cell Shape: A Comparative Analysis and Evaluation of the Two Popular Modeling Approximations. *Cellular Networks, Positioning, Performance Analysis, Reliability*, 103 - 122.

Nicoladie D. T. (2014). Hexagonal pixel-array for efficient spatial computation for motion-detection pre-processing of visual scenes. *Advances in Image and Video Processing, 2(2), 26 – 36.

Chapter 8

Analysis of the Quality of Pseudorandom Number Generators Based on Cellular Automata

ABSTRACT

The eighth chapter describes the studies of the presented generators using the ENT and NIST tests. For a complete description of the experiment, different initial settings were used. Tests were conducted for different sizes and for a different number of cells, which initially had a logical "1" states. Also, bit sequences of different lengths are formed. The results presented in this chapter indicate optimal sizes and optimal initial settings of cells of the cellular automaton. Generators are described on the basis of cellular automata with a Moore neighborhood. The obtained results are compared for all the pseudo-random number generators described earlier. Also, the generators were examined using graphical tests. The results of the graphical tests for the generators described in this manuscript are presented in this chapter. Test results are presented in tabular form and in graphical form.

DOI: 10.4018/978-1-5225-2773-2.ch008

ENT QUALITY ANALYZING TESTS OF PSEUDORANDOM NUMBER GENERATORS BASED ON CELLULAR AUTOMATA

The tests implemented in the program ENT (Walker, 2008) were used for the analysis and verification of the quality described generators and are posted on the website by John Walker in 2008. The program implements the five tests, which are intended for a statistical evaluation of the pseudo-random bit sequences. The tests aimed at processing bit files. The files are bit sequences, each element of which is formed by a bit sequence.

1. **Entropy:** This test is based on a calculation of entropy. Author of this program indicates the source of the description of the method (Richard, 1980). In accordance with this test is determined the size of a compression of the resulting file. If the file compression does not reducing its size, then the bit sequence is considered to be random. The program shows the result as the number of bits per character, and also identifies the size of the compression. The compression size displays the number of characters that reducing the file is an appropriate amount as a percentage.

2. **Chi-Square Test:** This test is the most commonly used test. This test is used to test the null hypothesis about the observed random variable subordinating to the specific theoretical distribution law. It is defined as the percentage that indicates how the calculated random sequence value exceeds the selection value. This percentage gives an estimate of randomness of the testing sequence. If the resulting percent value is greater than 99% or less than 1%, then the sequence is not considered to be random.

If the percentage value is obtained in the range from 5% to 99% or from 5% to 1%, then the sequence is considered as questionable and is aroused the suspicion and it may be a random. In addition, the sequence is considered to close to the suspect if the resulting percentage of the test conducted is in the range from 90% to 95% or from 5% to 10%. The remaining value of the received percent indicate on a sure random sequence. The author refers to the program information source (Knuth, 1969).

3. **Arithmetic Mean:** The simple arithmetic test that determines the value, which is being obtained by dividing the sum of the byte length on the

file. For a random sequences, this value approaching to the value of 0.5 on the output of the program.

4. **Monte Carlo Value for Pi:** The test determines the percentage of hits in the values of a circle is inscribed in a square. The number of π is calculated. If this number approaches the value 3.143580574, then the sequence is defined as random. To specify the the coordinates of a square the six bytes is used as 24 bit. The hitting to the inside circle is determined that in the given square is inscribed. This hit is taken as the target hit. To calculate the π the calculated the percentage of hitting the target is used.

5. **Serial Correlation Coefficient:** This approach in detail is described in the work (Knuth, 1969). This test evaluates the dependence of each byte from the previous one. For random sequences, this quantity tends to 0.

To testing of the described generators the following procedure are used.

1. The program generator models are selected.
2. For selected generators the initial installation are specified.
3. For each initial set the bit file has been formed, which by its structure indicated the formed a bit sequence.
4. Due to using of the ENT program the all generated bit files are processed.

For the implementation of the first action the generators with orthogonal coverage is used. As the first PRNG the PRNG with the orthogonal covering was selected, in which an additional bits was formed by the CA that changing its states through N×M time step (N×M – size of the CA). As the second PRNG the PRNG based on the CA, was selected, in which the CA itself during operation formed an additional bits. The third PRNG is based on a classic SCA with inhomogeneous cells.

Also for testing were chosen the PRNG on the basis of CA with a hexagonal coverage (GCA). From this family of the PRNGs based GCA the following PRNGs were selected:

1. The PRNG based on GCA with using an additional bit, which GCA itself forms during operation.
2. The PRNG is similar to the previous PRNG. The difference is that the cell, which forms an additional bits, inverts its state at each time step.
3. The PRNG based on classical GCA with heterogeneous cells.

As the initial settings are used:

- The CA size for CA with orthogonal cover;
- The number of cells which are set to logic "1" and their a location;
- Initial location of the active cells, which forms the bits of the bit sequence.

To test every bit sequence were formed by the generator for each the initial settings. The bit sequence with the following lengths have been formed 100, 1000, 10000, 1000000 bit.

Let us consider the results of passing the tests ENT by the first PRNG.

The software pattern of the initial states have been created to analyze the quality of the first PRNG. In the templates the sizes of a CA and the number of cells are used that at the initial step of time are in a logic "1" state. The templates of the initial states have been created for the following sizes of the ACA: 10×10, 15×15, 20×20, 25×25, 30×30.

For each ACA size the following number of ACA cells were installed. For size 10×10 were selected:

- The ACA with one cell that is in a logic state "1";
- The ACA with ten cells that are in a logic state "1";
- The ACA with fifty cells that are in a logic state "1".

Also, for each initial state by bit sequences of length 96 bits, 1000 bits, 10 000 bits, and 1 000 000 bits were formed.

An example of the initial state of the PRNG with an ACA, which has a size 15×15, is presented on the Figure 1.

On Figure 1 the white cells indicate that they are set to a logical "0" state. All generated sequences as a bit file with the extension «bb» were presented. A program that implements the ENT tests has tested these files. These tests have been described earlier. The result of the ENT test is presented on Figure 2.

In fact, for each initial state of the first pseudorandom number generator the four bit sequences as four bit files were formed. As a result of the ENT tests were formed the table of a dataset, which are grouped for each size of the PRNG and for each the initial ACA state.

For each size of the ACA and for each test the image histogram of quantitative values were constructed. These histograms allow us to assess the quality of pseudorandom number generator work and ACA behavior when the initial installations are given. The histograms are constructed in

Figure 1. An example of the initial state of the PRNG with an ACA, which has a size 15×15

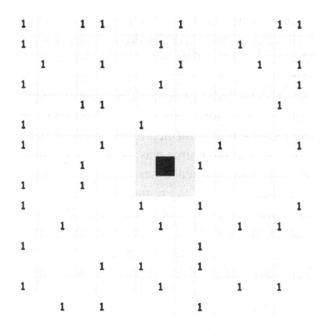

Figure 2. An example of the ENT tests implementation

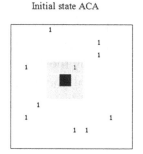

Initial state ACA   Implementation result of the ENT tests

such a way that the horizontal axis is the length of the sequences, and the vertical axis indicates the quantitative characteristic of the test. Each discrete sequence length corresponds to the number of values which are represented as columns that have the different color areas. The number of columns equals the number of initial settings of the PRNG who are tested. As a rule, in all figures the leftmost columns show values for the testing of a single cell, which is the initial time is set to a logic "1", the second column corresponds to 10 cells in the initial state set to logic "1", etc. The rightmost column of each length corresponding to the maximum number of cells, which at the initial time to a logic "1" state are installed. On Figure 3 are presented the results of passing of ENT tests for the first pseudorandom number generator that uses ACA size 10×10.

The entropy test (1st test) almost all the generated bit sequences are held. They have 0% volume reduction of the bit file. Only one sequence has the 2% of the file size reduction. It is formed by the ACA of size 10×10 and by the length of 96 bits. At the same time was the 10 cells, which have initially a logic "1" state. This same sequence has a poor distribution of ones and zeros, as well as the bad values of the remaining tests.

As a result, the visual analysis of the results of the PRNG with size of the ACA 10×10 we can conclude that the best performance gives the PRNG with the logic "1" cell states and more than 10 for sequences with a length of more than 100,000 bits. These sequences are selected to hold the following tests.

On Figures 4 - 7 the results of performing of the ENT tests are presented for other ACA sizes that for the experiment were used.

The analysis of results showed that the best and consistent results for the bit sequences more than 10000 bits are obtained. At the same time good results are propagated to the initial setting for all the ACA sizes. Also a good performance present when in the initial ACA settings are present cells that are at logical "1" state and their number is in the range from 30% to 70%.

The second PRNG showed more efficient operation during the formation of a pseudo-random bit sequence. The second PRNG has a smaller period of idling. About this indicates that the generated bit sequence by the length of 1000 bit also shows pseudorandom properties. However, not all the initial settings have given a positive result. A positive result showed a bit sequence that have been formed when the number of cells having a logical "1" state between 30% and 70%.

The second pseudorandom number generator ENT test results are shown on Figure 8.

Practically in all the generated bit sequences is not observed file compression. Therefore, the entropy test (1st ENT test) is not represented in the diagrams. As an initial settings of the ACA, were used same the initial settings that were in the first PRNG. Improving the characteristics of the second PRNG is related to the presence of dynamic changes in the cells of states that form the additional bit.

Figure 3. The histograms of the results of the ENT tests for the first pseudorandom number generator with ACA size 10×10

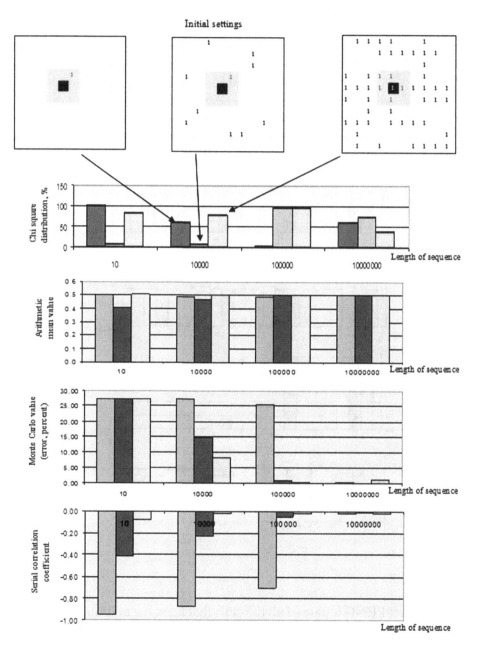

Figure 4. The results of implementation of the ENT tests of the first pseudorandom number generator based on the ACA size 15×15

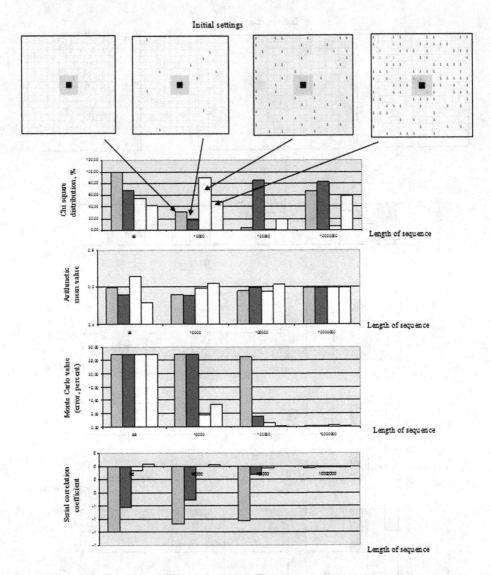

In the first PRNG a state of all the cells that form the additional bit, do not change during the N×M time steps. In the second PRNG a cell that generates additional bits across L time steps can change their condition more than once. It all depends on how many times the cell will become active during L time steps.

Figure 5. The results of implementation of the ENT tests of the first pseudorandom number generator based on the ACA size 20×20

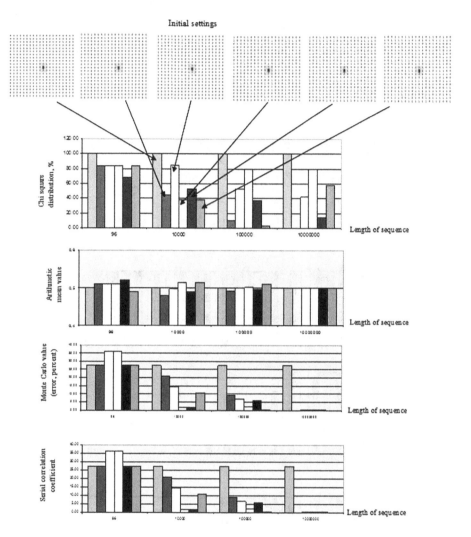

The ENT test analysis of the third PRNG takes more time. The third PRNG is based on CA, in which are selected cells with other local transfer functions or other neighborhood. These cells are called inhomogeneous cells. They are being placed in the field of a CA by the user.

The PRNG with varying amounts of the inhomogeneous cells were used for the experiment. At the same time the initial settings of KA are the same as for the first and second PRNGs have been used. For each the PRNG based on

Figure 6. The results of implementation of the ENT tests of the first pseudorandom number generator based on the ACA size 25×25

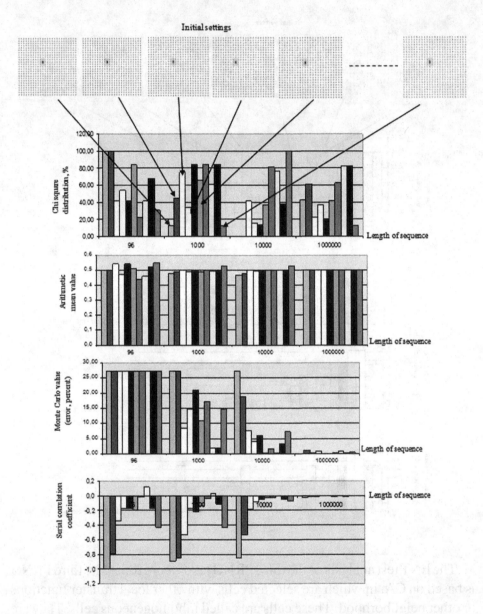

HCA the cells HCA dimension were selected: 10×10, 15×15, 20×20, 25×25, 30×30. For each HCA dimension from 1 to 4 an inhomogeneous cells have been selected. All heterogeneous cells in accordance with the dimension have the same coordinates for each the HCA.

Figure 7. The results of implementation of the ENT tests of the first pseudorandom number generator based on the ACA size 30×30

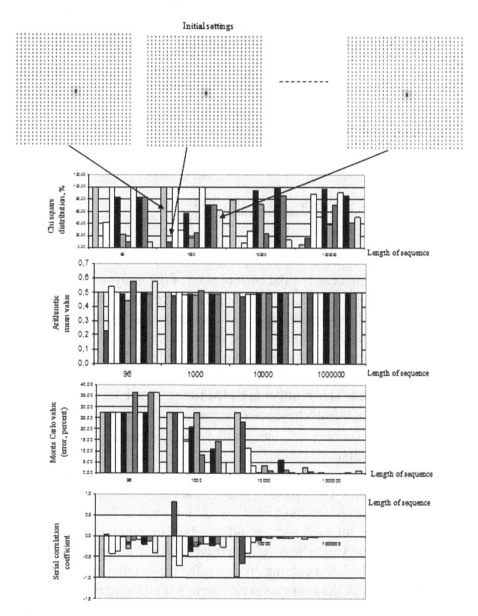

During operation, the third PRNG performs the memorization of the HCA state at each time step. At each time step, the state the generated an array of HCA cell states are being compared with states of the all previously generated arrays at previous time steps.

Figure 8. The ENT test results of the second pseudorandom number generator

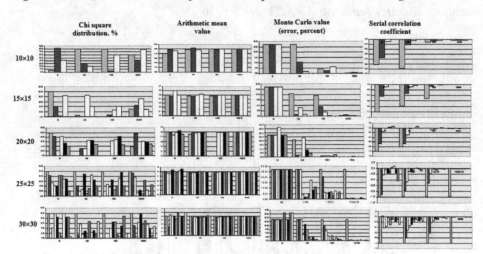

If there is a coincidence of the current state of the array of cells with one of the stored arrays of cells, the inhomogeneous cell coordinates are being change. In addition, the memorized arrays are deleted and a new accumulation of arrays of cells begins before the next coincidence.

In our experiment, the inhomogeneous cell coordinates have been changed as follows. The number of ones states of the cells in the neighborhood of each cell is counted. This number is added to the X and Y coordinates of a given cell. Those coordinates have been changed as a $X := X + L_1, Y := Y + L_1$ (where L_1 – the number of ones in the neighborhood of the selected inhomogeneous cells).

All the results have been displayed separately for each the number of the inhomogeneous cells. Third pseudorandom number generator test results are convenient to represent by the tables. Its table is created for each size, and in table the values for each test are indicated. Also the number of initially used inhomogeneous cells and cells that are initially at logical "1" states are indicated. In the latest column are indicated the number of coincidences in the comparison of the previous state arrays with the current CA state. In tables 1 –2 are presented the results of the third PRNG testing for size 10×10 and 20×20.

From the Table 1 and Table 2 can be seen that the number of coincidences decreases with increasing the size and number of an inhomogeneous cells. More a visual representation of the results can be presented in as graphical diagrams for each test parameter.

Table 1. ENT test results for the third pseudorandom number generator of size 10×10

The CA size	The Number of Inhomogeneous Cells	The Number of Cells That are in the Initial State of the Log. "1"	The Length of the Formed Sequence	The Number of "0"	The Number of "1"	The File Reducing Value %	The Excess of the Calculated Value, %	Arithmetic Mean	the Value of Monte Carlo method, %	Serial Correlation Coefficient	Number of Coincidences
10x10	1	1	104	58	46	0	23,93	0,44	27,32	0,064	>10
			1000	496	504	0	80,03	0,5	4,51	-0,004	>10
			10000	4947	5053	0	28,91	0,5	4,06	-0,008	>10
			1000000	493029	506971	0	0,01	0,5	4,66	-0,008	>10
		10	104	55	49	0	55,63	0,47	36,34	0,07	>10
			1000	474	526	0	10,01	0,52	1,86	0,009	>10
			10000	4970	5030	0	54,85	0,5	2,84	0,02	>10
			1000000	496796	503204	0	0,01	0,5	2,84	0,022	>10
		50	104	61	43	2	7,76	0,41	36,34	-0,03	>10
			1000	503	497	0	84,95	0,497	68,17	-0,22	>10
			10000	4922	5078	0	11,88	0,5	63,88	-0,2	>10
			1000000	490893	509107	0	0,01	0,5	62,87	-0,2	>10
	2	1	104	50	54	0	64,49	0,5	27,32	-0,001	0
			1000	527	473	0	8,77	0,47	8,23	0,09	>10
			10000	4102	5898	2	0,01	0,589	24,10	0,05	>10
			1000000	400232	599768	2	0,01	0,5	26,18	0,047	>10
		10	104	54	50	0	69,49	0,48	27,32	0,075	1
			1000	545	455	0	0,44	0,455	20,96	-0,06	>10
			10000	5723	4277	1	0,01	0,4277	15,08	0,09	>10
			1000000	573874	426126	1	0,01	0,42	14,0	0,111	>10

continued on following page

Table 1. Continued

The CA size	The Number of Inhomogeneous Cells	The Number of Cells That are in the Initial State of the Log. "1"	The Length of the Formed Sequence	The Number of "0"	The Number of "1"	The File Reducing Value %	The Excess of the Calculated Value, %	Arithmetic Mean	the Value of Monte Carlo method, %	Serial Correlation Coefficient	Number of Coincidences
	• 3	• 50	• 104	• 57	• 47	• 0	• 32,68	• 0,45	• 36,34	• -0,08	• 0
			• 1000	• 483	• 517	• 0	• 28,23	• 0,51	• 4,51	• -0,02	• 3
			• 10000	• 5370	• 4630	• 0	• 0,01	• 0,46	• 6,51	• -0,08	• >10
			• 1000000	• 576295	• 423705	• 1	• 0,01	• 0,4237	• 17,57	• -0,18	• >10
		• 1	• 104	• 59	• 45	• 1	• 16,98	• 0,43	• 27,32	• 0,02	• 0
			• 1000	• 480	• 520	• 0	• 20,59	• 0,52	• 17,24	• -0,05	• 0
			• 10000	• 5036	• 4964	• 0	• 47,15	• 0,49	• 2,67	• -0,04	• 5
			• 1000000	• 501014	• 498986	• 0	• 4,26	• 0,499	• 1,48	• 0,001	• >10
		• 10	• 104	• 48	• 56	• 0	• 43,28	• 0,53	• 36,34	• 0,07	• 0
			• 1000	• 491	• 509	• 0	• 56,92	• 0,5	• 14,59	• -0,048	• 0
			• 10000	• 5306	• 4694	• 0	• 0,91	• 0,46	• 8,96	• 0,055	• 7
			• 1000000	• 498864	• 501136	• 0	• 2,31	• 0,5	• 2,42	• 0,01	• 9
		• 50	• 104	• 58	• 46	• 0	• 23,93	• 0,44	• 100,0	• -0,09	• 0
			• 1000	• 524	• 476	• 0	• 12,90	• 0,47	• 1,86	• 0,0017	• 0
			• 10000	• 5040	• 4960	• 0	• 42,37	• 0,49	• 2,06	• 0,04	• 4
			• 1000000	• 501420	• 498580	• 0	• 0,45	• 0,49	• 2,27	• 0,003	• 7

continued on following page

Table 1. Continued

The CA size	The Number of Inhomogeneous Cells	The Number of Cells That are in the Initial State of the Log. "1"	The Length of the Formed Sequence	The Number of "0"	The Number of "1"	The File Reducing Value %	The Excess of the Calculated Value, %	Arithmetic Mean	the Value of Monte Carlo method, %	Serial Correlation Coefficient	Number of Coincidences
• 4	• 1		• 104	• 54	• 50	• 0	• 69,49	• 0,48	• 27,32	• 0,268	• 0
			• 1000	• 510	• 490	• 0	• 52,71	• 0,49	• 8,23	• 0,019	• 0
			• 10000	• 5060	• 4940	• 0	• 36,11	• 0,49	• 2,4	• 0,04	• 0
			• 1000000	• 501414	• 498586	• 0	• 0,47	• 0,498	• 1,02	• 0,0009	• 7
	• 10		• 104	• 64	• 40	• 3	• 1,86	• 0,38	• 27,32	• 0,065	• 0
			• 1000	• 501	• 499	• 0	• 94,96	• 0,499	• 10,87	• 0,0039	• 0
			• 10000	• 4957	• 5043	• 0	• 38,98	• 0,5	• 0,83	• 0,005	• 0
			• 1000000	• 501714	• 498286	• 0	• 0,06	• 0,498	• 2,16	• 0,006	• 7
	• 50		• 104	• 47	• 57	• 0	• 32,68	• 0,548	• 27,32	• -0,16	• 0
			• 1000	• 498	• 502	• 0	• 89,93	• 0,5	• 14,59	• -0,012	• 0
			• 10000	• 5043	• 4957	• 0	• 24,55	• 0,5	• 4,26	• -0,002	• 0
			• 1000000	• 494518	• 505482	• 0	• 0,01	• 0,5	• 0,92	• -0,002	• 7

Table 2. ENT test results for the third pseudorandom number generator of size 15×15

The CA Size	The Number of Inhomogeneous Cells	The Number of Cells That are in the Initial State of the Log. "1"	The Length of the Formed Sequence	The Number of "0"	The Number of "1"	The File reducing Value %	The Excess of the Calculated Value, %	Arithmetic Mean	The Value of Monte Carlo Method, %	Serial Correlation Coefficient	Number of Coincidences
15x15	1	1	104	54	50	0	69,49	0,48	27,32	-0,001	0
			1000	481	519	0	22,95	0,51	4,51	0,002	4
			10000	5089	4911	0	7,51	0,49	0,39	-0,0079	>10
			1000000	501151	498849	0	2,13	0,498	1,04	-0,0047	>10
		10	104	56	48	0	43,23	0,468	27,32	-0,0059	0
			1000	504	496	0	80,03	0,49	4,51	0,0079	1
			10000	5050	4950	0	31,73	0,495	4,06	-0,02	>10
			1000000	499753	500245	0	62,41	0,5	0,18	-0,00008	>10
		50	104	61	43	2	7,76	0,41	27,32	0,325	0
			1000	517	483	0	28,23	0,48	4,51	0,078	2
			10000	4997	5003	0	95,22	0,5	1,61	0,013	>10
			1000000	499639	500361	0	47,33	0,5	4,33	-0,0158	>10
		100	104	52	52	0	99,99	0,5	27,32	-0,076	0
			1000	493	507	0	65,80	0,5	4,51	0,0118	3
			10000	5089	4911	0	7,51	0,49	1,0	0,0108	>10
			1000000	498433	501567	0	0,17	0,5	2,56	-0,003	>10

continued on following page

Table 2. Continued

The CA Size	The Number of Inhomogeneous Cells	The Number of Cells That are in the Initial State of the Log. "1"	The Length of the Formed Sequence	The Number of "0"	The Number of "1"	The File reducing Value %	The Excess of the Calculated Value, %	Arithmetic Mean	The Value of Monte Carlo Method, %	Serial Correlation Coefficient	Number of Coincidences
• 2	• 2	• 1	• 104	• 56	• 48	• 0	• 43,28	• 0,46	• 27,32	• -0,04	• 0
			• 1000	• 497	• 503	• 0	• 84,95	• 0,50	• 4,51	• 0,019	• 0
			• 10000	• 5013	• 4987	• 0	• 79,49	• 0,498	• 0,83	• 0,007	• 0
			• 1000000	• 499934	• 500066	• 0	• 89,50	• 0,5	• 0,11	• -0,0013	• >10
		• 10	• 96	• 48	• 48	• 0	• 39,45	• 0,49	• 27,4	• 0,21	• 0
			• 1000	• 508	• 492	• 0	• 61,29	• 0,49	• 10,87	• 0,0037	• 0
			• 10000	• 5082	• 4918	• 0	• 10,1	• 0,49	• 7,12	• -0,0118	• 0
			• 1000000	• 499974	• 500026	• 0	• 95,85	• 0,5	• 0,05	• -0,0004	• 0
		• 50	• 104	• 59	• 45	• 1	• 16,98	• 0,43	• 27,32	• 0,099	• 0
			• 1000	• 519	• 481	• 0	• 22,95	• 0,48	• 8,23	• 0,0025	• 0
			• 10000	• 5037	• 4963	• 0	• 45,93	• 0,49	• 1,45	• 0,0039	• 0
			• 1000000	• 499974	• 500026	• 0	• 95,85	• 0,5	• 0,05	• -0,0004	• 2
		• 100	• 104	• 55	• 49	• 0	• 55,63	• 0,47	• 27,32	• -0,23	• 0
			• 1000	• 475	• 525	• 0	• 11,38	• 0,52	• 17,24	• -0,018	• 0
			• 10000	• 4999	• 5001	• 0	• 98,40	• 0,5	• 3,89	• -0,0036	• 0
			• 1000000	• 500308	• 499692	• 0	• 53,79	• 0,499	• 0,38	• -0,0001	• 2

continued on following page

173

Table 2. Continued

The CA Size	The Number of Inhomogeneous Cells	The Number of Cells That are in the Initial State of the Log. "1"	The Length of the Formed Sequence	The Number of "0"	The Number of "1"	The File reducing Value %	The Excess of the Calculated Value, %	Arithmetic Mean	The Value of Monte Carlo Method, %	Serial Correlation Coefficient	Number of Coincidences
	3	1	104	49	55	0	55,63	0,528	27,32	0,11	0
			1000	521	479	0	8,41	0,479	20,96	-0,04	0
			10000	5025	4975	0	61,71	0,497	5,9	-0,0028	0
			1000000	500115	499885	0	81,81	0,499	0,3	0,0007	0
		10	104	58	46	0	23,93	0,44	27,32	0,1	0
			1000	506	494	0	70,43	0,49	8,23	0,0078	0
			10000	4923	5077	0	12,36	0,5	2,67	-0,012	0
			1000000	499938	500062	0	90,13	0,5	0,23	-0,001	0
		50	104	61	43	2	7,76	0,41	27,32	0,008	0
			1000	527	473	0	8,77	0,47	1,86	0,001	0
			10000	5094	4906	0	6,01	0,49	4,67	-0,004	0
			1000000	499567	500433	0	38,65	0,5	0,43	0,00089	0
		100	104	63	41	3	3,10	0,39	27,32	-0,0065	0
			1000	511	489	0	48,66	0,489	14,59	0,007	0
			10000	5040	4960	0	42,37	0,49	4,67	0,0059	0
			1000000	500348	499652	0	48,64	0,499	0,09	-0,004	0

continued on following page

Table 2. Continued

The CA Size	The Number of Inhomogeneous Cells	The Number of Cells That are in the Initial State of the Log. "1"	The Length of the Formed Sequence	The Number of "0"	The Number of "1"	The File reducing Value %	The Excess of the Calculated Value, %	Arithmetic Mean	The Value of Monte Carlo Method, %	Serial Correlation Coefficient	Number of Coincidences
	• 4	• 1	• 104	• 51	• 53	• 0	• 84,45	• 0,5	• 27,32	• -0,038	• 0
			• 1000	• 507	• 493	• 0	• 65,8	• 0,49	• 10,87	• -0,008	• 0
			• 10000	• 5020	• 4980	• 0	• 68,92	• 0,49	• 2,06	• -0,000016	• 0
			• 1000000	• 500055	• 499945	• 0	• 91,24	• 0,499	• 0,1	• 0,0009	• 0
		• 10	• 104	• 55	• 49	• 0	• 55,63	• 0,47	• 27,32	• -0,003	• 0
			• 1000	• 506	• 494	• 0	• 70,43	• 0,49	• 8,23	• -0,008	• 0
			• 10000	• 5021	• 4979	• 0	• 67,45	• 0,49	• 2,67	• 0,0019	• 0
			• 1000000	• 499575	• 500425	• 0	• 39,53	• 0,5	• 0,11	• -0,0009	• 0
		• 50	• 104	• 57	• 47	• 0	• 32,68	• 0,45	• 27,32	• 0,029	• 0
			• 1000	• 515	• 485	• 0	• 34,28	• 0,48	• 20,96	• 0,023	• 0
			• 10000	• 4989	• 5011	• 0	• 82,59	• 0,5	• 2,23	• -0,014	• 0
			• 1000000	• 499950	• 500050	• 0	• 92,03	• 0,5	• 0,49	• -0,000024	• 0
		• 100	• 104	• 54	• 50	• 0	• 69,49	• 0,48	• 27,32	• -0,04	• 0
			• 1000	• 480	• 520	• 0	• 20,59	• 0,52	• 4,51	• -0,037	• 0
			• 10000	• 4910	• 5090	• 0	• 7,19	• 0,5	• 5,29	• -0,0059	• 0
			• 1000000	• 500872	• 499128	• 0	• 8,12	• 0,499	• 0,68	• -0,000043	• 0

On the Figure 9 are presented the distribution histogram of the ENT test results for the third pseudorandom number generator based on CA with inhomogeneous cells. The CA dimensions correspond to the 10×10 and 15×15.

Results of performance of the ENT tests for third pseudorandom number generator based on CA with inhomogeneous cells for sizes 20×20, 25×25 and 30×30 are presented in Tables 3 – 5.

On the Figures 10 - 12 are presented the distribution histogram of the ENT tests results for the third pseudorandom number generator based on CA with inhomogeneous cells.

The obtained histograms show that good results give the initial settings in which the number of cells that have a logical "1" states and they changing from 30% to 70% from all CA cells. In addition, good results are obtained by the use of of inhomogeneous cells, the number of which is more than 3.

The sustainable results give almost all the bit sequences with the different lengths through the use of more than 3 of inhomogeneous cells. To obtain such results the homogeneous cells perform the XOR function of the state signals of the neighborhood cell and their own status (automaton with memory). Inhomogeneous cells have been performing a majority function.

Figure 9. Results of performance of the ENT tests by third pseudorandom number generator based on CA with inhomogeneous cells for the CA sizes 10×10 and 15×15

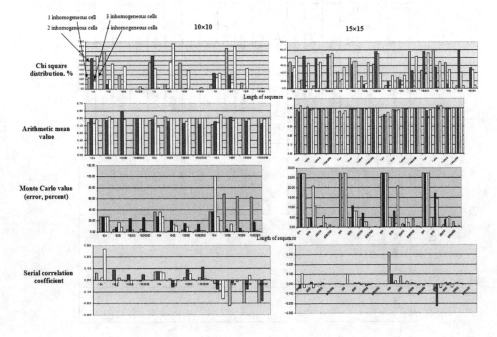

Table 3. Test ENT results for the third pseudorandom number generator of size 20×20

The CA Size	The Number of Inhomogeneous Cells	The Number of Cells That Are in the Initial State of the Log. "1"	The Length of the Formed Sequence	The Number of "0"	The Number of "1"	The File Reducing Value %	The Excess of the Calculated Value, %	Arithmetic Mean	The Value of Monte Carlo Method, %	Serial Correlation Coefficient	Number of Coincidences
20x20	1	1	104	61	43	2	7,76	0,41	27,32	-0,11	0
			1000	503	497	0	84,95	0,497	1,86	-0,04	0
			10000	4838	5162	0	0,12	0,51	5,73	0,0077	>10
			1000000	500248	499752	0	61,99	0,499	3,2	0,0006	>10
		10	104	56	48	0	43,28	0,46	27,32	-0,04	0
			1000	434	566	1	0,01	0,566	14,59	-0,017	1
			10000	4184	5816	1	0,01	0,58	26,10	-0,027	4
			1000000	499666	500334	0	50,41	0,5	1,19	-0,0048	>10
		50	104	56	48	0	43,28	0,46	27,32	0,226	1
			1000	478	522	0	16,41	0,52	27,32	-0,07	4
			10000	5124	4876	0	1,31	0,487	16,92	-0,119	>10
			1000000	503446	496554	0	0,01	0,49	1,23	-0,01	>10
		100	104	55	49	0	55,63	0,47	27,32	0,15	0
			1000	504	496	0	80,03	0,49	4,51	0,0799	1
			10000	5080	4920	0	10,96	0,49	9,4	0,017	6
			1000000	503934	496066	0	0,01	0,49	5,45	-0,019	>10
		200	104	53	51	0	84,45	0,49	27,32	-0,038	1
			1000	401	599	2	0,01	0,59	14,59	-0,278	7
			10000	3961	6039	3	0,01	0,6	18,14	-0,26	>10
			1000000	493802	506198	0	0,01	0,5	4,62	-0,002	>10

continued on following page

Table 3. Continued

The CA Size	The Number of Inhomogeneous Cells	The Number of Cells That Are in the Initial State of the Log. "1"	The Length of the Formed Sequence	The Number of "0"	The Number of "1"	The File Reducing Value %	The Excess of the Calculated Value, %	Arithmetic Mean	The Value of Monte Carlo Method, %	Serial Correlation Coefficient	Number of Coincidences
	2	250	104	41	63	3	3,1	0,6	100,0	-0,087	0
			1000	418	582	1	0,01	0,58	74,54	0,04	0
			10000	4861	5139	0	0,54	0,51	8,79	0,007	7
			1000000	503479	496521	0	0,01	0,49	3,87	-0,01	>10
		1	104	57	47	0	32,68	0,45	36,34	0,18	0
			1000	477	523	0	14,58	0,52	1,86	0,03	0
			10000	5030	4970	0	54,85	0,49	4,06	0,014	0
			1000000	501102	498898	0	2,75	0,49	0,43	0,0046	•
		10	104	51	53	0	84,45	0,5	100,0	0,15	0
			1000	503	497	0	84,95	0,49	100,87	0,039	0
			10000	4884	5116	0	2,03	0,51	1,61	0,01	0
			1000000	503110	496890	0	0,01	0,49	0,06	0,0018	•
		50	104	52	52	0	99,99	0,5	27,32	0,038	0
			1000	480	520	0	20,59	0,52	4,51	-0,02	0
			10000	4972	5028	0	57,55	0,5	5,73	-0,005	1
			1000000	493336	506664	0	0,01	0,5	0,27	-0,007	•
		100	104	65	39	4	1,08	0,32	27,32	0,056	0
			1000	486	514	0	37,59	0,51	4,51	0,015	0
			10000	4944	5056	0	26,27	0,5	5,73	-0,0037	0
			1000000	500218	499782	0	66,28	0,49	0,42	-0,001	•

continued on following page

Table 3. Continued

The CA Size	The Number of Inhomogeneous Cells	The Number of Cells That Are in the Initial State of the Log. "1"	The Length of the Formed Sequence	The Number of "0"	The Number of "1"	The File Reducing Value %	The Excess of the Calculated Value, %	Arithmetic Mean	The Value of Monte Carlo Method, %	Serial Correlation Coefficient	Number of Coincidences
	• 3	• 200	• 104	• 54	• 50	• 0	• 69,49	• 0,48	• 27,32	• 0,037	• 0
			• 1000	• 513	• 487	• 0	• 41,10	• 0,48	• 8,23	• -0,008	• 0
			• 10000	• 5025	• 4975	• 0	• 61,71	• 0,49	• 7,12	• -0,019	• 0
			• 1000000	• 500395	• 499605	• 0	• 42,95	• 0,49	• 0,17	• 0,00136	•
		• 250	• 104	• 58	• 46	• 0	• 23,93	• 0,44	• 27,32	• 0,1	• 0
			• 1000	• 511	• 489	• 0	• 48,66	• 0,489	• 4,51	• 0,03	• 0
			• 10000	• 4907	• 5093	• 0	• 6,29	• 0,5	• 4,51	• -0,0003	• 0
			• 1000000	• 498875	• 501125	• 0	• 2,44	• 0,5	• 1,36	• -0,0049	•
		• 1	• 104	• 48	• 56	• 0	• 43,28	• 0,53	• 27,32	• 0,03	• 0
			• 1000	• 481	• 519	• 0	• 22,95	• 0,51	• 8,23	• 0,01	• 0
			• 10000	• 4916	• 5084	• 0	• 9,3	• 0,5	• 0,39	• -0,008	• 0
			• 1000000	• 499172	• 500828	• 0	• 9,77	• 0,5	• 0,09	• 0,0006	• 0
		• 10	• 104	• 48	• 56	• 0	• 43,28	• 0,53	• 27,32	• 0,11	• 0
			• 1000	• 498	• 502	• 0	• 89,93	• 0,5	• 20,96	• 0,007	• 0
			• 10000	• 5091	• 4909	• 0	• 6,88	• 0,49	• 2,84	• -0,007	• 0
			• 1000000	• 500269	• 499731	• 0	• 59,06	• 0,49	• 0,9	• 0,001	• 0
		• 50	• 104	• 51	• 53	• 0	• 84,45	• 0,5	• 36,34	• 0,07	• 0
			• 1000	• 499	• 501	• 0	• 94,96	• 0,5	• 10,87	• -0,008	• 0
			• 10000	• 4988	• 5012	• 0	• 81,03	• 0,5	• 2,06	• -0,002	• 0
			• 1000000	• 500533	• 499467	• 0	• 28,64	• 0,49	• 0,29	• 0,0009	• 0

continued on following page

Table 3. Continued

The CA Size	The Number of Inhomogeneous Cells	The Number of Cells That Are in the Initial State of the Log. "1"	The Length of the Formed Sequence	The Number of "0"	The Number of "1"	The File Reducing Value %	The Excess of the Calculated Value, %	Arithmetic Mean	The Value of Monte Carlo Method, %	Serial Correlation Coefficient	Number of Coincidences
		• 100	• 104	• 53	• 51	• 0	• 84,45	• 0,49	• 36,34	• 0,038	• 0
			• 1000	• 509	• 491	• 0	• 56,92	• 0,49	• 8,23	• 0,03	• 0
			• 10000	• 5042	• 4958	• 0	• 40,09	• 0,49	• 2,23	• 0,0079	• 0
			• 1000000	• 565982	• 434018	• 1	• 0,01	• 0,43	• 21,6	• 0,25	• 0
		• 200	• 104	• 54	• 50	• 0	• 69,49	• 0,48	• 27,32	• -0,019	• 0
			• 1000	• 461	• 539	• 0	• 1,36	• 0,53	• 29,97	• 0,0097	• 0
			• 10000	• 4981	• 5019	• 0	• 70,39	• 0,5	• 2,06	• -0,002	• 0
			• 1000000	• 500481	• 499519	• 0	• 33,6	• 0,49	• 0,27	• -0,0007	• 0
		• 250	• 104	• 67	• 37	• 6	• 0,33	• 0,35	• 27,32	• 0,119	• 0
			• 1000	• 524	• 476	• 0	• 12,9	• 0,47	• 14,59	• -0,046	• 0
			• 10000	• 5036	• 4964	• 0	• 47,15	• 0,49	• 3,45	• 0,001	• 0
			• 1000000	• 499997	• 500003	• 0	• 99,52	• 0,5	• 0,28	• -0,0007	• 0
	• 4	• 1	• 104	• 50	• 54	• 0	• 69,40	• 0,51	• 27,32	• -0,078	• 0
			• 1000	• 491	• 509	• 0	• 56,92	• 0,5	• 4,51	• -0,08	• 0
			• 10000	• 5088	• 4912	• 0	• 7,84	• 0,49	• 4,67	• -0,019	• 0
			• 1000000	• 500108	• 499892	• 0	• 82,90	• 0,499	• 0,33	• 0,00048	• 0
		• 10	• 104	• 50	• 54	• 0	• 69,49	• 0,51	• 27,32	• -0,078	• 0
			• 1000	• 454	• 546	• 0	• 0,36	• 0,54	• 8,23	• -0,02	• 0
			• 10000	• 4936	• 5064	• 0	• 20,05	• 0,5	• 0,83	• 0,016	• 0
			• 1000000	• 499736	• 500264	• 0	• 59,75	• 0,5	• 0,78	• 0,0018	• 0

continued on following page

180

Table 3. Continued

The CA Size	The Number of Inhomogeneous Cells	The Number of Cells That Are in the Initial State of the Log. "1"	The Length of the Formed Sequence	The Number of "0"	The Number of "1"	The File Reducing Value %	The Excess of the Calculated Value, %	Arithmetic Mean	The Value of Monte Carlo Method, %	Serial Correlation Coefficient	Number of Coincidences
		• 50	• 104	• 53	• 51	• 0	• 84,45	• 0,49	• 27,32	• 0,112	• 0
			• 1000	• 495	• 505	• 0	• 75,18	• 0,5	• 14,59	• -0,012	• 0
			• 10000	• 5000	• 5000	• 0	• 99,99	• 0,5	• 4,67	• -0,0048	• 0
			• 1000000	• 499787	• 500213	• 0	• 67,01	• 0,5	• 0,18	• 0,000168	• 0
		• 100	• 104	• 59	• 45	• 1	• 16,98	• 0,43	• 36,34	• 0,138	• 0
			• 1000	• 514	• 486	• 0	• 37,54	• 0,48	• 4,51	• -0,016	• 0
			• 10000	• 5039	• 4961	• 0	• 43,54	• 0,49	• 2,23	• 0,01	• 0
			• 1000000	• 500102	• 499898	• 0	• 83,84	• 0,499	• 0,12	• 0,0005	• 0
		• 200	• 104	• 57	• 47	• 0	• 32,62	• 0,45	• 27,32	• 0,18	• 0
			• 1000	• 486	• 514	• 0	• 67,59	• 0,51	• 14,59	• 0,003	• 0
			• 10000	• 5023	• 4977	• 0	• 64,55	• 0,497	• 5,29	• -0,0096	• 0
			• 1000000	• 498865	• 501135	• 0	• 2,32	• 0,5	• 0,84	• 0,0005	• 0
		• 250	• 104	• 53	• 51	• 0	• 84,45	• 0,49	• 27,32	• -0,077	• 0
			• 1000	• 483	• 517	• 0	• 28,23	• 0,51	• 1,86	• -0,029	• 0
			• 10000	• 5011	• 4989	• 0	• 82,59	• 0,49	• 3,89	• -0,006	• 0
			• 1000000	• 498850	• 501150	• 0	• 2,01	• 0,5	• 0,68	• 0,0003	• 0

Table 4. ENT test results for the third pseudorandom number generator of size 25×25

The CA size	The Number of Inhomogeneous Cells	The Number Of cells That are in the Initial State of the Log. "1"	The Length of the Formed Sequence	The Number of "0"	The Number of "1"	The File Reducing Value %	The Excess of the Calculated Value, %	Arithmetic Mean	The Value of Monte Carlo Method, %	Serial Correlation Coefficient	Number of Coincidences
25x25	1	1	104	52	52	0	99,99	0,5	36,34	-0,115	0
			1000	491	509	0	56,92	0,5	10,87	-0,028	0
			10000	4950	5050	0	31,73	0,5	3,45	0,0079	0
			1000000	499554	500446	0	39,72	0,5	1,83	0,0002	0
		10	104	59	45	1	16,98	0,43	27,32	-0,018	0
			1000	535	465	0	2,69	0,46	8,23	-0,07	0
			10000	4963	5037	0	45,93	0,5	0,83	-0,00005	0
			1000000	500934	499066	0	41,23	0,49	0,17	-0,0002	0
		50	104	57	47	0	32,68	0,45	36,34	-0,048	0
			1000	500	500	0	99,99	0,5	4,51	0,016	0
			10000	4940	5060	0	23,01	0,5	7,57	0,006	0
			1000000	499456	500544	0	52,17	0,5	0,34	0,0001	0
		100	104	48	56	0	43,28	0,53	27,32	0,226	0
			1000	518	482	0	25,49	0,48	8,23	0,032	0
			10000	4981	5019	0	70,39	0,5	1,0	0,007	0
			1000000	499715	500285	0	47,12	0,5	0,87	0,0001	0
		200	104	53	51	0	24,45	0,49	27,32	0,07	0
			1000	511	489	0	48,66	0,489	4,51	0,027	0
			10000	4955	5045	0	36,81	0,5	0,22	-0,0012	0
			1000000	499613	500387	0	44,72	0,5	0,46	0,0004	0

continued on following page

Table 4. Continued

The CA size	The Number of Inhomogeneous Cells	The Number Of cells That are in the Initial State of the Log. "1"	The Length of the Formed Sequence	The Number of "0"	The Number of "1"	The File Reducing Value %	The Excess of the Calculated Value, %	Arithmetic Mean	The Value of Monte Carlo Method, %	Serial Correlation Coefficient	Number of Coincidences
		250	104	55	49	0	55,63	0,47	36,34	0,459	0
			1000	496	504	0	80,03	0,5	17,24	-0,06	0
			10000	5009	4991	0	85,72	0,49	2,84	-0,01	0
			1000000	499613	500387	0	44,72	0,5	0,46	-0,0004	0
		300	104	52	52	0	99,99	0,5	36,34	0,076	0
			1000	523	477	0	14,58	0,477	4,51	0,017	0
			10000	4940	5060	0	23,01	0,5	6,96	-0,0017	0
			1000000	499613	500387	0	44,72	0,5	0,46	0,0004	0
		400	104	53	51	0	84,45	0,49	36,34	0,038	0
			1000	513	487	0	41,10	0,487	23,61	0,055	0
			10000	5077	4923	0	12,36	0,49	4,51	-0,004	0
			1000000	499293	500707	0	11,65	0,5	0,25	-0,0004	0
		500	104	56	48	0	43,28	0,46	27,32	-0,0059	0
			1000	488	512	0	44,79	0,51	8,23	0,007	0
			10000	4977	5023	0	64,55	0,5	0,22	-0,004	0
			1000000	499041	500959	0	4,23	0,5	0,31	-0,0006	0
		600	104	50	54	0	69,49	0,51	36,34	-0,001	0
			1000	506	494	0	70,43	0,49	10,87	-0,028	0
			10000	4971	5029	0	56,19	0,5	2,06	-0,016	0
			1000000	499613	500387	0	44,72	0,5	0,46	-0,0004	0

continued on following page

Table 4. Continued

The CA size	The Number of Inhomogeneous Cells	The Number Of cells That are in the Initial State of the Log. "1"	The Length of the Formed Sequence	The Number of "0"	The Number of "1"	The File Reducing Value %	The Excess of the Calculated Value, %	Arithmetic Mean	The Value of Monte Carlo Method, %	Serial Correlation Coefficient	Number of Coincidences
	2	1	104	57	47	0	32,68	0,45	27,32	-0,16	0
			1000	492	508	0	61,29	0,5	14,59	0,0037	0
			10000	5030	4970	0	54,85	0,49	5,9	-0,01	0
			1000000	499566	500434	0	59,07	0,5	1,41	-0,0002	0
		10	104	63	41	3	3,10	0,39	27,32	-0,04	0
			1000	520	480	0	20,59	0,48	1,86	-0,02	0
			10000	5098	4902	0	5,0	0,49	2,06	0,004	0
			1000000	500347	499653	0	56,15	0,5	4,18	0,006	0
		50	104	58	46	0	23,93	0,44	36,34	0,1	0
			1000	515	485	0	34,28	0,48	23,61	-0,0129	0
			10000	5015	4985	0	76,42	0,498	0,22	-0,0012	0
			1000000	500280	499720	0	52,65	0,5	0,73	0,003	0
		100	104	52	52	0	99,99	0,5	27,32	0,23	0
			1000	497	503	0	84,95	0,5	8,23	-0,05	0
			10000	5065	4935	0	19,36	0,49	1,61	0,009	0
			1000000	499538	500462	0	21,35	0,5	0,18	-0,0002	0
		200	104	60	44	1	11,67	0,42	27,32	-0,024	0
			1000	494	506	0	70,43	0,5	4,51	0,031	0
			10000	4996	5004	0	93,62	0,5	2,84	0,000799	0
			1000000	499688	500312	0	48,15	0,5	2,11	0,0002	0

continued on following page

Table 4. Continued

The CA size	The Number of Inhomogeneous Cells	The Number Of cells That are in the Initial State of the Log. "1"	The Length of the Formed Sequence	The Number of "0"	The Number of "1"	The File Reducing Value %	The Excess of the Calculated Value, %	Arithmetic Mean	The Value of Monte Carlo Method, %	Serial Correlation Coefficient	Number of Coincidences
		• 250	• 104	• 47	• 57	• 0	• 32,68	• 0,54	• 36,34	• -0,048	• 0
			• 1000	• 499	• 501	• 0	• 94,96	• 0,5	• 14,59	• 0,03	• 0
			• 10000	• 5008	• 4992	• 0	• 87,29	• 0,499	• 4,51	• -0,0016	• 0
			• 1000000	• 500624	• 499376	• 0	• 41,31	• 0,5	• 0,16	• 0,0001	• 0
		• 300	• 104	• 50	• 54	• 0	• 81,56	• 0,5	• 25,22	• -0,00027	• 0
			• 1000	• 507	• 493	• 0	• 65,8	• 0,49	• 1,86	• -0,008	• 0
			• 10000	• 5030	• 4970	• 0	• 54,85	• 0,49	• 2,84	• 0,0059	• 0
			• 1000000	• 499645	• 500355	• 0	• 48,26	• 0,5	• 2,73	• 0,00002	• 0
		• 400	• 104	• 51	• 53	• 0	• 84,45	• 0,5	• 27,32	• -0,00037	• 0
			• 1000	• 494	• 506	• 0	• 70,43	• 0,5	• 14,59	• -0,02	• 0
			• 10000	• 5048	• 4952	• 0	• 33,71	• 0,49	• 2,84	• -0,0056	• 0
			• 1000000	• 500427	• 499573	• 0	• 24,33	• 0,5	• 3,24	• -0,0001	• 0
		• 500	• 104	• 48	• 56	• 0	• 43,28	• 0,53	• 27,32	• -0,044	• 0
			• 1000	• 501	• 499	• 0	• 94,96	• 0,49	• 2,23	• 0,031	• 0
			• 10000	• 5048	• 4952	• 0	• 33,71	• 0,49	• 0,22	• 0,017	• 0
			• 1000000	• 499552	• 500448	• 0	• 28,56	• 0,5	• 0,69	• 0,0004	• 0
		• 600	• 104	• 50	• 54	• 0	• 69,49	• 0,519	• 27,32	• 0,037	• 0
			• 1000	• 505	• 495	• 0	• 75,18	• 0,495	• 8,23	• -0,012	• 0
			• 10000	• 4974	• 5026	• 0	• 60,31	• 0,5	• 1,61	• 0,00517	• 0
			• 1000000	500380	499620	0	12,22	0,499	3,25	-0,0001	• 0

continued on following page

Table 4. Continued

The CA size	The Number of Inhomogeneous Cells	The Number Of cells That are in the Initial State of the Log. "1"	The Length of the Formed Sequence	The Number of "0"	The Number of "1"	The File Reducing Value %	The Excess of the Calculated Value, %	Arithmetic Mean	The Value of Monte Carlo Method, %	Serial Correlation Coefficient	Number of Coincidences
3	3	1	104	57	47	0	32,68	0,45	27,32	-0,048	0
			1000	480	520	0	20,59	0,52	1,86	-0,0016	0
			10000	470	5030	0	54,85	0,5	2,23	0,0027	0
			1000000	500470	499530	0	34,72	0,499	0,25	-0,0002	0
		10	104	61	43	2	7,76	0,41	27,32	0,008	0
			1000	491	509	0	56,92	0,5	20,96	0,0076	0
			10000	4876	5124	0	1,31	0,51	2,84	0,016	0
			1000000	499300	500700	0	16,15	0,5	0,02	-0,00013	0
		50	104	54	50	0	69,49	0,48	27,32	-0,117	0
			1000	454	546	0	0,36	0,54	1,86	-0,02	0
			10000	4957	5043	0	38,09	0,5	2,84	0,0019	0
			1000000	500780	499214	0	11,60	0,499	0,25	0,000678	0
		100	104	58	46	0	23,93	0,44	27,32	-0,13	0
			1000	522	478	0	16,41	0,478	17,24	-0,017	0
			10000	5052	4948	0	29,83	0,49	3,28	0,001	0
			1000000	499784	500216	0	66,57	0,5	0,21	0,00006	0
		200	104	58	46	0	23,93	0,44	27,32	0,1	0
			1000	476	524	0	12,90	0,52	4,51	-0,01	0
			10000	4943	5057	0	25,43	0,5	7,57	-0,026	0
			1000000	499261	500739	0	13,94	0,5	0,26	-0,0015	0

continued on following page

Table 4. Continued

The CA size	The Number of Inhomogeneous Cells	The Number Of cells That are in the Initial State of the Log. "1"	The Length of the Formed Sequence	The Number of "0"	The Number of "1"	The File Reducing Value %	The Excess of the Calculated Value, %	Arithmetic Mean	The Value of Monte Carlo Method, %	Serial Correlation Coefficient	Number of Coincidences
		250	104	54	50	0	69,49	0,48	27,32	0,114	0
			1000	531	469	0	4,99	0,469	4,51	0,016	0
			10000	4995	5005	0	92,03	0,5	1,0	-0,003	0
			1000000	499235	500765	0	12,60	0,5	0,31	-0,0009	0
		300	104	52	52	0	59,45	0,38	27,32	-0,217	0
			1000	505	495	0	75,18	0,49	14,59	0,027	0
			10000	5006	4994	0	90,45	0,499	2,67	0,0019	0
			1000000	498481	501519	0	0,24	0,5	0,46	-0,0016	0
		400	104	51	53	0	97,89	0,5	33,37	0,018	0
			1000	495	505	0	75,18	0,5	1,86	0,0119	0
			10000	483	517	0	53,36	0,5	8,83	-0,04	0
			1000000	499342	500658	0	18,82	0,5	0,19	-0,0016	0
		500	104	52	52	0	99,99	0,5	36,34	0,038	0
			1000	489	511	0	48,66	0,51	10,87	-0,07	0
			10000	5061	4939	0	22,25	0,49	0,23	-0,0025	0
			1000000	499047	500953	0	5,67	0,5	0,01	-0,0005	0
		600	104	59	45	1	16,98	0,43	36,34	0,17	0
			1000	484	516	0	31,16	0,51	4,51	0,01	0
			10000	5005	4995	0	92,3	0,499	3,89	-0,014	0
			1000000	499291	500709	0	15,62	0,5	0,15	-0,0006	0

continued on following page

Table 4. Continued

The CA size	The Number of Inhomogeneous Cells	The Number Of cells That are in the Initial State of the Log. "1"	The Length of the Formed Sequence	The Number of "0"	The Number of "1"	The File Reducing Value %	The Excess of the Calculated Value, %	Arithmetic Mean	The Value of Monte Carlo Method, %	Serial Correlation Coefficient	Number of Coincidences
		1	104	53	51	0	84,45	0,49	27,32	0,115	0
			1000	500	500	0	99,99	0,5	29,97	0,008	0
			10000	4893	5107	0	3,24	0,51	5,73	-0,0096	0
			1000000	499195	500805	0	16,21	0,5	0,38	0,00018	0
		10	104	52	52	0	99,99	0,5	27,32	0,153	0
			1000	502	498	0	36,75	0,5	14,68	0,24	0
			10000	5008	4992	0	87,29	0,499	0,39	0,027	0
			1000000	500939	499061	0	6,04	0,499	0,06	-0,00019	0
	4	50	104	62	42	2	4,99	0,4	27,32	0,0015	0
			1000	512	488	0	44,79	0,488	4,51	-0,0085	0
			10000	5021	4979	0	67,45	0,4979	2,67	-0,002	0
			1000000	499887	500113	0	82,12	0,5	0,06	-0,00007	0
		100	104	47	57	0	32,68	0,548	27,32	-0,048	0
			1000	498	502	0	89,93	0,5	4,51	-0,07	0
			10000	5083	4917	0	9,69	0,49	0,83	-0,009	0
			1000000	500805	499195	0	10,74	0,499	0,37	0,002	0
		200	104	57	47	0	32,68	0,45	27,32	-0,2	0
			1000	499	501	0	99,96	0,5	8,23	-0,032	0
			10000	5031	4969	0	53,53	0,49	1,45	0,009	0
			1000000	499296	500704	0	15,91	0,5	0,16	0,00028	0

continued on following page

Table 4. Continued

The CA size	The Number of Inhomogeneous Cells	The Number Of cells That are in the Initial State of the Log. "1"	The Length of the Formed Sequence	The Number of "0"	The Number of "1"	The File Reducing Value %	The Excess of the Calculated Value, %	Arithmetic Mean	The Value of Monte Carlo Method, %	Serial Correlation Coefficient	Number of Coincidences
		250	104	57	47	0	32,62	0,45	27,32	-0,2	0
			1000	499	501	0	94,96	0,5	8,23	-0,032	0
			10000	5031	4969	0	53,53	0,49	1,45	-0,009	0
			1000000	499296	500704	0	15,91	0,5	0,18	0,00028	0
		300	104	57	47	0	32,68	0,45	27,32	0,068	0
			1000	486	514	0	37,59	0,51	1,86	-0,0047	0
			10000	4950	5050	0	31,73	0,5	3,45	-0,0001	0
			1000000	499959	500041	0	93,46	0,5	0,23	0,0002	0
		400	104	53	51	0	84,45	0,49	27,32	-0,00037	0
			1000	501	499	0	58,11	0,5	2,04	-0,0032	0
			10000	49991	5009	0	85,72	0,5	2,67	-0,0004	0
			1000000	499387	500613	0	22,02	0,5	0,48	0,00007	0
		500	104	50	54	0	69,49	0,51	36,34	0,037	0
			1000	487	513	0	41,1	0,51	10,87	-0,0006	0
			10000	4952	5048	0	33,71	0,5	3,89	0,0087	0
			1000000	499954	500046	0	92,67	0,5	0,25	0,0002	0
		600	104	49	55	0	55,63	0,528	36,34	0,112	0
			1000	475	525	0	11,38	0,52	17,24	0,009	0
			10000	4919	5081	0	10,52	0,5	0,83	0,024	0
			1000000	499645	500355	0	47,77	0,5	0,14	-0,011	0

Table 5. Test results for the third pseudorandom number generator of size 30×30

The CA Size	The Number of Inhomogeneous cells	The Number of Cells That Are in the Initial State of the Log. "1"	The Length of the Formed Sequence	The Number of "0"	The Number of "1"	The File reducing Value %	The Excess of the Calculated Value, %	Arithmetic mean	The Value of Monte Carlo Method, %	Serial Correlation Coefficient	Number of Coincidences
30x30	1	1	104	57	47	0	32,68	0,45	27,32	-0,086	1
			1000	511	489	0	48,66	0,489	4,51	0,031	0
			10000	4967	5033	0	50,93	0,5	4,51	0,0019	2
			1000000	501644	498356	0	0,1	0,498	1,55	0,00018	>10
		10	104	55	49	0	55,63	0,47	27,32	0,112	0
			1000	483	517	0	28,23	0,5	1,86	0,034	2
			10000	4987	5013	0	79	0,5	1,0	-0,017	2
			1000000	495555	504445	0	0,01	0,5	0,99	-0,0019	8
		50	104	48	56	0	43,28	0,538	36,34	0,148	1
			1000	479	521	0	18,41	0,52	4,51	0,020	1
			10000	4992	5058	0	24,6	0,5	2,67	0,005	2
			1000000	500800	499200	0	10,96	0,50	0,08	0,003	4
		100	104	55	49	0	55,63	0,47	36,34	-0,157	0
			1000	515	485	0	34,28	0,485	14,59	-0,0049	1
			10000	5087	4913	0	8,19	0,49	3,28	0,001	4
			1000000	502755	497245	0	0,01	0,50	2,79	-0,016	>10
		200	104	53	51	0	84,45	0,49	36,34	0,038	0
			1000	503	497	0	84,95	0,49	8,23	-0,076	1
			10000	4677	5323	0	0,01	0,53	16,31	-0,1	2
			1000000	498271	501729	0	0,05	0,50	0,11	0,000	8

continued on following page

Table 5. Continued

The CA Size	The Number of Inhomogeneous cells	The Number of Cells That Are in the Initial State of the Log. "1"	The Length of the Formed Sequence	The Number of "0"	The Number of "1"	The File reducing Value %	The Excess of the Calculated Value, %	Arithmetic mean	The Value of Monte Carlo Method, %	Serial Correlation Coefficient	Number of Coincidences
		• 300	• 104	• 48	• 56	• 0	• 43,28	• 0,53	• 100,00	• 0,07	• 0
			• 1000	• 495	• 505	• 0	• 75,18	• 0,5	• 23,61	• 0,023	• 0
			• 10000	• 5007	• 4993	• 0	• 88,87	• 0,499	• 0,83	• 0,0047	• 1
			• 1000000	• 499501	• 500499	• 0	• 12,22	• 0,5	• 0,16	• 0,0004	• 0
		• 400	• 104	• 48	• 56	• 0	• 43,28	• 0,538	• 27,32	• -0,08	• 0
			• 1000	• 503	• 497	• 0	• 84,95	• 0,497	• 1,86	• -0,008	• 0
			• 10000	• 5069	• 4931	• 0	• 16,76	• 0,49	• 1,61	• -0,008	• 0
			• 1000000	• 500324	• 500676	• 0	• 7,43	• 0,5	• 1,68	• 0,0002	• 0
		• 500	• 104	• 51	• 53	• 0	• 84,45	• 0,5	• 27,32	• -0,19	• 0
			• 1000	• 487	• 513	• 0	• 41,10	• 0,51	• 4,51	• -0,04	• 0
			• 10000	• 5014	• 4986	• 0	• 77,95	• 0,498	• 4,06	• 0,004	• 0
			• 1000000	• 499823	• 500177	• 0	• 33,45	• 0,5	• 0,65	• 0,00007	• 0
		• 600	• 104	• 59	• 45	• 1	• 16,98	• 0,43	• 36,34	• -0,09	• 0
			• 1000	• 517	• 483	• 0	• 28,23	• 0,48	• 23,61	• 0,01	• 0
			• 10000	• 5009	• 4991	• 0	• 68,49	• 0,499	• 3,97	• 0,0097	• 0
			• 1000000	• 499746	• 500254	• 0	• 47,25	• 0,5	• 0,88	• 0,0005	• 0
		• 700	• 104	• 51	• 53	• 0	• 84,45	• 0,5	• 36,34	• 0,19	• 0
			• 1000	• 477	• 523	• 0	• 14,58	• 0,52	• 10,87	• 0,02	• 0
			• 10000	• 5013	• 4987	• 0	• 79,49	• 0,498	• 2,67	• 0,009	• 0
			• 1000000	• 500016	• 499984	• 0	• 28,49	• 0,5	• 4,23	• 0,0003	• 0

continued on following page

191

Table 5. Continued

The CA Size	The Number of Inhomogeneous cells	The Number of Cells That Are in the Initial State of the Log. "1"	The Length of the Formed Sequence	The Number of "0"	The Number of "1"	The File reducing Value %	The Excess of the Calculated Value, %	Arithmetic mean	The Value of Monte Carlo Method, %	Serial Correlation Coefficient	Number of Coincidences
	2	800	104	59	45	1	16,98	0,43	100,0	-0,05	0
			1000	520	480	0	20,50	0,48	1,86	-0,057	0
			10000	5017	4983	0	73,39	0,498	3,89	-0,03	0
			1000000	499224	500776	0	28,36	0,5	1,53	-0,00015	0
		1	104	56	48	0	43,28	0,46	27,32	-0,12	0
			1000	490	510	0	52,71	0,51	14,59	0,05	0
			10000	5015	4985	0	76,42	0,498	1,0	0,005	0
			1000000	500222	499778	0	43,14	0,5	0,29	0,0005	0
		10	104	63	41	3	3,10	0,39	36,34	-0,006	0
			1000	501	499	0	94,96	0,499	36,34	0,007	0
			10000	4975	5025	0	73,12	0,51	3,54	-0,0003	0
			1000000	499558	500442	0	40,75	0,5	0,58	0,0005	0
		50	104	57	47	0	32,68	0,45	27,32	0,068	0
			1000	533	467	0	3,69	0,467	4,51	-0,02	0
			10000	5076	4924	0	12,85	0,49	2,23	-0,0014	0
			1000000	499297	500703	0	5,91	0,5	0,17	0,0005	0
		100	104	49	55	0	55,63	0,528	100,0	0,035	0
			1000	499	501	0	94,96	0,5	23,61	-0,024	0
			10000	5020	4980	0	68,92	0,49	0,22	-0,0136	0
			1000000	499465	500535	0	37,25	0,5	0,32	-0,0001	0

continued on following page

Table 5. Continued

The CA Size	The Number of Inhomogeneous cells	The Number of Cells That Are in the Initial State of the Log. "1"	The Length of the Formed Sequence	The Number of "0"	The Number of "1"	The File reducing Value %	The Excess of the Calculated Value, %	Arithmetic mean	The Value of Monte Carlo Method, %	Serial Correlation Coefficient	Number of Coincidences
		• 200	• 104	• 54	• 50	• 0	• 69,49	• 0,48	• 27,32	• -0,078	• 0
			• 1000	• 505	• 495	• 0	• 75,18	• 0,495	• 8,23	• -0,06	• 0
			• 10000	• 4981	• 5019	• 0	• 70,39	• 0,5	• 2,67	• 0,007	• 0
			• 1000000	• 499354	• 500646	• 0	• 26,54	• 0,5	• 0,78	• 0,0007	• 0
		• 300	• 104	• 54	• 50	• 0	• 69,49	• 0,48	• 36,34	• -0,15	• 0
			• 1000	• 501	• 499	• 0	• 94,96	• 0,499	• 8,23	• 0,0079	• 0
			• 10000	• 5012	• 4988	• 0	• 81,03	• 0,498	• 3,28	• 0,0139	• 0
			• 1000000	500386	499614	0	43,83	0,499	0,17	-0,0001	• 0
		• 400	• 104	• 50	• 54	• 0	• 69,49	• 0,519	• 27,32	• -0,04	• 0
			• 1000	• 523	• 477	• 0	• 14,58	• 0,477	• 10,87	• 0,037	• 0
			• 10000	• 5022	• 4978	• 0	• 65,99	• 0,497	• 1,61	• 0,0039	• 0
			• 1000000	499291	500709	0	12,9	0,5	0,14	0,0004	• 0
		• 500	• 104	• 55	• 49	• 0	• 55,63	• 0,47	• 27,32	• -0,04	• 0
			• 1000	• 511	• 489	• 0	• 48,66	• 0,489	• 17,24	• 0,003	• 0
			• 10000	• 5084	• 4916	• 0	• 9,3	• 0,49	• 0,22	• 0,0025	• 0
			• 1000000	• 500801	• 499199	• 0	• 9,72	• 0,499	• 0,28	• 0,002	• 0
		• 600	• 104	• 60	• 44	• 1	• 11,67	• 0,42	• 36,34	• 0,09	• 0
			• 1000	• 507	• 493	• 0	• 65,80	• 0,49	• 8,23	• 0,06	• 0
			• 10000	• 5001	• 4999	• 0	• 98,4	• 0,499	• 1,61	• 0,005	• 0
			• 1000000	• 500184	• 499816	• 0	• 74,74	• 0,48	• 0,29	• -0,00007	• 0

continued on following page

Table 5. Continued

The CA Size	The Number of Inhomogeneous cells	The Number of Cells That Are in the Initial State of the Log. "1"	The Length of the Formed Sequence	The Number of "0"	The Number of "1"	The File reducing Value %	The Excess of the Calculated Value, %	Arithmetic mean	The Value of Monte Carlo Method, %	Serial Correlation Coefficient	Number of Coincidences
		700	104	50	54	0	69,49	0,51	36,34	0,19	0
			1000	479	521	0	18,41	0,52	23,61	-0,025	0
			10000	4993	5007	0	88,87	0,5	0,83	0,0035	0
			1000000	499385	500615	0	19,52	0,5	0,12	0,0002	0
		800	104	55	49	0	55,63	0,47	36,34	-0,0033	0
			1000	480	520	0	20,59	0,52	17,24	-0,0056	0
			10000	4964	5036	0	47,15	0,5	3,45	-0,0088	0
			1000000	499554	500446	0	39,65	0,5	0,48	0,0006	0
	3	1	104	57	47	0	32,68	0,45	27,32	-0,16	0
			1000	512	488	0	44,79	0,488	10,87	-0,028	0
			10000	5026	4974	0	60,31	0,497	4,51	-0,0016	0
			1000000	499172	500828	0	9,77	0,5	0,09	0,0006	0
		10	104	55	49	0	55,63	0,47	27,32	-0,04	0
			1000	488	512	0	27,16	0,51	11,23	-0,004	0
			10000	5020	4980	0	68,09	0,498	2,06	0,0047	0
			1000000	499603	500397	0	42,72	0,5	0,45	0,0007	0
		50	104	50	54	0	69,49	0,51	27,32	-0,04	0
			1000	480	520	0	20,59	0,52	4,51	0,022	0
			10000	4964	5036	0	47,15	0,5	5,73	0,0023	0
			1000000	499915	500085	0	86,50	0,5	0,0	0,001	0

continued on following page

Table 5. Continued

The CA Size	The Number of Inhomogeneous cells	The Number of Cells That Are in the Initial State of the Log. "1"	The Length of the Formed Sequence	The Number of "0"	The Number of "1"	The File reducing Value %	The Excess of the Calculated Value, %	Arithmetic mean	The Value of Monte Carlo Method, %	Serial Correlation Coefficient	Number of Coincidences
		• 100	• 104	• 54	• 50	• 0	• 69,49	• 0,48	• 36,34	• -0,070	• 0
			• 1000	• 502	• 498	• 0	• 89,93	• 0,498	• 1,86	• -0,04	• 0
			• 10000	• 4953	• 5047	• 0	• 34,72	• 0,5	• 3,28	• -0,00048	• 0
			• 1000000	• 500208	• 499792	• 0	• 67,74	• 0,499	• 0,17	• -0,00018	• 0
		• 200	• 104	• 46	• 58	• 0	• 23,93	• 0,55	• 36,34	• 0,18	• 0
			• 1000	• 499	• 501	• 0	• 56,65	• 0,51	• 6,11	• -0,002	• 0
			• 10000	• 5012	• 4988	• 0	• 81,03	• 0,498	• 4,51	• 0,004	• 0
			• 1000000	• 499859	• 500141	• 0	• 77,79	• 0,5	• 0,54	• -0,002	• 0
		• 300	• 104	• 50	• 54	• 0	• 69,49	• 0,51	• 100,0	• -0,04	• 0
			• 1000	• 489	• 511	• 0	• 48,66	• 0,51	• 8,23	• -0,012	• 0
			• 10000	• 5055	• 4945	• 0	• 27,13	• 0,49	• 3,45	• 0,005	• 0
			• 1000000	• 499469	• 500531	• 0	• 28,82	• 0,5	• 0,12	• -0,0009	• 0
		• 400	• 104	• 52	• 52	• 0	• 99,99	• 0,5	• 27,32	• 0,0	• 0
			• 1000	• 501	• 499	• 0	• 99,96	• 0,499	• 14,59	• -0,012	• 0
			• 10000	• 4987	• 5013	• 0	• 79,49	• 0,5	• 0,39	• 0,005	• 0
			• 1000000	• 500222	• 499778	• 0	• 65,70	• 0,499	• 0,34	• -0,0009	• 0
		• 500	• 104	• 53	• 51	• 0	• 84,45	• 0,49	• 36,34	• 0,076	• 0
			• 1000	• 508	• 492	• 0	• 61,29	• 0,49	• 10,87	• -0,04	• 0
			• 10000	• 5067	• 4933	• 0	• 18,02	• 0,49	• 4,67	• -0,0008	• 0
			• 1000000	• 500181	• 499819	• 0	• 71,74	• 0,499	• 0,29	• -0,00018	• 0

continued on following page

Table 5. Continued

The CA Size	The Number of Inhomogeneous cells	The Number of Cells That Are in the Initial State of the Log. "1"	The Length of the Formed Sequence	The Number of "0"	The Number of "1"	The File reducing Value %	The Excess of the Calculated Value, %	Arithmetic mean	The Value of Monte Carlo Method, %	Serial Correlation Coefficient	Number of Coincidences
		600	104	48	56	0	43,28	0,53	36,34	-0,0059	0
			1000	465	535	0	2,69	0,53	4,51	-0,0089	0
			10000	4823	5177	0	0,04	0,517	3,28	-0,01	0
			1000000	500371	499629	0	45,81	0,499	0,13	-0,001	0
		700	104	53	51	0	31,77	0,456	36,24	-0,0198	0
			1000	486	514	0	37,59	0,51	0,45	-0,04	0
			10000	4991	5009	0	85,72	0,5	0,39	0,009	0
			1000000	499808	500192	0	70,1	0,5	0,16	0,001	0
		800	104	57	47	0	32,68	0,45	36,34	-0,009	0
			1000	546	454	0	0,36	0,45	8,23	-0,05	0
			10000	5046	4954	0	35,76	0,495	1,45	-0,004	0
	4		1000000	498725	501275	0	1,08	0,5	0,51	0,000001	0
		1	104	63	41	3	3,10	0,39	27,32	-0,08	0
			1000	489	511	0	48,66	0,51	17,24	0,019	0
			10000	5036	4964	0	47,15	0,49	7,74	0,008	0
			1000000	499343	500657	0	18,88	0,5	0,59	0,0005	0
		10	104	54	50	0	69,49	0,48	36,34	-0,001	0
			1000	491	509	0	56,92	0,5	4,51	-0,008	0
			10000	4988	5012	0	81,03	0,5	5,73	0,0039	0
			1000000	49938	500617	0	21,72	0,5	0,11	0,0002	0

continued on following page

Table 5. Continued

The CA Size	The Number of Inhomogeneous cells	The Number of Cells That Are in the Initial State of the Log. "1"	The Length of the Formed Sequence	The Number of "0"	The Number of "1"	The File reducing Value %	The Excess of the Calculated Value, %	Arithmetic mean	The Value of Monte Carlo Method, %	Serial Correlation Coefficient	Number of Coincidences
		• 50	• 104	• 56	• 48	• 0	• 43,28	• 0,46	• 27,32	• 0,11	• 0
			• 1000	• 505	• 495	• 0	• 75,18	• 0,495	• 20,96	• -0,04	• 0
			• 10000	• 4968	• 5032	• 0	• 52,22	• 0,5	• 3,28	• -0,004	• 0
			• 1000000	• 500376	• 499624	• 0	• 45,21	• 0,499	• 0,21	• -0,0017	• 0
		• 100	• 104	• 59	• 45	• 1	• 16,98	• 0,43	• 36,34	• -0,05	• 0
			• 1000	• 504	• 496	• 0	• 80,03	• 0,49	• 17,24	• 0,0079	• 0
			• 10000	• 4999	• 5001	• 0	• 98,4	• 0,5	• 3,89	• 0,012	• 0
			• 1000000	• 499596	• 500404	• 0	• 41,91	• 0,5	• 0,19	• -0,00068	• 0
		• 200	• 104	• 5	• 51	• 0	• 84,45	• 0,49	• 36,34	• -0,00037	• 0
			• 1000	• 508	• 492	• 0	• 61,29	• 0,49	• 8,23	• 0,011	• 0
			• 10000	• 4942	• 5058	• 0	• 24,60	• 0,5	• 2,67	• -0,005	• 0
			• 1000000	• 500450	• 499550	• 0	• 36,81	• 0,499	• 0,05	• 0,0012	• 0
		• 300	• 104	• 50	• 54	• 0	• 69,49	• 0,51	• 36,34	• 0,037	• 0
			• 1000	• 494	• 506	• 0	• 70,43	• 0,5	• 4,51	• -0,012	• 0
			• 10000	• 4942	• 5058	• 0	• 24,60	• 0,5	• 2,06	• -0,0057	• 0
			• 1000000	• 500338	• 499662	• 0	• 49,9	• 0,499	• 0,18	• -0,00076	• 0
		• 400	• 104	• 52	• 52	• 0	• 99,99	• 0,5	• 27,32	• -0,15	• 0
			• 1000	• 528	• 472	• 0	• 7,66	• 0,47	• 1,86	• 0,028	• 0
			• 10000	• 5003	• 4997	• 0	• 95,22	• 0,499	• 2,23	• -0,004	• 0
			• 1000000	• 500351	• 499649	• 0	• 48,27	• 0,499	• 0,18	• 0,001	• 0

continued on following page

Table 5. Continued

The CA Size	The Number of Inhomogeneous cells	The Number of Cells That Are in the Initial State of the Log. "1"	The Length of the Formed Sequence	The Number of "0"	The Number of "1"	The File reducing Value %	The Excess of the Calculated Value, %	Arithmetic mean	The Value of Monte Carlo Method, %	Serial Correlation Coefficient	Number of Coincidences
		500	104	55	49	0	55,63	0,47	27,32	0,228	0
			1000	502	498	0	89,93	0,498	1,86	-0,000016	0
			10000	5029	4971	0	56,19	0,497	2,67	0,006	0
			1000000	500371	499629	0	46	0,499	0,56	-0,00066	0
		600	104	55	49	0	55,63	0,47	36,34	0,07	0
			1000	503	497	0	84,95	0,497	1,86	0,011	0
			10000	5068	4932	0	17,38	0,49	5,9	0,0078	0
			1000000	500181	499819	0	71,74	0,499	0,3	0,00008	0
		700	104	48	56	0	43,28	0,538	36,34	0,07	0
			1000	474	526	0	10,01	0,52	1,86	0,025	0
			10000	4974	5026	0	60,31	0,5	1,61	-0,011	0
			1000000	498977	501023	0	4,08	0,5	0,16	-0,00069	0
		800	104	57	47	0	32,68	0,45	36,34	0,107	0
			1000	491	509	0	56,92	0,5	1,86	-0,012	0
			10000	4940	5060	0	23,01	0,5	6,96	-0,0149	0
			1000000	500073	499927	0	88,39	0,499	0,38	-0,0001	0

Figure 10. Results of performance of the ENT tests by third pseudorandom number generator based on CA with inhomogeneous cells for the CA size 20×20

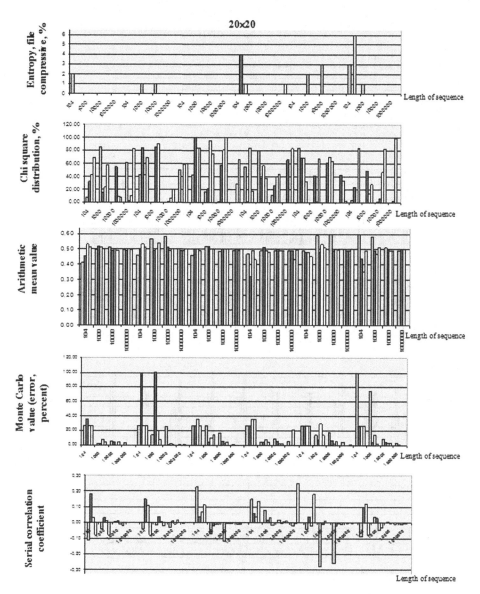

At each time step the inhomogeneous cell has been setting to a logical "1" state, if the previous time step, the number of neighborhood cells that have a logic "1" state was more than a neighborhood of the cells that were in a state of logical "0". This number includes the state of the inhomogeneous cell.

Figure 11. Results of performance of the ENT tests by third pseudorandom number generator based on CA with inhomogeneous cells for the CA size 25×25

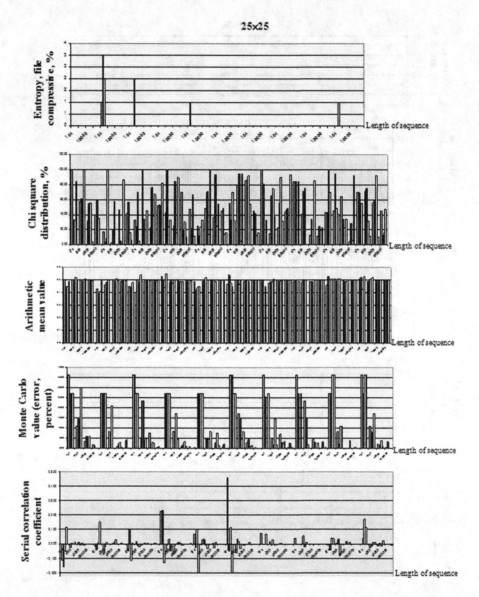

The fourth pseudorandom number generator, which was subjected to testing was the pseudorandom number generator based ACA with a hexagonal cover (HACA). The dimension 16×16 has been selected. For the experiment were used the initial installation of HACA, which contain 1, 10, 50, 100 and 200 cells that initially set to logic "1" state. Their location is being chosen arbitrarily

Figure 12. Results of performance of the ENT tests by third pseudorandom number generator based on CA with inhomogeneous cells for the CA size 30×30

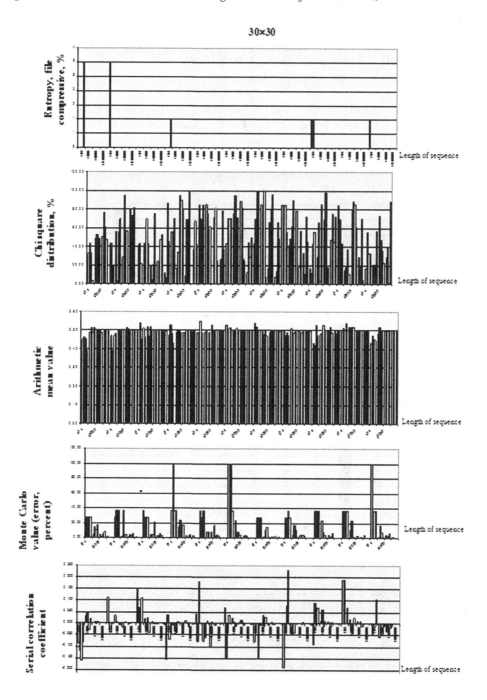

by the user. On the Figure 13 are presented the distribution histogram of the results of ENT tests application to the fourth generator.

For this generator the test for the compression is not considered, since the test showed compression 0% for all sequences. An additional bit is formed by row from left to right and from top to bottom.

Figure 13. The ENT tests results of the fourth pseudorandom number generator based on the HACA

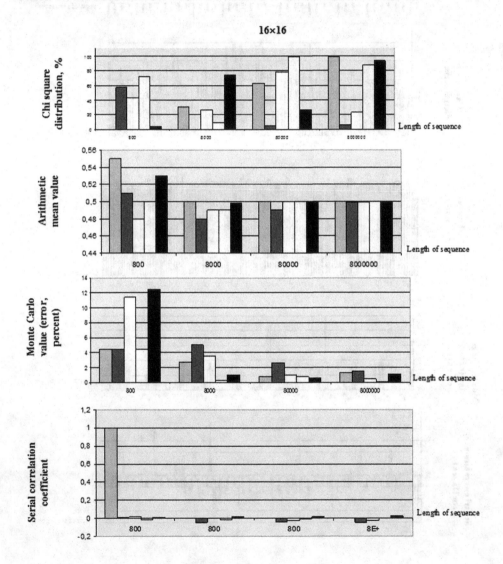

For a more extensive analysis was used the pseudorandom number generator, wherein the cell that generates an additional bit inverted on its the opposite state after how an additional bit was formed. The results of this analysis for the fifth pseudorandom number generator are shown on the Figure 14.

As seen from the Figure 14 the generator with inversion cells that forming an additional bit does not give a better result than the previous generator.

Figure 14. The results of passing the ENT tests by the fifth pseudorandom number generator based on HACA with inversion of the cell states, which form an additional bit at each time step

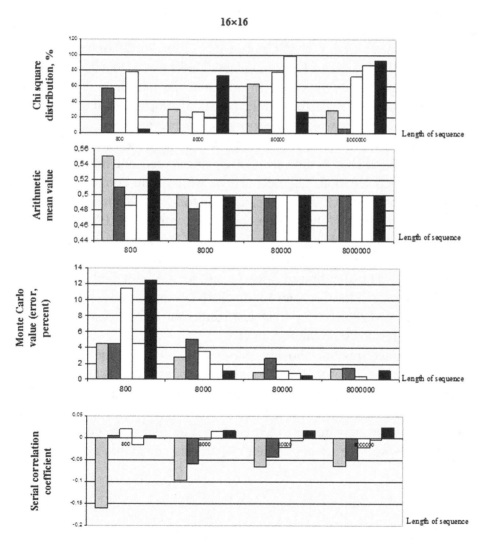

Only under of separate initial settings and the length of the sequence it won the first test. Basically the previous pseudorandom number generator has good features on the great lengths of a bit sequences. The increase the GCA dimension does not degrade the feature of the formed bit sequence.

The last pseudorandom number generator, which was subjected to testing is the pseudorandom number generator, which is implemented in the GCA and it functions as a third pseudorandom number generator, which is built on the basis of SCA with the orthogonal mosaics. In the pseudorandom number generator based SCA all the cells perform the same local transition function and have the same a neighborhood structure. The cells that perform different local transition function are being selected. These cells are called inhomogeneous. The programming model, which allows you to resize the GCA field is also implemented. The pseudorandom number generator have been investigated based on a HGCA size 10×10 and 20×20 of the area cells. For each size the 1, 2, 3 and 4 inhomogeneous cells was used inhomogeneous cell carried a majority function. In addition, the pseudorandom number generator based HGCA performed the constant comparison of arrays of the previous HGCA states, which were formed at the previous time steps. If some of their previous arrays coincide with HGCA state at the current time step, all previous stored HGCA state arrays are being zeroed, and inhomogeneous cell change their location. The new arrays, which were compared with the current state of each HGCA have been began to form. The main cell was set originally, and it formed the bit sequence at the output. The ENT test results for pseudorandom number generator based HGCA size 10×10 are presented in Table 6 and the basic value of its indicators is reduced to the Figure 15.

The obtained results showed a good result for CA with 4 inhomogeneous cells. The impact of the CA sizes for this PRNG was also investigated on the CA with the size 20×20. The ENT test results for PRNG based on the CA size 20×20 are shown on the Figure 16.

The obtained results showed good indicators for the CA with 4 inhomogeneous cells at the great length sequences. This fact confirms the presence of a certain time, which is used to obtain a normal distribution of sequence elements. This time is greater for small quantities of the cells which at the initial time step are set to logical "1" state. For more quantity of the primary cells with the state of logical "1" the test indicators are improved.

Table 6. Test results for the sixth pseudorandom number generator of size 10×10

The CA Size	The Number of Inhomogeneous Cells	The Number of Cells That Are in the Initial State of the Log. "1"	The Length Of The Formed Sequence	The Number of "0"	The Number of "1"	The File Reducing Value %	The Excess of the Calculated Value, %	Arithmetic Mean	The Value of Monte Carlo Method, %	Serial Correlation Coefficient
10x10	•1	•1	•800	•403	•397	•0	•83,20	•0,49	•19,37	•0,02
			•8000	•4051	•3949	•0	•25,41	•0,49	•5,85	•0,0051
			•80000	•40904	•39096	•0	•0,01	•0,48	•1,65	•-0,014
			•8000000	•3995933	•4004067	•0	•0,10	•0,5	•2,29	•-0,0001
		•10	•800	•372	•428	•0	•47,70	•0,53	•36,34	•0,0051
			•8000	•3977	•4023	•0	•60,70	•0,5	•1,46	•-0,010
			•80000	•39133	•40867	•0	•0,01	•0,5	•1,95	•0,009
			•8000000	•3999999	•4000001	•0	•99,94	•0,47	•27,32	•-0,26
		•50	•800	•421	•379	•0	•13,76	•0,48	•11,41	•0,05
			•8000	•4081	•3919	•0	•70,01	•0,48	•0,22	•0,046
			•80000	•39888	•40112	•0	•49,80	•0,5	•2,18	•-0,02
			•8000000	•3984570	•4015440	•0	•0,01	•0,5	•1,92	•0,0004
	•2	•1	•800	•404	•396	•0	•77,73	•0,49	•20,42	•-0,03
			•8000	•3999	•4001	•0	•98,22	•0,5	•0,48	•-0,003
			•80000	•37596	•42404	•0	•0,01	•0,53	•7,07	•0,0026
			•8000000	•3980791	•4019209	•0	•0,01	•0,5	•1,12	•0,001
		•10	•800	•386	•414	•0	•32,22	•0,51	•3,45	•-0,006
			•8000	•3974	•4026	•0	•56,16	•0,5	•2,59	•0,03
			•80000	•38344	•41656	•0	•0,01	•0,52	•5,23	•0,003
			•8000000	•3973069	•4026931	•0	•0,01	•0,5	•2,12	•0,0001

continued on following page

Table 6. Continued

The CA Size	The Number of Inhomogeneous Cells	The Number of Cells That Are in the Initial State of the Log. "1"	The Length Of The Formed Sequence	The Number of "0"	The Number of "1"	The File Reducing Value %	The Excess of the Calculated Value, %	Arithmetic Mean	The Value of Monte Carlo Method, %	Serial Correlation Coefficient
		• 50	• 800	• 411	• 389	• 0	• 43,67	• 0,48	• 11,41	• 0,02
			• 8000	• 3938	• 4062	• 0	• 16,56	• 0,5	• 0,29	• 0,01
			• 80000	• 39929	• 40071	• 0	• 61,56	• 0,5	• 1,19	• -0,0027
			• 8000000	• 3981346	• 4018654	• 0	• 0,01	• 0,5	• 0,7	• 0,0045
		• 1	• 800	• 397	• 403	• 0	• 83,20	• 0,5	• 12,46	• -0,04
			• 8000	• 3974	• 4026	• 0	• 56,16	• 0,5	• 1,82	• -0,009
			• 80000	• 40051	• 39949	• 0	• 71,84	• 0,499	• 1,11	• 0,005
	• 3		• 8000000	• 4001733	• 3998267	• 0	• 22,04	• 0,49	• 0,02	• -0,0008
		• 10	• 800	• 405	• 395	• 0	• 72,37	• 0,49	• 3,45	• -0,035
			• 8000	• 3974	• 4026	• 0	• 56,16	• 0,5	• 0,29	• -0,002
			• 80000	• 39982	• 40018	• 0	• 89,87	• 0,5	• 0,8	• -0,003
			• 8000000	• 2315322	• 2317870	• 0	• 23,65	• 0,5	• 0,18	• 0,00003
		• 50	• 800	• 357	• 443	• 0	• 0,24	• 0,55	• 4,51	• 0,008
			• 8000	• 3998	• 4002	• 0	• 96,43	• 0,5	• 4,31	• 0,0005
			• 80000	• 39999	• 40001	• 0	• 99,44	• 0,5	• 0,27	• -0,008
			• 8000000	• 799492	• 800528	• 0	• 40,38	• 0,5	• 0,15	• -0,0016

continued on following page

Table 6. Continued

The CA Size	The Number of Inhomogeneous Cells	The Number of Cells That Are in the Initial State of the Log. "1"	The Length Of The Formed Sequence	The Number of "0"	The Number of "1"	The File Reducing Value %	The Excess of the Calculated Value, %	Arithmetic Mean	The Value of Monte Carlo Method, %	Serial Correlation Coefficient
• 4	• 4	• 1	• 800	• 405	• 395	• 0	• 72,37	• 0,49	• 11,41	• -0,05
			• 8000	• 3922	• 4078	• 0	• 8,11	• 0,5	• 4,89	• -0,009
			• 80000	• 39763	• 40237	• 0	• 9,38	• 0,5	• 0,27	• 0,006
			• 8000000	• 2581317	• 2580899	• 0	• 85,40	• 0,5	• 0,09	• 0,0005
		• 10	• 800	• 420	• 380	• 0	• 15,73	• 0,47	• 3,45	• 0,0025
			• 8000	• 4083	• 3917	• 0	• 6,35	• 0,48	• 2,78	• 0,003
			• 80000	• 39735	• 40265	• 0	• 6,10	• 0,5	• 1,64	• 0,001
			• 8000000	• 799853	• 800147	• 0	• 81,62	• 0,5	• 0,01	• 0,0005
		• 50	• 800	• 381	• 419	• 0	• 17,91	• 0,52	• 3,45	• -0,02
			• 8000	• 3933	• 4067	• 0	• 13,41	• 0,5	• 2,59	• 0,005
			• 80000	• 40027	• 39973	• 0	• 84,86	• 0,499	• 2,49	• 0,002
			• 8000000	• 800674	• 799326	• 0	• 28,66	• 0,499	• 0,27	• -0,00047

Figure 15. The ENT tests results for sixth PRNG based HGCA size 10×10. The results are shown for 1, 2, 3 and 4 of inhomogeneous cells

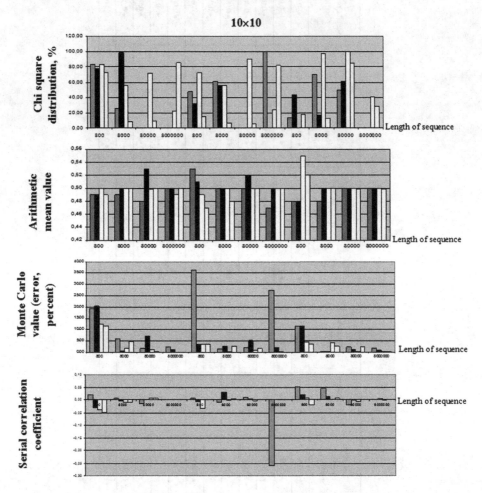

NIST QUALITY ANALYZING TESTS OF PSEUDORANDOM NUMBER GENERATORS BASED ON CELLULAR AUTOMATA

Today the problem of estimating the statistical properties of the pseudorandom number generator is widely studied. There are many methods for assessing the statistical properties pseudorandom number generator and professionals today are looking for new approaches to solving this problem. The methods

Figure 16. The ENT tests results for sixth PRNG based HGCA size 20×20. The results are shown for 1, 2, 3 and 4 of inhomogeneous cells

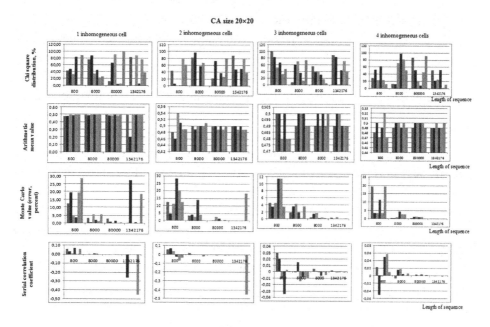

and techniques that are developed using in the form of a set of tests. These tests can have both mathematical and graphical content. They are meant to give developers pseudorandom number generator as much information for decision making on quality pseudorandom number generator.

The pseudorandom number generator considered acceptable for use if it has passed a large number of tests with positive results. We believe that the tests allow us to determine the extent of the proximity to the existing random sequence of numbers. The main characteristics of the developers take into account characteristics such as uniformity of distribution of numbers in sequence, a large length of time delay and other characteristics. These characteristics suggest that any element of the formed sequence can not be predicted on the basis of the existing elements of the previous interim steps.

Currently, among the most common statistical tests of the properties PRNG are the most popular the NIST tests (USA) (NIST Special Publications 800-22, 2001; NIST Special Publications 800-22, 2010). The NIST tests are used to analyze of the pseudorandom number generator that in further are planning for cryptographic use.

Tests were built so that they take into account such proposals.

1. The number of ones and zeros must be equal in sequence.
2. The probability of the appearance of 0 is probability of the appearance 1 at any time step during the sequence formation.
3. Each test can be applied to arbitrary sequences formed by any of its subsequence.
4. Tests should be applied to pseudorandom number generator with different initial settings. Initial installation must have significant differences.

Tests NIST used the following approach for decision making.

To test statistics the corresponding value of the probability are calculated. Statistic test is regarded as the realization of a random variable that obeys the known distribution law. According to statistics the big test values shall indicate the value indicating the reasons for the decision that the sequence is not random. The calculated value of a probability P_{value} in this case exceeds the accepted value that indicates that the sequence is random. If P_{value} takes a value less than the value α taken for random sequences $\left(P_{value} < \alpha \right)$, it is taken as evidence that the sequence is not random. The value of α is recommended to choose the interval [0,001÷0,01].

The sequence of steps to assess the quality pseudorandom number generator consists of four steps.

1. Formulation of hypothesis. It is believed that the sequence is random.
2. Calculate the test statistic sequence. Testing is performed on the bit level.
3. The P_{value}. $P_{value} \in [0;1]$ are calculated.
4. The P_{value} с α ($\alpha \in [0,001; 0,01]$) are compared.

If the $P_{value} \geq \alpha$ - tests passed.

Typically to calculate P_{value} following functions are used:

- $\varphi(z) = \dfrac{1}{2\pi} \displaystyle\int\limits_{-\infty}^{z} e^{-\frac{u^2}{2}} du$ - the function of the standard normal distribution;

- $erfc = \dfrac{2}{\sqrt{\pi}} \displaystyle\int\limits_{-z}^{\infty} e^{-u^2} du$ - additional error function;

- $\theta(a, x) = \dfrac{1}{\Gamma(a)} \displaystyle\int\limits_{x}^{\infty} e^{-t} t^{a-t} dt$ - incomplete gamma - function.

The structure of NIST guidance includes the following tests.

1. The Frequency (Monobit) Test.
2. The Frequency Test within a Block.
3. The Runs Test.
4. Test for the Longest-Run-of-Ones in a Block.
5. The Binary Matrix Rank Test.
6. The Discrete Fourier Transform (Spectral) Test.
7. The Non-overlapping Template Matching Test.
8. The Overlapping Template Matching Test.
9. Maurer's «Universal Statistical» Test.
10. The Lempel–Ziv Compression Test.
11. The Linear Complexity Test.
12. The Serial Test.
13. The Approximate Entropy Test.
14. The Cumulative Sums Test.
15. The Random Excursions Test.
16. The Random Excursions Variant Test.

The first test is designed to determine the number of zeros and ones in the sequence. For a positive result the number of zeros and ones must be the same or have tolerance. The recommended length sequence - at least 100 bits.

The second test determines the number of zeros and ones in the subsequence. This test allows to determine the uniformity of a distribution of 0 and 1. Recommended settings of testing: the length of sequence - at least 100 bits.. $n > MN, M \geq 20, M > 0,01n, N < 100$ (where M - the length of subsequence, $N = \dfrac{n}{M}$).

The third test detects fluctuations in the flow of bits. For this case the subsequences by the number of zeros and ones are determined. The recommended length sequence - at least 100 bits.

The fourth test detects abnormalities in the uniform distribution of zeros and ones in the subsequences. The ratios is used to determine the length of the sequences are presented in Table 7.

Recommended length of sequence - at least 100 bits.

The fifth test detects deviation matrix of rank distribution for a truly random sequence. Recommended length sequence - at least $38 \cdot M \cdot Q$ bit (where M×Q - size matrix).

Table 7. The relation between M and the minimum length of the sequence

Min n	M
• 128	• 8
• 6272	• 218
• 750000	• 10^4

A spectral test assesses property of periodic secuence. The analyses allow to estimate of the reduction height of the Fourier transform.

Seventh test determines the appearance frequency of non-periodic patterns. Templates are defined in advance. Recommended settings of testing: $N \le 100$, $M > 0,01n$. The value of the template from the tables are selected..

The eighth test determines the frequency of m - bit sequences of ones. Recommended settings of testing: $n \ge MN$, $N \cdot \min(\pi_i) > 5$, $\lambda \approx 2$, $m \approx \log_2 M$, $K \approx 2\lambda$.

Ninth test determine the compressibility of the test sequence. We analyze the distance between the sequences. Analyzed parameters are selected from the tables under the guide of NIST.

The tenth test determines the amount of excess compressibility under value of the compressibility of the truly random sequence. Recommended length sequence: $n = 1\ 000\ 000$.

The eleventh test determines the deviation of the distribution of linear complexity for finite length of a row. The linear complexity of the subsequences are analyzed. Recommended settings of testing: $n \ge 1\ 000\ 000$, $500 \le M \le 5000$, $N \ge 200$.

The twelfth test determines the uneven distribution of *m* - bit subsequences. The recommended settings of testing: $m < \lceil \log_2 n \rceil - 2$.

The thirteenth test determines the frequency of an appearance of m - bit subsequence. The recommended settings of testing: $m < \lceil \log_2 n \rceil - 2$.

Fourteenth test reveals a large number of ones and zeros at the beginning of the sequence. The maximum deviation of sum amount of elements of the normalized sequence from 0 is analyzed. The recommended length sequence: $n \ge 100$.

Fifteenth test makes it possible to determine the amount of deviation of the sum of elements of the normalized sequence from zero. The recommended length sequence: $n \ge 10^6$.

The sixteenth test allows you to calculate the deviation value from the distribution of the number of occurrences of subsequences of the certain species. This test extends the capabilities of the previous test.

To perform the NIST tests the bit sequences are used, which for performance tests ENT are generated. Since each test NIST proposed recommendations on length sequence tests were conducted for the corresponding bit sequences that were formed at the same initial settings as in the tests ENT. The data in a table 8 we display. The proposed six pseudorandom number generators successfully passed the first NIST test.

Table 8. The results of performance of the first NIST test for the second pseudorandom number generator by sizes 20×20 and 25×25

The CA Size	The Number of Cells That Are in the Initial State of the Log. "1"	The Length of the Formed Sequence	The Number of "0"	The Number of "1"	The Test Result (Positive / Negative)
20x20	• 1	• 96	• 48	• 48	• positive
		• 1000	• 540	• 460	• positive
		• 1000000	• 500436	• 499564	• positive
	• 10	• 96	• 49	• 47	• positive
		• 1000	• 516	• 484	• positive
		• 1000000	• 500032	• 499978	• positive
	• 50	• 96	• 54	• 42	• positive
		• 1000	• 516	• 484	• positive
		• 10000	• 5023	• 4977	• positive
		• 1000000	• 499744	• 500256	• positive
	• 100	• 96	• 49	• 47	• positive
		• 1000	• 507	• 493	• positive
		• 10000	• 5019	• 4981	• positive
		• 1000000	• 500246	• 499754	• positive
	• 200	• 96	• 45	• 51	• positive
		• 1000	• 507	• 493	• positive
		• 10000	• 4989	• 5011	• positive
		• 1000000	• 500275	• 499725	• positive
	• 250	• 96	• 52	• 44	• positive
		• 1000	• 511	• 489	• positive
		• 10000	• 4964	• 5036	• positive
		• 1000000	• 499657	• 500343	• positive

continued on following page

Table 8. Continued

The CA Size	The Number of Cells That Are in the Initial State of the Log. "1"	The Length of the Formed Sequence	The Number of "0"	The Number of "1"	The Test Result (Positive / Negative)
25x25	• 1	• 96	• 48	• 48	• positive
		• 1000	• 500	• 500	• positive
		• 10000	• 5000	• 5000	• positive
		• 1000000	• 500000	• 500000	• positive
	• 10	• 96	• 47	• 49	• positive
		• 1000	• 513	• 487	• positive
		• 10000	• 5191	• 4809	• positive
		• 1000000	• 499950	• 500050	• positive
	• 50	• 96	• 51	• 45	• positive
		• 1000	• 520	• 480	• positive
		• 10000	• 5036	• 4964	• positive
		• 1000000	• 500157	• 499843	• positive
	• 100	• 96	• 52	• 44	• positive
		• 1000	• 517	• 483	• positive
		• 10000	• 4954	• 5046	• positive
		• 1000000	• 499249	• 500751	• positive
	• 200	• 96	• 44	• 52	• positive
		• 10000	• 502	• 498	• positive
		• 100000	• 5023	• 4977	• positive
		• 10000000	• 500597	• 499403	• positive
	• 250	• 96	• 47	• 49	• positive
		• 1000	• 525	• 475	• positive
		• 10000	• 5056	• 4944	• positive
		• 1000000	• 500843	• 499157	• positive
	• 300	• 96	• 47	• 49	• positive
		• 1000	• 484	• 516	• positive
		• 10000	• 5040	• 4960	• positive
		• 1000000	• 499756	• 500244	• positive
	• 400	• 96	• 50	• 46	• positive
		• 1000	• 497	• 503	• positive
		• 10000	• 5017	• 4983	• The positive
		• 1000000	• 499408	• 500592	• positive
	• 500	• 96	• 46	• 50	• positive
		• 1000	• 493	• 507	• positive
		• 10000	• 5003	• 4997	• positive
		• 1000000	• 501117	• 498883	• positive

continued on following page

Table 8. Continued

The CA Size	The Number of Cells That Are in the Initial State of the Log. "1"	The Length of the Formed Sequence	The Number of "0"	The Number of "1"	The Test Result (Positive / Negative)
	• 600	• 96	• 42	• 54	• negative
		• 1000	• 513	• 481	• positive
		• 10000	• 5040	• 4960	• positive
		• 1000000	• 500370	• 499630	• positive

The practically all of the generated bit sequences gave a positive result on the first NIST test. The bit sequences formed with too small and too large amount of cells that have the logical "1" state as well as for large cellular automata sizes, gave the negative result.

To perform of the second NIST the test bit sequences, whose length is greater than 100 bits are used. Also the following size of M unit according to the conditions was being selected $M \geq 20$, $M > 0,01n$, $N < 100$. The results of the second test for the part of the sequences shown in Table 9.

Table 9. The results of the second NIST test passing for the selected bit sequences and for different cellular automata sizes

The Cellular Automata Size	The Number of Cells That Are in the Initial State of the Log. "1"	The Number of Inhomogeneous Cells	The Length of the Formed Sequence	The Block Length	The Number of Blocks	The Test Result (Positive / Negative)
• The First Pseudorandom Number Generator						
15x15	• 10	•	• 1000000	• 10000	• 100	• positive
	• 50	•	• 10000	• 1000	• 10	• positive
20x20	• 50	•	• 10000	• 1000	• 10	• positive
	• 100	•	• 1000000	• 10000	• 100	• negative
25x25	• 200	•	• 1000	• 100	• 10	• positive
	• 500	•	• 10000	• 1000	• 10	• positive
30x30	• 10	•	• 1000000	• 10000	• 100	• negative
	• 300	•	• 10000	• 1000	• 10	• положительный
• The Second Pseudorandom Number Generator						
10x10	• 50	•	• 1000000	• 10000	• 100	• positive
15x15	• 10	•	• 1000	• 100	• 10	• positive
20x20	• 50	•	• 10000	• 1000	• 10	• positive
25x25	• 500	•	• 10000	• 1000	• 10	• positive
30x30	• 10	•	• 10000	• 1000	• 10	• negative
	• 600	•	• 10000	• 1000	• 10	• positive

continued on following page

Table 9. Continued

The Cellular Automata Size	The Number of Cells That Are in the Initial State of the Log. "1"	The Number of Inhomogeneous Cells	The Length of the Formed Sequence	The Block Length	The Number of Blocks	The Test Result (Positive / Negative)
	• The Third Pseudorandom Number Generator					
10x10	• 1	• 1	• 10000	• 1000	• 10	• positive
	• 10	• 2	• 1000	• 100	• 10	• positive
	• 50	• 3	• 1000000	• 10000	• 100	• negative
	• 50	• 4	• 1000	• 100	• 10	• positive
15x15	• 10	• 1	• 1000	• 100	• 10	• positive
	• 100	• 2	• 10000	• 1000	• 10	• positive
	• 50	• 3	• 10000	• 1001	• 10	• positive
	• 4	• 1	• 10000	• 1002	• 10	• positive
20x20	• 50	• 1	• 1000000	• 10002	• 100	• negative
	• 250	• 1	• 10000	• 1010	• 10	• negative
	• 10	• 2	• 1000	• 105	• 10	• positive
	• 100	• 2	• 10000	• 1010	• 10	• positive
	• 50	• 3	• 10000	• 1020	• 10	• positive
	• 1	• 4	• 10000	• 1002	• 10	• positive
25x25	• 10	• 1	• 1000	• 105	• 10	• positive
	• 50	• 2	• 10000	• 1020	• 10	• positive
	• 600	• 3	• 10000	• 1001	• 10	• positive
	• 200	• 4	• 1000	• 108	• 9	• positive
30x30	• 300	• 1	• 10000	• 1008	• 10	• positive
	• 1	• 2	• 10000	• 1002	• 10	• positive
	• 300	• 3	• 1000000	• 100000	• 10	• positive
	• 500	• 3	• 10000	• 1004	• 10	• positive
	• 700	• 4	• 10000	• 1006	• 10	• positive
	• The Fourth Pseudorandom Number Generator					
16x16	• 10	•	• 80000	• 1100	• 72	• positive
	• 50	•	• 8000	• 1000	• 8	• positive
	• 100	•	• 80000	• 10000	• 8	• positive
	• 200	•	• 8000	• 100	• 80	• positive
	• The Fifth Pseudorandom Number Generator					
16x16	• 1		• 8000	• 100	• 80	• positive
	• 50		• 80000	• 10000	• 8	• positive
	• The Sixth Pseudorandom Number Generator					
10x10	• 1	• 1	• 80000	• 1000	• 80	• negative
	• 10	• 2	• 8000	• 100	• 80	• negative
	• 50	• 3	• 1600000	• 10000	• 160	• negative
	• 50	• 4	• 8000	• 102	• 78	• negative

continued on following page

Table 9. Continued

The Cellular Automata Size	The Number of Cells That Are in the Initial State of the Log. "1"	The Number of Inhomogeneous Cells	The Length of the Formed Sequence	The Block Length	The Number of Blocks	The Test Result (Positive / Negative)
20x20	• 50			• 1004	• 80	• positive
	• 200	• 1	• 80000	• 1010	• 79	• positive
	• 300			• 1002	• 80	• positive
	• 10		• 8000	• 105	• 76	• negative
	• 100	• 2		• 1004	• 79	• positive
	• 200			• 1004	• 79	• positive
	• 50			• 1020	• 78	• negative
	• 200	• 3		• 1010	• 79	• positive
	• 300		• 80000	• 1010	• 79	• positive
	• 10			• 1008	• 79	• positive
	• 50	• 4		• 1002	• 79	• positive
	• 200			• 1002	• 79	• positive
	• 300			• 1004	• 79	• positive

Successfully tests have been completed for most bit sequences. Especially good results sequence with the great M have shown and with a small amount of blocks N.

The all generators was successfully passed the third NIST test. The third and sixth pseudorandom number generator have shown Good results with using of the inhomogeneous cells. However, the first, second, fourth and fifth pseudorandom number generators passed the third test under certain conditions.

The number of cells, which have initially a logic "1" state should be in the range from 30% to 70%. Table 10 shows the results of the passage of the runs test.

As a result of the passage of a fourth NIST test, the first and second pseudorandom number generator yielded positive results with the initial number of cells having a logic "1" state for more than 30%. The third pseudorandom number generator showed poor quality of the generated pseudo-random bit sequences with inhomogeneous cells and for sizes 10×10 and 20×20. At the same time to the size 10×10 the fourth NIST test gave a negative result using two inhomogeneous cells. The fourth and fifth generators have shown positive results for practically all the initial settings. The sixth pseudorandom number generator has shown positive results.

Table 10. The results of passing of the third test by all generators (the partial selection bit sequences)

The Cellular Automata Size	The Number of Cells That Are in the Initial State of the Log. "1"	The number of Inhomogeneous Cells	The Length of the Formed Sequence	The Test Result (Positive / Negative)
• The First Pseudorandom Number Generator				
10x10	• 1, 50		• 1000	• positive
15x15	• 10		• 1000000	• positive
	• 50		• 96	• positive
	• 100		• 1000	• positive
20x20	• 10		• 10000	• negative
	• 50		• 1000	• negative
	• 100		• 1000	• positive
	• 200		• 1000	• positive
	• 200		• 10000	• positive
	• 250		• 1000	• positive
25x25	• 1		• 10000	• positive
	• 100		• 1000	• positive
	• 200		• 1000	• negative
	• 300		• 1000	• positive
	• 400		• 10000	• positive
	• 500		• 10000	• positive
30x30	• 50		• 1000	• positive
	• 300		• 1000	• negative
	• 400		• 10000	• negative
	• 700		• 10000	• negative
• The Second Pseudorandom Number Generator				
10x10	• 10		• 10000	• negative
	• 10		• 1000	• negative
	• 50		• 1000	• negative
15x15	• 10		• 1000	• negative
	• 50		• 1000	• negative
	• 100		• 1000	• positive
	• 100		• 10000	• positive
20x20	• 50		• 10000	• negative
	• 100		• 1000	• positive
	• 200		• 1000	• positive
	• 250		• 1000	• positive

continued on following page

Table 10. Continued

The Cellular Automata Size	The Number of Cells That Are in the Initial State of the Log. "1"	The number of Inhomogeneous Cells	The Length of the Formed Sequence	The Test Result (Positive / Negative)
25x25	• 100		• 1000	• negative
	• 250		• 1000	• negative
	• 300		• 1000	• positive
	• 400		• 10000	• positive
	• 500		• 10000	• positive
30x30	• 10		• 10000	• negative
	• 400		• 1000	• positive
	• 500		• 1000	• negative
	• 500		• 10000	• positive
	• 600		• 10000	• negative
• The Third Pseudorandom Number Generator				
10x10	• 1	• 1	• 10000	• positive
	• 10	• 2	• 1000	• positive
	• 50	• 3	• 1000000	• negative
	• 50	• 4	• 1000	• positive
15x15	• 10	• 1	• 1000	• positive
	• 100	• 2	• 10000	• positive
	• 50	• 3	• 10000	• positive
	• 4	• 1	• 10000	• positive
20x20	• 50	• 1	• 1000000	• positive
	• 250	• 1	• 10000	• positive
	• 10	• 2	• 1000	• positive
	• 100	• 2	• 10000	• positive
	• 50	• 3	• 10000	• positive
	• 1	• 4	• 10000	• positive
25x25	• 10	• 1	• 1000	• positive
	• 50	• 2	• 10000	• positive
	• 600	• 3	• 10000	• positive
	• 200	• 4	• 1000	• positive
30x30	• 300	• 1	• 10000	• positive
	• 1	• 2	• 10000	• positive
	• 300	• 3	• 1000000	• positive
	• 500	• 3	• 10000	• positive
	• 700	• 4	• 10000	• positive

continued on following page

Table 10. Continued

The Cellular Automata Size	The Number of Cells That Are in the Initial State of the Log. "1"	The number of Inhomogeneous Cells	The Length of the Formed Sequence	The Test Result (Positive / Negative)
• The Fourth Pseudorandom Number Generator				
16x16	• 1		• 8000	• negative
	• 10		• 80000	• negative
	• 50		• 8000	• positive
	• 100		• 80000	• positive
	• 200		• 8000	• positive
• The Fifth Pseudorandom Number Generator				
16x16	• 1		• 8000	• negative
	• 10		• 8000	• negative
	• 50		• 8000	• positive
	• 100		• 8000	• positive
	• 200		• 8000	• positive
	• 200		• 80000	• positive
• The Sixth Pseudorandom Number Generator				
10x10	• 1	• 1	• 80000	• negative
	• 10	• 2	• 8000	• negative
	• 50	• 3	• 1600000	• positive
	• 50	• 4	• 8000	• positive
20x20	• 50	• 1	• 1600000	• positive
	• 300	• 1	• 80000	• positive
	• 10	• 2	• 8000	• positive
	• 100	• 2	• 80000	• positive
	• 50	• 3	• 80000	• positive
	• 1	• 4	• 80000	• negative
	• 50	• 4	• 8000	• positive
	• 200	• 4	• 80000	• positive

For testing the bit sequence by length the 6272 bits was generated. In this case the block length corresponds to 128 bits. The partial results are presented in Table 11. Total has been tested more than 300 bit sequences.

The fifth NIST test was performed for sequences of length 10000 bits. The matrix 5×5 size was used. The results were positive for sizes 25×25 and 30×30 with an initial amount of cells having a logic "1" state from 50% to 70%. The third pseudorandom number generators tested positive for the same size and with four inhomogeneous cells. Fourth and fifth pseudorandom number generators showed good results for the initial 50% of cells that have logical

Table 11. The results of the passage of the fourth NIST test by all the generators (for a selected number of bit sequences)

The Cellular Automata Size	The Number of Cells That Are in the Initial State of the Log. "1"	The Number of Inhomogeneous Cells	The Length of the Formed Sequence	The Test Result (Positive / Negative)
• The First Pseudorandom Number Generator				
10x10	• 1		• 6272	• negative
	• 10		• 6272	• positive
	• 50		• 6272	• positive
15x15	• 1		• 6272	• negative
	• 10		• 6272	• positive
	• 50		• 6272	• positive
	• 100		• 6272	• positive
20x20	• 1		• 6272	• negative
	• 10		• 6272	• negative
	• 50		• 6272	• positive
25x25	• 10		• 6272	• negative
	• 50		• 6272	• negative
	• 100		• 6272	• positive
	• 200		• 6272	• positive
	• 300		• 6272	• positive
	• 400		• 6272	• positive
	• 500		• 6272	• positive
	• 600		• 6272	• positive
30x30	• 1		• 6272	• negative
	• 10		• 6272	• negative
	• 50		• 6272	• negative
	• 100, 200, 300, 400, 500, 600, 700, 800		• 6272	• positive
• The Second Pseudorandom Number Generator				
10x10	• 1, 10, 50		• 6272	• positive
15x15	• 1		• 6272	• negative
	• 10, 50, 100		• 6272	• positive
20x20	• 1, 10		• 6272	• negative
	• 50, 100, 200, 250		• 6272	• positive
25x25	• 1, 10, 50		• 6272	• negative
	• 100, 200, 250, 300, 400, 500, 600		• 6272	• positive
30x30	• 1, 10, 50, 100, 200		• 6272	• negative
	• 300, 400, 500, 600, 700, 800		• 6272	• positive

continued on following page

Table 11. Continued

The Cellular Automata Size	The Number of Cells That Are in the Initial State of the Log. "1"	The Number of Inhomogeneous Cells	The Length of the Formed Sequence	The Test Result (Positive / Negative)
• The Third Pseudorandom Number Generator				
10x10	• 1	• 1	• 6272	• negative
	• 10	• 1	• 6272	• negative
	• 50	• 1	• 6272	• negative
	• 1	• 2	• 6272	• negative
	• 10	• 2	• 6272	• negative
	• 50	• 2	• 6272	• negative
	• 1	• 3	• 6272	• positive
	• 10	• 3	• 6272	• positive
	• 50	• 3	• 6272	• negative
	• 1	• 4	• 6272	• positive
	• 10	• 4	• 6272	• positive
	• 50	• 4	• 6272	• positive
15x15	• 1	• 1, 2, 3, 4	• 6272	• positive
	• 10	• 1, 2, 3, 4	• 6272	• positive
	• 50	• 1, 2, 3, 4	• 6272	• positive
	• 100	• 1, 2, 3, 4	• 6272	• positive
20x20	• 1, 10, 50, 100, 200	• 1	• 6272	• negative
	• 250	• 1	• 6272	• positive
	• 1, 10, 50, 100, 200, 250	• 2, 3, 4	• 6272	• positive
25x25	• 1, 10, 50, 100, 200, 300, 400, 500, 600	• 1, 2, 3, 4	• 6272	• positive
30x30	• 50, 200	• 1	• 6272	• negative
	• 1, 10, 100, 300, 400, 500, 600, 700, 800	• 1	• 6272	• positive
	• 1, 10, 50, 100, 200, 300, 400, 500, 600, 700, 800	• 2, 3, 4	• 6272	• positive
• The Fourth Pseudorandom Number Generator				
16x16	• 1, 10, 50, 100, 200	•	• 6272	• positive
• The Fifth Pseudorandom Number Generator				
16x16	• 1		• 6272	• negative
	• 10, 50, 100, 200, 300		• 6272	• positive
• The Sixth Pseudorandom Number Generator				
10x10	• 1, 10, 50	• 1, 2, 3, 4	• 6272	• positive
20x20	• 1, 10, 50, 100, 200, 300	• 1, 2, 3, 4	• 6272	

"1" states. The sixth pseudorandom number generator also showed positive results. Results of performance of fifth NIST test are shown in Table 12.

The sixth NIST test based on The Discrete Fourier Transform has shown positive results for all the pseudorandom number generators. The sixth NIST test results for all the pseudorandom number generators and the selected sequences generated are shown in Table 13.

To pass the test were chosen the bit sequence by length of 10000 bits, and 8000 bits for the fourth, fifth and sixth pseudorandom number generators.

Table 12. The results of the fifth NIST test passing by all the generators (partially)

The Cellular Automata Size	The Number of Inhomogeneous Cells	The Number of Cells That Are in the Initial State of the Log. "1"	The Length of the Formed Sequence	The Matrix Size	The Test Result (Positive / Negative)
• The First Pseudorandom Number Generator					
10x10		• 1	• 1000	• 5×5	• negative
		• 10, 50	• 1000	• 5×5	• positive
15x15		• 1, 10	• 1000	• 5×5	• negative
		• 50, 100	• 1000	• 5×5	• positive
20x20		• 1, 10, 50, 200	• 1000	• 5×5	• negative
		• 100, 250	• 1000	• 5×5	• positive
25x25		• 1, 10, 50, 300, 400, 600	• 1000	• 5×5	• negative
		• 100, 200, 250, 500	• 1000	• 5×5	• positive
30x30		• 1, 10, 50, 100, 200	• 1000	• 5×5	• negative
		• 300, 400, 500, 600, 700, 800	• 1000	• 5×5	• positive
• The Second Pseudorandom Number Generator					
10x10		• 1, 10	• 1000	• 5×5	• negative
		• 50	• 1000	• 5×5	• positive
15x15		• 1, 50, 100	• 1000	• 5×5	• negative
		• 10	• 1000	• 5×5	• positive
20x20		• 1, 10, 50, 100, 200	• 1000	• 5×5	• negative
		• 250	• 1000	• 5×5	• positive
25x25		• 1, 50, 100, 200, 250, 500	• 1000	• 5×5	• negative
		• 100, 300, 400, 600	• 1000	• 5×5	• positive
30x30		• 1, 10, 50, 200, 300, 400, 700, 800	• 1000	• 5×5	• negative
		• 100, 500, 600	• 1000	• 5×5	• positive

continued on following page

Table 12. Continued

The Cellular Automata Size	The Number of Inhomogeneous Cells	The Number of Cells That Are in the Initial State of the Log. "1"	The Length of the Formed Sequence	The Matrix Size	The Test Result (Positive / Negative)
* The Third Pseudorandom Number Generator					
10x10	• 1	• 1, 10, 50	• 1000	• 5×5	• negative
	• 2	• 1, 10, 50	• 1000	• 5×5	• negative
	• 3	• 1, 10, 50	• 1000	• 5×5	• negative
	• 4	• 1, 10, 50	• 1000	• 5×5	• negative
15x15	• 1	• 1, 10, 50, 100	• 1000	• 5×5	• positive
	• 2	• 1, 10, 50	• 1000	• 5×5	• positive
		• 100	• 1000	• 5×5	• negative
	• 3	• 1, 10, 50, 100	• 1000	• 5×5	• positive
	• 4	• 1, 10, 50	• 1000	• 5×5	• positive
		• 100	• 1000	• 5×5	• negative
20x20	• 1	• 1, 10, 50, 100, 250	• 1000	• 5×5	• negative
		• 200	• 1000	• 5×5	• positive
	• 2	• 1, 100	• 1000	• 5×5	• positive
		• 10, 50, 200, 250	• 1000	• 5×5	• negative
	• 3	• 1, 10, 50, 100, 200	• 1000	• 5×5	• negative
		• 250	• 1000	• 5×5	• positive
	• 4	• 1, 50, 100, 200, 250	• 1000	• 5×5	• positive
		• 10, 200	• 1000	• 5×5	• negative
25x25	• 1	• 1, 300	• 1000	• 5×5	• positive
		• 10, 50,100, 200, 250, 400, 500, 600	• 1000	• 5×5	• positive
	• 2	• 1, 10, 50, 250, 300, 500	• 1000	• 5×5	• positive
		• 100, 200, 400, 600	• 1000	• 5×5	• negative
	• 3	• 1, 250, 400, 500	• 1000	• 5×5	• positive
		• 10, 50, 100, 200, 300, 600	• 1000	• 5×5	• negative
	• 4	• 1, 10, 50, 250, 400, 500	• 1000	• 5×5	• positive
		• 100, 200, 300, 600	• 1000	• 5×5	• negative

continued on following page

Table 12. Continued

The Cellular Automata Size	The Number of Inhomogeneous Cells		The Number of Cells That Are in the Initial State of the Log. "1"	The Length of the Formed Sequence	The Matrix Size	The Test Result (Positive / Negative)
30x30	• 1		• 1, 10, 50, 200 800	• 1000	• 5×5	• positive
			• 100, 300, 400, 500, 600, 700	• 1000	• 5×5	• negative
	• 2		• 1, 10, 100, 300, 600	• 1000	• 5×5	• negative
			• 50, 200, 400, 500, 700, 800	• 1000	• 5×5	• positive
	• 3		• 1, 10, 100, 200, 300, 400, 500, 700, 800	• 1000	• 5×5	• positive
			• 50, 600	• 1000	• 5×5	• negative
	• 4		• 1, 10, 100, 200, 300, 400, 700, 800	• 1000	• 5×5	• positive
			• 50, 500, 600	• 1000	• 5×5	• negative
• The Fourth Pseudorandom Number Generator						
16x16			• 1, 10, 50, 200	• 800	• 4×4	• positive
			• 100	• 800	• 4×4	• negative
• The Fifth Pseudorandom Number Generator						
16x16 inv			• 1, 10, 50, 200	• 800	• 4×4	• positive
			• 100	• 800	• 4×4	• negative
• The Sixth Pseudorandom Number Generator						
10x10	• 1		• 1	• 800	• 5×5	• positive
			• 10	• 800	• 5×5	• negative
			• 50	• 800	• 5×5	• positive
	• 2		• 1	• 800	• 5×5	• positive
			• 10	• 800	• 5×5	• positive
			• 50	• 800	• 5×5	• positive
	• 3		• 1	• 800	• 5×5	• positive
			• 10	• 800	• 5×5	• positive
			• 50	• 800	• 5×5	• negative
	• 4		• 1	• 800	• 5×5	• negative
			• 10	• 800	• 5×5	• negative
			• 50	• 800	• 5×5	• negative

continued on following page

Table 12. Continued

The Cellular Automata Size	The Number of Inhomogeneous Cells	The Number of Cells That Are in the Initial State of the Log. "1"	The Length of the Formed Sequence	The Matrix Size	The Test Result (Positive / Negative)
20x20	• 1	• 1	• 800	• 5×5	• positive
		• 10	• 800	• 5×5	• positive
		• 50	• 800	• 5×5	• negative
		• 100	• 800	• 5×5	• negative
		• 200	• 800	• 5×5	• positive
		• 300	• 800	• 5×5	• positive
	• 2	• 1	• 800	• 5×5	• negative
		• 10	• 800	• 5×5	• positive
		• 50	• 800	• 5×5	• negative
		• 100	• 800	• 5×5	• negative
		• 200	• 800	• 5×5	• positive
		• 300	• 800	• 5×5	• positive
	• 3	• 1	• 800	• 5×5	• positive
		• 10, 50	• 800	• 5×5	• negative
		• 100, 200, 300	• 800	• 5×5	• positive
	• 4	• 1, 10, 100, 300	• 800	• 5×5	• negative
		• 50, 200	• 800	• 5×5	• positive

Table 13. Results of performance of the six NIST test by all generators (partially)

The Cellular Automata Size	The Number of Inhomogeneous Cells	The Number of Cells That Are in the Initial State of the Log. "1"	The Length of the Formed Sequence	The Test Result (Positive / Negative)
• The First Pseudorandom Number Generator				
10x10		• 1	• 10000	• negative
		• 10, 50	• 10000	• positive
15x15		• 1	• 10000	• negative
		• 10, 50, 100	• 10000	• positive
20x20		• 1	• 10000	• negative
		• 10, 50, 100, 200, 250	• 10000	• positive
25x25		• 1, 10	• 10000	• negative
		• 50, 100, 200, 300, 400, 500, 600	• 10000	• positive
30x30		• 1, 10	• 10000	• negative
		• 50, 100, 200, 300, 400, 500, 600, 700, 800	• 10000	• positive

continued on following page

Table 13. Continued

The Cellular Automata Size	The Number of Inhomogeneous Cells	The Number of Cells That Are in the Initial State of the Log. "1"	The Length of the Formed Sequence	The Test Result (Positive / Negative)
• The Second Pseudorandom Number Generator				
10x10		• 1, 10, 50	• 1000	• positive
15x15		• 1	• 1000	• negative
		• 10, 50, 100	• 1000	• positive
20x20		• 1, 10	• 1000	• negative
		• 50, 100, 200, 250	• 1000	• positive
25x25		• 1, 10	• 1000	• negative
		• 50, 100, 200, 250, 300, 400, 500, 600	• 1000	• positive
30x30		• 1, 10, 800	• 1000	• negative
		• 50, 100, 200, 250, 300, 400, 500, 600, 700	• 1000	• positive
• The Third Pseudorandom Number Generator				
10x10	• 1	• 1, 10, 50	• 10000	• negative
	• 2	• 1, 10, 50	• 10000	• negative
	• 3	• 1, 50	• 10000	• positive
		• 10	• 10000	• negative
	• 4	• 1, 10, 50	• 10000	• positive
15x15	• 1	• 1, 10, 50, 100	• 10000	• positive
	• 2	• 1, 10, 50, 100	• 10000	• positive
	• 3	• 1, 10, 50, 100	• 10000	• positive
	• 4	• 1, 10, 50, 100	• 10000	• positive
20x20	• 1	• 1, 250	• 10000	• positive
		• 10, 50, 100, 200	• 10000	• negative
	• 2	• 1, 10, 50, 100, 200, 250	• 10000	• positive
	• 3	• 1, 10, 50, 100, 200, 250	• 10000	• positive
	• 4	• 1, 10, 50, 100, 200, 250	• 10000	• positive
25x25	• 1	• 1, 10, 100, 250, 300, 400, 500, 600	• 10000	• positive
		• 50, 200	• 10000	• negative
	• 2	• 1, 10, 50, 100, 200, 250, 300, 400, 500, 600	• 10000	• positive
	• 3	• 1, 250, 400, 500	• 10000	• positive
		• 10, 50, 100, 300, 600	• 10000	• negative
	• 4	• 1, 10, 50, 250, 400, 500	• 10000	• positive
		• 100, 200, 300, 600	• 10000	• negative

continued on following page

Table 13. Continued

The Cellular Automata Size	The Number of Inhomogeneous Cells	The Number of Cells That Are in the Initial State of the Log. "1"	The Length of the Formed Sequence	The Test Result (Positive / Negative)
30x30	• 1	• 1, 10	• 10000	• negative
		• 50, 100, 200, 300, 400, 500, 600, 700, 800	• 10000	• positive
	• 2	• 1	• 10000	• negative
		• 10, 50, 100, 200, 300, 400, 500, 600, 700, 800	• 10000	• positive
	• 3	• 1, 10, 50, 100, 200, 300, 400, 500, 600, 700, 800	• 10000	• positive
	• 4	• 1, 10, 50, 100, 200, 300, 400, 500, 600, 700, 800	• 10000	• positive
• The Fourth Pseudorandom Number Generator				
16x16		• 1, 10, 50, 100, 200	• 80000	• positive
• The Fifth Pseudorandom Number Generator				
16x16 inv		• 1, 10, 50, 100, 200	• 80000	• positive
• The Sixth Pseudorandom Number Generator				
10x10	1	• 1, 10	• 80000	• positive
		• 50	• 80000	• negative
	2, 3, 4	• 1, 10, 50	• 80000	• positive
20x20	1, 2, 3, 4	• 1, 10, 50, 100, 200, 300	• 80000	• positive

The seventh test also showed the positive results for the selected template. Basically test sequences are divided into the 1428 or 2000 blocks. The length of the template has 9 bits. The results of passing the seventh NIST test by the developed pseudorandom number generators are presented in Table 14.

All the pseudorandom number generator also successfully passed the eighth test. However, the number of blocks was selected in 2314. The length of the chosen template 10, 11 bits, and the length of the generated sequences were chosen by length 8000, 10000 and 80000 bits. The results of the passage of all 8 NIST test by the generators are shown in Table 15.

The ninth NIST test assesses the degree of compression of the generated bit sequence. For the NIST test were formed the bit sequences by length 387840 bits for each variant of the pseudorandom number generator. All the pseudorandom number generators successfully passed the test and tested positive for the compressive. The results are presented in Table 16.

The Lempel–Ziv Compression Test also all the generators passed for certain an initial conditions. These conditions and restrictions remain for almost all the NIST tests. At the same time for dimension 16x16 the fourth and fifth the pseudorandom number generators the NIST tests have not passed. A

Table 14. The results of passing the seventh NIST test by the all designed generators (partially)

The Cellular Automata Size	The Number Of Inhomogeneous Cells	The Number of Cells That Are in the Initial State of the log. "1"	The Length Of The Formed Sequence	The Block Form	The Number Of Blocks	The Test Result (Positive / Negative)
		• The First Pseudorandom Number Generator				
10x10		• 1	• 10000	• 000000001	• 2000	• positive
		• 1	• 10000	• 101000110	• 2000	• positive
		• 10	• 10000	• 111000001	• 2000	• positive
		• 50	• 10000	• 111010000	• 2000	• positive
15x15		• 1	• 10000	• 111010000	• 2000	• positive
		• 10	• 10000	• 110011000	• 1428	• positive
		• 50	• 10000	• 110011000	• 1428	• positive
		• 100	• 10000	• 111111110	• 1428	• positive
20x20		• 1	• 10000	• 110101000	• 1428	• negative
		• 10	• 10000	• 110101000	• 1428	• positive
		• 50	• 10000	• 000111111	• 1428	• positive
		• 100	• 10000	• 010000111	• 1428	• positive
		• 200	• 10000	• 010000111	• 1428	• positive
		• 250	• 10000	• 100000000	• 1428	• positive
25x25		• 1	• 10000	• 100000000	• 1428	• positive
		• 10	• 10000	• 010000111	• 1428	• positive
		• 50	• 10000	• 010000111	• 1428	• positive
		• 100	• 10000	• 001011111	• 1428	• positive
		• 200	• 10000	• 001011111	• 1428	• positive
		• 250	• 10000	• 001011111	• 1100	• positive
		• 300	• 10000	• 001011111	• 1100	• positive
		• 400	• 10000	• 100100000	• 1428	• positive
		• 500	• 10000	• 100100000	• 1428	• positive
		• 600	• 10000	• 100100000	• 1428	• positive
30x30		• 1	• 10000	• 101111000	• 1428	• negative
		• 10	• 10000	• 101111000	• 1428	• negative
		• 50	• 10000	• 101111000	• 1428	• positive
		• 100	• 10000	• 101111000	• 1428	• positive
		• 200	• 10000	• 101111000	• 1428	• positive
		• 300	• 10000	• 101111000	• 1428	• positive
		• 400	• 10000	• 011111111	• 1428	• positive
		• 500	• 10000	• 011111111	• 1428	• positive
		• 600	• 10000	• 100110000	• 1428	• positive
		• 700	• 10000	• 100110000	• 1428	• positive
		• 800	• 10000	• 100110000	• 1428	• positive

continued on following page

Table 14. Continued

The Cellular Automata Size	The Number Of Inhomogeneous Cells	The Number of Cells That Are in the Initial State of the log. "1"	The Length Of The Formed Sequence	The Block Form	The Number Of Blocks	The Test Result (Positive / Negative)
• The Second Pseudorandom Number Generator						
1000		• 1	• 10000	• 000000001	• 1428	• negative
		• 10	• 10000	• 101000110	• 1428	• negative
		• 50	• 10000	• 111000001	• 1428	• positive
15x15		• 1	• 10000	• 111010000	• 1428	• negative
		• 10	• 10000	• 111010000	• 1428	• positive
		• 50	• 10000	• 110011000	• 1428	• positive
		• 100	• 10000	• 110011000	• 1428	• positive
20x20		• 1	• 10000	• 111111110	• 1428	• negative
		• 10	• 10000	• 110101000	• 1428	• positive
		• 50	• 10000	• 110101000	• 1428	• positive
		• 100	• 10000	• 000111111	• 1428	• positive
		• 200	• 10000	• 010000111	• 1428	• negative
		• 250	• 10000	• 010000111	• 1428	• positive
25x25		• 1	• 10000	• 100000000	• 1428	• negative
		• 10	• 10000	• 100000000	• 1428	• negative
		• 50	• 10000	• 010000111	• 1428	• positive
		• 100	• 10000	• 010000111	• 1428	• positive
		• 200	• 10000	• 001011111	• 1428	• positive
		• 250	• 10000	• 001011111	• 1428	• positive
		• 300	• 10000	• 001011111	• 1100	• positive
		• 400	• 10000	• 001011111	• 1100	• positive
		• 500	• 10000	• 100100000	• 1428	• positive
		• 600	• 10000	• 100100000	• 1428	• positive
30x30		• 1	• 10000	• 100100000	• 1428	• negative
		• 10	• 10000	• 101111000	• 1428	• positive
		• 50	• 10000	• 101111000	• 1428	• positive
		• 100	• 10000	• 101111000	• 1428	• positive
		• 200	• 10000	• 101111000	• 1428	• positive
		• 300	• 10000	• 101111000	• 1428	• positive
		• 400	• 10000	• 101111000	• 1428	• positive
		• 500	• 10000	• 011111111	• 1428	• negative
		• 600	• 10000	• 011111111	• 1428	• positive
		• 700	• 10000	• 100110000	• 1428	• positive
		• 800	• 10000	• 100110000	• 1428	• positive

continued on following page

Table 14. Continued

The Cellular Automata Size	The Number Of Inhomogeneous Cells	The Number of Cells That Are in the Initial State of the log. "1"	The Length Of The Formed Sequence	The Block Form	The Number Of Blocks	The Test Result (Positive / Negative)
			• The Third Pseudorandom Number Generator			
10x10	1	• 1	• 10000	• 100110000	• 1428	• negative
		• 10	• 10000	• 101110000	• 1428	• negative
		• 50	• 10000	• 111111100	• 1428	• positive
	2	• 1	• 10000	• 111111100	• 1428	• positive
		• 10	• 10000	• 100011100	• 1428	• positive
		• 50	• 10000	• 000000001	• 1428	• positive
	3	• 1	• 10000	• 000000001	• 1428	• positive
		• 10	• 10000	• 011000001	• 1428	• positive
		• 50	• 10000	• 011000001	• 1428	• positive
	4	• 1	• 10000	• 111001100	• 1428	• positive
		• 10	• 10000	• 111001100	• 1428	• positive
		• 50	• 10000	• 111001100	• 1428	• positive
15x15	1	• 1	• 10000	• 111110000	• 1428	• positive
		• 10	• 10000	• 111110000	• 1428	• positive
		• 50	• 10000	• 111111110	• 1428	• negative
		• 100	• 10000	• 111111110	• 1428	• positive
	2	• 1	• 10000	• 111111110	• 1428	• positive
		• 10	• 10000	• 101111110	• 1428	• positive
		• 50	• 10000	• 101111110	• 1428	• positive
		• 100	• 10000	• 110010010	• 1428	• negative
	3	• 1	• 10000	• 110010010	• 1428	• positive
		• 10	• 10000	• 110011010	• 1428	• positive
		• 50	• 10000	• 110011010	• 1428	• positive
		• 100	• 10000	• 110011010	• 1428	• positive
	4	• 1	• 10000	• 110011110	• 1428	• positive
		• 10	• 10000	• 110011110	• 1428	• positive
		• 50	• 10000	• 110011110	• 1428	• positive
		• 100	• 10000	• 110011110	• 1428	• positive

continued on following page

Table 14. Continued

The Cellular Automata Size	The Number Of Inhomogeneous Cells	The Number of Cells That Are in the Initial State of the log. "1"	The Length Of The Formed Sequence	The Block Form	The Number Of Blocks	The Test Result (Positive / Negative)
20x20	1	• 1	• 10000	• 110011110	• 1428	• positive
		• 10	• 10000	• 111011111	• 1428	• positive
		• 50	• 10000	• 111011111	• 1428	• positive
		• 100	• 10000	• 101011111	• 1428	• positive
		• 200	• 10000	• 101011111	• 1428	• positive
		• 250	• 10000	• 100000000	• 1428	• positive
	2	• 1	• 10000	• 100000000	• 1428	• positive
		• 10	• 10000	• 100000000	• 1428	• positive
		• 50	• 10000	• 101000000	• 1428	• positive
		• 100	• 10000	• 101000000	• 1428	• positive
		• 200	• 10000	• 101000000	• 1428	• positive
		• 250	• 10000	• 101010000	• 1428	• positive
	3	• 1	• 10000	• 101010000	• 1428	• positive
		• 10	• 10000	• 101010000	• 1428	• positive
		• 50	• 10000	• 101110000	• 1428	• positive
		• 100	• 10000	• 101110000	• 1428	• positive
		• 200	• 10000	• 101110000	• 1428	• positive
		• 250	• 10000	• 111110000	• 1428	• positive
	4	• 1	• 10000	• 111110000	• 1428	• positive
		• 10	• 10000	• 111110000	• 1428	• positive
		• 50	• 10000	• 111110001	• 1428	• positive
		• 100	• 10000	• 111110001	• 1428	• positive
		• 200	• 10000	• 111110011	• 1428	• positive
		• 250	• 10000	• 111110011	• 1428	• positive
25x25	1	• 1	• 10000	• 111110011	• 1428	• positive
		• 10	• 10000	• 111110011	• 1428	• positive
		• 50	• 10000	• 111110011	• 1428	• positive
		• 100	• 10000	• 111110011	• 1428	• positive
		• 200	• 10000	• 111111011	• 1428	• positive
		• 250	• 10000	• 111111011	• 1428	• positive
		• 300	• 10000	• 111111011	• 1428	• positive
		• 400	• 10000	• 000000011	• 1428	• positive
		• 500	• 10000	• 000000011	• 1428	• positive
		• 600	• 10000	• 000000011	• 1428	• positive

continued on following page

Table 14. Continued

The Cellular Automata Size	The Number Of Inhomogeneous Cells	The Number of Cells That Are in the Initial State of the log. "1"	The Length Of The Formed Sequence	The Block Form	The Number Of Blocks	The Test Result (Positive / Negative)
	2	• 1	• 10000	• 000000011	• 1428	• positive
		• 10	• 10000	• 000000011	• 1428	• positive
		• 50	• 10000	• 111000000	• 1428	• positive
		• 100	• 10000	• 111000000	• 1428	• positive
		• 200	• 10000	• 111000000	• 1428	• positive
		• 250	• 10000	• 111000000	• 1428	• positive
		• 300	• 10000	• 111010000	• 1428	• positive
		• 400	• 10000	• 111010000	• 1428	• positive
		• 500	• 10000	• 111010100	• 1428	• positive
		• 600	• 10000	• 111010100	• 1428	• positive
	3	• 1	• 10000	• 111010100	• 1428	• positive
		• 10	• 10000	• 111010100	• 1428	• positive
		• 50	• 10000	• 111010100	• 1428	• positive
		• 100	• 10000	• 111110100	• 1428	• positive
		• 200	• 10000	• 111110100	• 1428	• positive
		• 250	• 10000	• 111110100	• 1428	• positive
		• 300	• 10000	• 111110100	• 1428	• positive
		• 400	• 10000	• 111111100	• 1428	• positive
		• 500	• 10000	• 111111100	• 1428	• positive
		• 600	• 10000	• 111111110	• 1428	• positive
	4	• 1	• 10000	• 111111110	• 1428	• positive
		• 10	• 10000	• 111111110	• 1428	• positive
		• 50	• 10000	• 111111110	• 1428	• positive
		• 100	• 10000	• 001111110	• 1428	• positive
		• 200	• 10000	• 001111110	• 1428	• positive
		• 250	• 10000	• 001111110	• 1428	• positive
		• 300	• 10000	• 101111110	• 1428	• positive
		• 400	• 10000	• 101111110	• 1428	• positive
		• 500	• 10000	• 101011110	• 1428	• positive
		• 600	• 10000	• 101011110	• 1428	• positive

continued on following page

Table 14. Continued

The Cellular Automata Size	The Number Of Inhomogeneous Cells	The Number of Cells That Are in the Initial State of the log. "1"	The Length Of The Formed Sequence	The Block Form	The Number Of Blocks	The Test Result (Positive / Negative)
30x30	• 1	• 1	• 10000	• 101011110	• 1428	• positive
		• 10	• 10000	• 101011110	• 1428	• positive
		• 50	• 10000	• 101011110	• 1428	• positive
		• 100	• 10000	• 101010110	• 1428	• positive
		• 200	• 10000	• 101010110	• 1428	• positive
		• 300	• 10000	• 101010110	• 1428	• positive
		• 400	• 10000	• 101010110	• 1428	• positive
		• 500	• 10000	• 101010100	• 1428	• positive
		• 600	• 10000	• 101010100	• 1428	• positive
		• 700	• 10000	• 101010100	• 1428	• positive
		• 800	• 10000	• 000010100	• 1428	• positive
	• 2	• 1	• 10000	• 000010100	• 1428	• positive
		• 10	• 10000	• 000000100	• 1428	• negative
		• 50	• 10000	• 000000101	• 1428	• positive
		• 100	• 10000	• 000000101	• 1428	• negative
		• 200	• 10000	• 000000101	• 1428	• positive
		• 300	• 10000	• 000000101	• 1428	• negative
		• 400	• 10000	• 000000101	• 1428	• positive
		• 500	• 10000	• 000010100	• 1428	• positive
		• 600	• 10000	• 000000101	• 1428	• negative
		• 700	• 10000	• 000000100	• 1428	• positive
		• 800	• 10000	• 001100101	• 1428	• positive
	• 3	• 1	• 10000	• 000000110	• 1428	• positive
		• 10	• 10000	• 000010100	• 1428	• positive
		• 50	• 10000	• 001111110	• 1428	• negative
		• 100	• 10000	• 101111110	• 1428	• positive
		• 200	• 10000	• 101111110	• 1428	• positive
		• 300	• 10000	• 101011110	• 1428	• positive
		• 400	• 10000	• 101011110	• 1428	• positive
		• 500	• 10000	• 101011110´	• 1428	• positive
		• 600	• 10000	• 101011110	• 1428	• negative
		• 700	• 10000	• 101011110	• 1428	• positive
		• 800	• 10000	• 101010110	• 1428	• positive

continued on following page

Table 14. Continued

The Cellular Automata Size	The Number Of Inhomogeneous Cells	The Number of Cells That Are in the Initial State of the log. "1"	The Length Of The Formed Sequence	The Block Form	The Number Of Blocks	The Test Result (Positive / Negative)
		• 1	• 10000	• 101010110	• 1428	• positive
		• 10	• 10000	• 101010110	• 1428	• positive
		• 50	• 10000	• 001111110	• 1428	• positive
		• 100	• 10000	• 101111110	• 1428	• positive
		• 200	• 10000	• 101111110	• 1428	• positive
	• 4	• 300	• 10000	• 000011101	• 1428	• positive
		• 500	• 10000	• 000011101	• 1428	• negative
		• 600	• 10000	• 000011101	• 1428	• negative
		• 700	• 10000	• 000000001	• 1428	• positive
		• 800	• 10000	• 000000001	• 1428	• positive
• The Fourth Pseudorandom Number Generator						
16x16		• 1	• 8000	• 000011101	• 1428	• positive
		• 10	• 8000	• 000011101	• 1428	• positive
		• 50	• 8000	• 000000001	• 1428	• positive
		• 100	• 8000	• 000000001	• 1428	• negative
		• 200	• 8000	• 000000011	• 1428	• positive
• The Fifth Pseudorandom Number Generator						
16x16 inv		• 1	• 8000	• 000000011	• 1428	• negative
		• 10	• 8000	• 000000011	• 1428	• positive
		• 50	• 8000	• 000001011	• 1428	• positive
		• 100	• 8000	• 000001011	• 1428	• positive
		• 200	• 8000	• 000001011	• 1428	• positive
• The Sixth Pseudorandom Number Generator						
10x10	• 1	• 1	• 80000	• 100110000	• 11428	• negative
		• 10	• 80000	• 101110000	• 11428	• negative
		• 50	• 80000	• 111111100	• 11428	• positive
	• 2	• 1	• 80000	• 111111100	• 11428	• negative
		• 10	• 80000	• 100011100	• 11428	• positive
		• 50	• 80000	• 000000001	• 11428	• positive
	• 3	• 1	• 80000	• 000000001	• 11428	• positive
		• 10	• 80000	• 011000001	• 11428	• positive
		• 50	• 80000	• 011000001	• 11428	• negative
	• 4	• 1	• 80000	• 111001100	• 11428	• positive
		• 10	• 80000	• 111001100	• 11428	• positive
		• 50	• 80000	• 111001100	• 11428	• positive

continued on following page

Table 14. Continued

The Cellular Automata Size	The Number Of Inhomogeneous Cells	The Number of Cells That Are in the Initial State of the log. "1"	The Length Of The Formed Sequence	The Block Form	The Number Of Blocks	The Test Result (Positive / Negative)
20x20	• 1	• 1	• 80000	• 110011110	• 11428	• positive
		• 10	• 80000	• 111011111	• 11428	• positive
		• 50	• 80000	• 111011111	• 11428	• positive
		• 100	• 80000	• 101011111	• 11428	• positive
		• 200	• 80000	• 101011111	• 11428	• positive
		• 300	• 80000	• 100000000	• 11428	• positive
	• 2	• 1	• 80000	• 100000000	• 11428	• positive
		• 10	• 80000	• 100000000	• 11428	• positive
		• 50	• 80000	• 101000000	• 11428	• positive
		• 100	• 80000	• 101000000	• 11428	• positive
		• 200	• 80000	• 101000000	• 11428	• positive
		• 300	• 80000	• 101010000	• 11428	• positive
	• 3	• 1	• 80000	• 101010000	• 11428	• positive
		• 10	• 80000	• 101010000	• 11428	• positive
		• 50	• 80000	• 101110000	• 11428	• positive
		• 100	• 80000	• 101110000	• 11428	• positive
		• 200	• 80000	• 101110000	• 11428	• positive
		• 300	• 80000	• 111110000	• 11428	• positive
	• 4	• 1	• 80000	• 111110000	• 11428	• negative
		• 10	• 80000	• 111110000	• 11428	• positive
		• 50	• 80000	• 111110001	• 11428	• positive
		• 100	• 80000	• 111110001	• 11428	• positive
		• 200	• 80000	• 111110011	• 11428	• positive
		• 300	• 80000	• 111110011	• 11428	• positive

negative result was obtained for these generators. The results of the passage of the tenth NIST test are shown in Table 17.

The eleventh test focuses on finding LFSR in the structure of the random number generator, which is being tested. For this by its linear complexity is determined. Methods carries out the analysis the generated bit sequence, according to which the smallest polynomial is searched. The smallest shift register is determined. According to its length is determined whether the random bit sequence. The results of the passage of the eleventh NIST test are shown in Table 18.

Table 15. The results of the passage of the eighth NIST test by all the designed generators (in part)

The Cellular Automata Size	The Number of Inhomogeneous Cells	The Number of Cells That Are in the Initial State of the Log. "1"	The Length of the Formed Sequence	The Block Length	The Number of Blocks	The Test Result (Positive / Negative)
• The First Pseudorandom Number Generator						
10x10		• 1	• 10000	• 0000000011	• 2314	• positive
		• 1	• 10000	• 0000000011	• 2314	• positive
		• 10	• 10000	• 00000010111	• 2314	• positive
		• 50	• 10000	• 00000010111	• 2314	• positive
15x15		• 1	• 10000	• 00000010111	• 2314	• positive
		• 10	• 10000	• 00001010111	• 2314	• positive
		• 100	• 10000	• 00001010111	• 2314	• positive
20x20		• 10	• 10000	• 10000000000	• 2314	• positive
		• 200	• 10000	• 10000000000	• 2314	• positive
25x25		• 1	• 10000	• 11111111110	• 2314	• positive
		• 200	• 10000	• 11111111110	• 2314	• positive
		• 500	• 10000	• 11111111010	• 2314	• positive
30x30		• 50	• 10000	• 11111111010	• 2314	• positive
		• 400	• 10000	• 11111101010	• 2314	• positive
		• 700	• 10000	• 11111101010	• 2314	• positive
• The Second Pseudorandom Number Generator						
10x10		• 10	• 10000	• 11111101010	• 2314	• positive
15x15		• 10, 100	• 10000	• 10111101010	• 2314	• positive
20x20		• 50	• 10000	• 10111101011	• 2314	• positive
		• 250	• 10000	• 10111101011	• 2314	• positive
25x25		• 10	• 10000	• 00011111111	• 2314	• positive
		• 300	• 10000	• 00010111111	• 2314	• positive
30x30		• 1, 200, 600	• 10000	• 00010100111	• 2314	• positive
• The Third Pseudorandom Number Generator						
10x10	• 1	• 50	• 10000	• 10010100111	• 2314	• positive
	• 2	• 10	• 10000	• 10110100111	• 2314	• positive
	• 3	• 1	• 10000	• 10110100101	• 2314	• positive
	• 4	• 10	• 10000	• 10110100101	• 2314	• positive
15x15	• 1	• 10	• 10000	• 10110100101	• 2314	• positive
	• 2	• 1	• 10000	• 11111111100	• 2314	• positive
	• 3	• 10	• 10000	• 11111111100	• 2314	• positive
	• 4	• 10	• 10000	• 11111101100	• 2314	• positive

continued on following page

Table 15. Continued

The Cellular Automata Size	The Number of Inhomogeneous Cells	The Number of Cells That Are in the Initial State of the Log. "1"	The Length of the Formed Sequence	The Block Length	The Number of Blocks	The Test Result (Positive / Negative)
20x20	• 1	• 50	• 10000	• 11111101100	• 2314	• positive
	• 2	• 1	• 10000	• 11111001100	• 2314	• positive
		• 200	• 10000	• 10111001100	• 2314	• positive
	• 3	• 10	• 10000	• 10111001100	• 2314	• positive
	• 4	• 100	• 10000	• 10111001000	• 2314	• positive
25x25	• 1	• 10	• 10000	• 10111001000	• 2314	• positive
		• 400	• 10000	• 00000001111	• 2314	• positive
	• 2	• 50	• 10000	• 00000001111	• 2314	• positive
		• 500	• 10000	• 00011001111	• 2314	• positive
	• 3	• 1	• 10000	• 00011001111	• 2314	• positive
		• 300	• 10000	• 10011001111	• 2314	• positive
	• 4	• 100	• 10000	• 10011001111	• 2314	• positive
		• 400	• 10000	• 10011011111	• 2314	• positive
30x30	• 1	• 10	• 10000	• 10011011111	• 2314	• positive
		• 500	• 10000	• 10000000000	• 2314	• positive
	• 2	• 400	• 10000	• 10000000000	• 2314	• positive
	• 3	• 1	• 10000	• 10000000000	• 2314	• positive
		• 600	• 10000	• 10011110000	• 2314	• negative
	• 4	• 50	• 10000	• 10011110000	• 2314	• negative
		• 400	• 10000	• 10011110100	• 2314	• positive
• The Fourth Pseudorandom Number Generator						
16x16		• 1	• 8000	• 1101001000	• 2314	• negative
		• 10	• 8000	• 1101001010	• 2314	• positive
		• 50	• 80000	• 10011110100	• 3000	• positive
		• 100	• 80000	• 00000000011	• 3000	• positive
		• 200	• 80000	• 00000010011	• 3000	• negative
• The Fifth Pseudorandom Number Generator						
16x16 inv		• 1	• 8000	• 1100000000	• 1000	• positive
		• 10	• 80000	• 00000100111	• 1000	• positive
		• 50	• 8000	• 1101000000	• 1000	• positive
		• 100	• 8000	• 1101000000	• 1000	(• positive)
		• 200	• 8000	• 1101001000	• 1000	• positive
• The Sixth Pseudorandom Number Generator						
10x10	• 1	• 50	• 80000	• 10010100111	• 2314	• positive
	• 2	• 10	• 80000	• 10110100111	• 2314	• positive
	• 3	• 1	• 80000	• 10110100101	• 2314	• positive
	• 4	• 10	• 80000	• 10110100101	• 2314	• negative

continued on following page

Table 15. Continued

The Cellular Automata Size	The Number of Inhomogeneous Cells	The Number of Cells That Are in the Initial State of the Log. "1"	The Length of the Formed Sequence	The Block Length	The Number of Blocks	The Test Result (Positive / Negative)
20x20	• 1	• 50	• 80000	• 11111101100	• 2314	• negative
	• 2	• 1	• 80000	• 11111001100	• 2314	• negative
		• 200	• 80000	• 10111001100	• 2314	• positive
	• 3	• 10	• 80000	• 10111001100	• 2314	• negative
		• 300	• 80000	• 111110000	• 2314	• positive
	• 4	• 100	• 80000	• 10111001000	• 2314	• negative

Table 16. The results of the passage of the ninth NIST test by the all designed generators (in part)

The Cellular Automata Size	The Number of Inhomogeneous Cells	The Number of Cells That Are in the Initial State of the Log. "1"	The Length of the Formed Sequence	The Number of Initialization Blocks	The Number of Test Blocks	The Test Result (Positive / Negative)
• The First Pseudorandom Number Generator						
10x10		• 10	• 387840	• 640	• 64000	• negative
15x15		• 50	• 387840	• 640	• 64000	• positive
20x20		• 50	• 387840	• 640	• 64000	• positive
25x25		• 200	• 387840	• 640	• 64000	• positive
30x30		• 500	• 387840	• 640	• 64000	• positive
• The Second Pseudorandom Number Generator						
10x10		• 50	• 387840	• 640	• 64000	• negative
15x15		• 50	• 387840	• 640	• 64000	• positive
20x20		• 10	• 387840	• 640	• 64000	• negative
25x25		• 300	• 387840	• 640	• 64000	• positive
30x30		• 500	• 387840	• 640	• 64000	• positive
• The Third Pseudorandom Number Generator						
10x10	• 1	• 50	• 387840	• 640	• 64000	• negative
	• 2	• 10	• 387840	• 640	• 64000	• negative
	• 3	• 1	• 387840	• 640	• 64000	• negative
	• 4	• 10	• 387840	• 640	• 64000	• negative
15x15	• 1	• 50	• 387840	• 640	• 64000	• negative
	• 2	• 10	• 387840	• 640	• 64000	• negative
	• 3	• 100	• 387840	• 640	• 64000	• positive
	• 4	• 10	• 387840	• 640	• 64000	• positive

continued on following page

Table 16. Continued

The Cellular Automata Size	The Number of Inhomogeneous Cells	The Number of Cells That Are in the Initial State of the Log. "1"	The Length of the Formed Sequence	The Number of Initialization Blocks	The Number of Test Blocks	The Test Result (Positive / Negative)
20x20	• 1	• 200	• 387840	• 640	• 64000	• negative
	• 2	• 50	• 387840	• 640	• 64000	• negative
	• 3	• 50	• 387840	• 640	• 64000	• positive
	• 4	• 200	• 387840	• 640	• 64000	• positive
25x25	• 1	• 300	• 387840	• 640	• 64000	• positive
	• 2	• 100	• 387840	• 640	• 64000	• positive
	• 3	• 200	• 387840	• 640	• 64000	• positive
	• 4	• 400	• 387840	• 640	• 64000	• positive
30x30	• 1	• 200	• 387840	• 640	• 64000	• negative
	• 2	• 400	• 387840	• 640	• 64000	• positive
	• 3	• 100	• 387840	• 640	• 64000	• positive
	• 4	• 300	• 387840	• 640	• 64000	• positive
• The Fourth Pseudorandom Number Generator						
16x16		• 1	• 387840	• 640	• 64000	• negative
		• 10	• 387840	• 640	• 64000	• positive
		• 50	• 387840	• 640	• 64000	• negative
		• 100	• 387840	• 640	• 64000	• positive
		• 200	• 387840	• 640	• 64000	• negative
• The Fifth Pseudorandom Number Generator						
16x16 inv		• 1, 10,	• 387840	• 640	• 64000	• negative
		• 50, 100, 200	• 387840	• 640	• 64000	• positive
• The Sixth Pseudorandom Number Generator						
10x10	• 1	• 1	• 387840	• 640	• 64000	• negative
	• 2	• 10	• 387840	• 640	• 64000	• negative
	• 3	• 50	• 387840	• 640	• 64000	• positive
	• 4	• 10	• 387840	• 640	• 64000	• positive
20x20	• 1	• 50	• 387840	• 640	• 64000	• positive
		• 100	• 387840	• 640	• 64000	• negative
	• 2	• 1, 10, 100, 200, 300	• 387840	• 640	• 64000	• positive
		• 50	• 387840	• 640	• 64000	• negative
	• 3	• 1, 10, 50, 100	• 387840	• 640	• 64000	• positive
	• 4	• 100, 200, 300	• 387840	• 640	• 64000	• positive

Table 17. The results of the passage of The Lempel-Ziv Compression Test by all the designed generators (in part)

The Cellular Automata Size	The Number of Inhomogeneous Cells	The Number of Cells That Are in the Initial State of the Log. "1"	The Length of the Formed Sequence	The Test Result (Positive / Negative)
• The First Pseudorandom Number Generator				
10x10		• 1	• 1000000	• negative
		• 10	• 1000000	• negative
		• 50	• 1000001	• negative
15x15		• 1	• 1000000	• negative
		• 10	• 1000000	• negative
		• 50	• 1000000	• positive
		• 100	• 1000000	• positive
20x20		• 1, 10, 100	• 1000000	• negative
		• 50, 200, 250	• 1000000	• positive
25x25		• 1, 10, 50	• 1000000	• negative
		• 100, 200, 300, 400, 500	• 1000000	• positive
30x30		• 10, 50, 200	• 1000000	• negative
		• 100, 300, 400, 500	• 1000000	• положительный
• The Second Pseudorandom Number Generator				
10x10		• 1, 50	• 1000000	• negative
15x15		• 10, 100	• 1000000	• positive
20x20		• 50	• 1000000	• negative
		• 200	• 1000000	• positive
25x25		• 100	• 1000000	• positive
30x30		• 300	• 1000000	• positive
• The Third Pseudorandom Number Generator				
10x10	• 1	• 1, 10, 50	• 1000000	• negative
	• 2	• 1, 10, 50	• 1000000	• negative
	• 3	• 1	• 1000000	• positive
		• 50	• 1000000	• negative
	• 4	• 10	• 1000000	• negative
15x15	• 1	• 10	• 1000000	• negative
	• 2	• 50	• 1000000	• positive
	• 3	• 10	• 1000000	• positive
	• 4	• 100	• 1000000	• positive
20x20	• 1	• 100	• 1000000	• negative
	• 2	• 100	• 1000000	• negative
	• 3	• 100	• 1000000	• negative
	• 4	• 200	• 1000000	• positive

continued on following page

Table 17. Continued

The Cellular Automata Size	The Number of Inhomogeneous Cells	The Number of Cells That Are in the Initial State of the Log. "1"	The Length of the Formed Sequence	The Test Result (Positive / Negative)
25x25	• 1	• 1	• 1000000	• negative
	• 2	• 100	• 1000000	• positive
	• 3	• 200	• 1000000	• positive
	• 4	• 300	• 1000000	• positive
30x30	• 1	• 300	• 1000000	• negative
	• 2	• 300	• 1000000	• negative
	• 3	• 400	• 1000000	• positive
	• 4	• 300	• 1000000	• positive
• The Fourth Pseudorandom Number Generator				
16x16		• 1, 10, 50, 100, 200	• 80000	• negative
• The Fifth Pseudorandom Number Generator				
16x16 inv		• 1, 10, 50, 200	• 80000	• negative
		• 100	• 80000	• positive
• The Sixth Pseudorandom Number Generator				
10x10	• 3	• 10	• 1000000	• positive
	• 4	• 50	• 1000000	• negative
20x20	• 2	• 10	• 1000000	• positive
	• 3	• 50	• 1000000	• positive
	• 4	• 100	• 1000000	• negative

Table 18. The results of the passage of the eleventh NIST test by all the designed generators (in part)

The Cellular Automata Size	The Number of Inhomogeneous Cells	The Number of Cells That Are in the Initial State of the Log. "1"	The Length of the Formed Sequence	The Block Length	The Number of Blocks	The Test Result (Positive / Negative)
• The First Pseudorandom Number Generator						
10x10		• 1, 10, 50	• 1000000	• 5000	• 200	• positive
15x15		• 1, 10, 50, 100	• 1000000	• 5000	• 200	• positive
20x20		• 1	• 1000000	• 5000	• 200	• negative
		• 10, 50, 100, 200	• 1000000	• 5000	• 200	• positive
25x25		• 1, 10, 50, 100, 200, 300, 400, 500, 600	• 1000000	• 5000	• 200	• positive
30x30		• 1	• 1000000	• 5000	• 200	• negative
		• 10, 50, 100, 200, 300, 400, 500, 600, 700, 800	• 1000000	• 5000	• 200	• positive

continued on following page

Table 18. Continued

The Cellular Automata Size	The Number of Inhomogeneous Cells	The Number of Cells That Are in the Initial State of the Log. "1"	The Length of the Formed Sequence	The Block Length	The Number of Blocks	The Test Result (Positive / Negative)
• The Second Pseudorandom Number Generator						
10x10		• 1	• 1000	• 5000	• 200	• negative
		• 10, 50	• 1000	• 5000	• 200	• positive
15x15		• 1, 10, 50, 100	• 1000	• 5000	• 200	• positive
20x20		• 1, 10, 50, 100, 200, 250	• 1000	• 5000	• 200	• positive
25x25		• 1	• 1000	• 5000	• 200	• negative
		• 10, 50, 100, 200, 300, 400, 500, 600	• 1000	• 5000	• 200	• positive
30x30		• 1	• 1000	• 5000	• 200	• negative
		• 10, 50, 100, 200, 300, 400, 500, 600, 700, 800	• 1000	• 5000	• 200	• positive
• The Third Pseudorandom Number Generator						
10x10	• 1	• 1, 10, 50	• 1000000	• 5000	• 200	• negative
	• 2	• 1, 50	• 1000000	• 5000	• 200	• negative
		• 10	• 1000000	• 5000	• 200	• positive
	• 3	• 1, 10, 50	• 1000000	• 5000	• 200	• positive
	• 4	• 1, 10, 50	• 1000000	• 5000	• 200	• positive
15x15	• 1	• 1, 50	• 1000000	• 5000	• 200	• negative
		• 10, 100	• 1000000	• 5000	• 200	• positive
	• 2	• 1, 10, 50, 100	• 1000000	• 5000	• 200	• positive
	• 3	• 1, 10, 50, 100	• 1000000	• 5000	• 200	• positive
	• 4	• 1, 10, 50, 100	• 1000000	• 5000	• 200	• positive
20x20	• 1	• 1, 10, 50, 100, 200	• 1000000	• 5000	• 200	• negative
	• 2	• 1, 10, 100, 200	• 1000000	• 5000	• 200	• positive
		• 50	• 1000000	• 5000	• 200	• negative
	• 3	• 1, 10, 50, 200	• 1000000	• 5000	• 200	• positive
		• 100	• 1000000	• 5000	• 200	• negative
	• 4	• 1, 10, 50, 100, 200	• 1000000	• 5000	• 200	• positive
25x25	• 3	• 1, 10, 50, 100, 200, 300, 400, 500, 600	• 1000000	• 5000	• 200	• positive
	• 4	• 1, 10, 50, 100, 200, 300, 400, 500, 600	• 1000000	• 5000	• 200	• positive
30x30	• 1	• 1, 10, 50, 200, 500	• 1000000	• 5000	• 200	• positive
		• 100, 300, 400, 600, 700, 800	• 1000000	• 5000	• 200	• negative
	• 3	• 1, 10, 100, 200, 300, 400, 500, 600, 700, 800	• 1000000	• 5000	• 200	• positive
		• 50	• 1000000	• 5000	• 200	• negative
	• 4	• 1, 10, 50, 100, 200, 300, 400, 500, 600, 700, 800	• 1000000	• 5000	• 200	• positive

continued on following page

Table 18. Continued

The Cellular Automata Size	The Number of Inhomogeneous Cells	The Number of Cells That Are in the Initial State of the Log. "1"	The Length of the Formed Sequence	The Block Length	The Number of Blocks	The Test Result (Positive / Negative)
• The Fourth Pseudorandom Number Generator						
16x16		• 1, 10, 50, 100, 200	• 1120008	• 5000	• 200	• positive
• The Fifth Pseudorandom Number Generator						
16x16 inv		• 1, 10, 50, 100, 200	• 1120008	• 5000	• 200	• positive
• The Sixth Pseudorandom Number Generator						
10x10	• 1	• 1, 10, 50	• 8000000	• 5000	• 200	• negative
	• 2	• 1, 10	• 8000000	• 5000	• 200	• negative
	• 3	• 50	• 1600000	• 8000	• 200	• positive
	• 4	• 10, 50	• 1600000	• 8000	• 200	• positive
20x20	• 1	• 1, 50, 100, 200, 300	• 1600000	• 8000	• 200	• positive
		• 10	• 1120000	• 5600	• 200	• negative
	• 2	• 1, 10, 50, 100, 200, 300	• 1600000	• 8000	• 200	• positive
	• 3	• 1, 10, 50, 100, 200, 300	• 1600000	• 8000	• 200	• positive
	• 4	• 1, 10, 50, 100, 200, 300	• 1600000	• 8000	• 200	• positive

The twelfth NIST test showed good results for all the pseudorandom number generators. As a result of the test it was determined that blocks with a smaller length of 5 and 4 bits in almost all cases gave a positive result in the analysis of the bit sequence of length 1000 bits. The results of the passage of the twelfth NIST test are shown in Table 19.

Thirteenth NIST test also showed good results for all the pseudorandom number generators. As a result of the test it was determined that blocks with a smaller length of 5 and 4 bits in almost all cases gave a positive result in the analysis of the bit sequence of length 1000 bits. The fourth and fifth pseudorandom number generators showed conflicting results. The results of the passage of the thirteenth NIST test in Table 20 are shown.

Good results with the help of the fourteenth NIST test for all the pseudorandom number generators were obtained. All the pseudorandom number generators showed stable results. The results of the passage of the fourteenth NIST test in Table 21 are shown.

The fifteenth NIST test was carried out for a number of the bit sequences equal to 100,000 or more. The pseudorandom number generator gives satisfactory results, which have large dimensions (more then 20x20). For the pseudorandom number generator based on CA with inhomogeneous cells the best results were obtained from CA with a large number of the inhomogeneous

Table 19. The results of the passage of the twelfth NIST test by all the designed generators

The Cellular Automata Size	The Number of Inhomogeneous Cells	The Number of Cells That Are in the Initial State of the Log. "1"	The Length of the Formed Sequence	The Block Length	The Test Result (Positive / Negative)
• The First Pseudorandom Number Generator					
10x10		• 1, 10, 50	• 1000	• 5	• negative
15x15		• 1, 10	• 1000	• 6	• negative
		• 50, 100	• 1000	• 5	• positive
20x20		• 1, 10, 50, 100	• 1000	• 5, 6	• negative
		• 200	• 1000	• 5, 6	• positive
25x25		• 1, 10, 50, 100, 200, 500, 600	• 1000	• 5, 6	• negative
		• 250, 300, 400	• 1000	• 5, 6	• positive
30x30		• 1, 10, 50, 100, 500, 600, 700, 800	• 1000	• 5	• negative
		• 200, 300, 400	• 1000	• 5	• positive
• The Second Pseudorandom Number Generator					
10x10		• 1, 10	• 1000	• 5	• negative
		• 50	• 1000	• 5	• positive
15x15		• 1, 10, 50	• 1000	• 5	• negative
		• 100	• 1000	• 5	• positive
20x20		• 1, 10, 50, 100	• 1000	• 5	• negative
		• 200, 250	• 1000	• 5	• positive
25x25		• 1, 10, 50, 100, 600	• 1000	• 5	• negative
		• 200, 250, 300, 400, 500	• 1000	• 5	• positive
30x30		• 1, 10, 50, 100, 200, 300, 600	• 1000	• 5	• negative
		• 400, 500	• 1000	• 5	• positive
• The Third Pseudorandom Number Generator					
10x10	• 1	• 1, 10	• 1000	• 5	• negative
		• 50	• 1000	• 5	• positive
	• 2	• 1, 10, 30	• 1000	• 5	• negative
	• 3	• 1, 10, 30	• 1000	• 5	• positive
	• 4	• 1, 50	• 1000	• 5	• positive
		• 10	• 1000	• 5	• negative
15x15	• 1	• 1, 10, 100	• 1000	• 5	• positive
		• 50	• 1000	• 5	• negative
	• 2	• 1, 10, 50	• 1000	• 5	• positive
		• 100	• 1000	• 5	• negative
	• 3	• 1, 10, 50, 100	• 1000	• 5	• positive
	• 4	• 1, 10, 50, 100	• 1000	• 5	• positive

continued on following page

Table 19. Continued

The Cellular Automata Size	The Number of Inhomogeneous Cells	The Number of Cells That Are in the Initial State of the Log. "1"	The Length of the Formed Sequence	The Block Length	The Test Result (Positive / Negative)
20x20	• 1	• 1, 100	• 1000	• 5	• positive
		• 10, 50, 200, 250	• 1000	• 5	• negative
	• 2	• 1, 50, 100, 200, 250	• 1000	• 5	• positive
		• 10	• 1000	• 5	• negative
	• 3	• 1, 200	• 1000	• 5	• negative
		• 10, 50, 100, 250	• 1000	• 5	• positive
	• 4	• 1	• 1000	• 5	• negative
		• 10, 50, 100, 200, 250	• 1000	• 5	• positive
25x25	• 1	• 1, 10, 50, 100, 200, 250, 300, 400	• 1000	• 5	• positive
		• 500, 600	• 1000	• 5	• negative
	• 2	• 1, 10, 50, 100, 200, 250, 300, 400, 600	• 1000	• 5	• positive
		• 500	• 1000	• 5	• negative
	• 3	• 1, 10, 400	• 1000	• 5	• negative
		• 50, 100, 200, 250, 300, 500, 600	• 1000	• 5	• positive
	• 4	• 1, 600	• 1000	• 5	• negative
		• 10, 50, 100, 200, 250, 300, 400, 500	• 1000	• 5	• positive
30x30	• 1	• 1, 100, 400	• 1000	• 5	• positive
		• 10, 50, 200, 300, 500, 600, 700, 800	• 1000	• 5	• negative
	• 2	• 1, 50, 100, 200, 400, 500, 600, 700	• 1000	• 5	• positive
		• 10, 300, 800	• 1000	• 5	• negative
	• 3	• 1, 10, 50, 100, 400, 500, 600	• 1000	• 5	• positive
		• 200, 300, 700, 800	• 1000	• 5	• negative
	• 4	• 1, 10, 50, 100, 300, 400, 500, 600, 800	• 1000	• 5	• positive
		• 200, 700	• 1000	• 5	• negative
• The Fourth Pseudorandom Number Generator					
16x16		• 1, 10, 50, 200	• 800	• 5	• negative
		• 100	• 800	• 5	• positive
• The Fifth Pseudorandom Number Generator					
16x16 inv		• 1, 10, 200	• 800	• 5	• negative
		• 50, 100	• 800	• 5	• positive
• The Sixth Pseudorandom Number Generator					
10x10	• 1	• 1, 10	• 800	• 6	• positive
		• 50	• 800	• 6	• negative
	• 2	• 1, 10, 50	• 800	• 6	• positive
	• 3	• 1, 10, 50	• 800	• 6	• negative
	• 4	• 1, 10, 50	• 800	• 6	• positive

continued on following page

Table 19. Continued

The Cellular Automata Size	The Number of Inhomogeneous Cells	The Number of Cells That Are in the Initial State of the Log. "1"	The Length of the Formed Sequence	The Block Length	The Test Result (Positive / Negative)
20x20	• 1	• 1, 10, 50, 200	• 800	• 6	• negative
		• 100, 300	• 800	• 6	• positive
	• 2	• 1, 10, 200	• 800	• 6	• positive
		• 50, 100, 300	• 800	• 6	• negative
	• 3	• 1	• 800	• 6	• negative
		• 10, 50, 100, 200, 300	• 800	• 6	• positive
	• 4	• 1, 200, 300	• 800	• 6	• negative
		• 10, 50, 100	• 800	• 6	• positive

Table 20. The results of the passage of the thirteenth NIST test by all the designed pseudorandom number generators

The Cellular Automata Size	The Number of Inhomogeneous Cells	The Number of Cells That Are in the Initial State of the Log. "1"	The Length of the Formed Sequence	The Block Length	The Test Result (Positive / Negative)
		• The First Pseudorandom Number Generator			
10x10		• 1, 10	• 1000	• 5	• negative
		• 50	• 1000	• 5	• positive
15x15		• 1, 10, 100	• 1000	• 5	• negative
		• 50	• 1000	• 5	• positive
20x20		• 1	• 1000	• 5	• negative
		• 10, 50	• 1000	• 5	• negative
		• 100, 200, 250	• 1000	• 5	• positive
25x25		• 10, 50, 100, 200, 250, 600	• 1000	• 5	• negative
		• 300, 400, 500	• 1000	• 5	• positive
30x30		• 1, 10, 50, 100, 200, 300, 400, 500, 600, 700, 800	• 1000	• 5	• negative
		• The Second Pseudorandom Number Generator			
10x10		• 1, 10	• 1000	• 5	• negative
		• 50	• 1000	• 5	• positive
15x15		• 1	• 1000	• 5	• negative
		• 10, 50, 100	• 1000	• 5	• positive
20x20		• 1, 10, 50	• 1000	• 5	• negative
		• 100, 200, 250	• 1000	• 5	• positive
25x25		• 1, 10, 50, 100, 600	• 1000	• 5	• negative
		• 200, 250, 300, 400, 500	• 1000	• 5	• positive

continued on following page

Table 20. Continued

The Cellular Automata Size	The Number of Inhomogeneous Cells	The Number of Cells That Are in the Initial State of the Log. "1"	The Length of the Formed Sequence	The Block Length	The Test Result (Positive / Negative)
30x30		• 1, 10, 50, 100, 200, 300, 600, 700	• 1000	• 5	• negative
		• 400, 500, 800	• 1000	• 5	• positive
• The Third Pseudorandom Number Generator					
10x10	• 1	• 1, 50	• 1000	• 5	• negative
		• 10	• 1000	• 5	• positive
	• 2	• 1, 10	• 1000	• 5	• negative
		• 50	• 1000	• 5	• positive
	• 3	• 1, 10, 50	• 1000	• 5	• positive
	• 4	• 1, 10, 50	• 1000	• 5	• positive
15x15	• 1	• 1, 10, 50	• 1000	• 5	• positive
		• 100	• 1000	• 5	• negative
	• 2	• 1, 10, 50	• 1000	• 5	• positive
		• 100	• 1000	• 5	• negative
	• 3	• 1, 10, 50, 100	• 1000	• 5	• positive
	• 4	• 1, 10, 50, 100	• 1000	• 5	• positive
20x20	• 1	• 1, 100	• 1000	• 5	• positive
		• 10, 50, 200, 250	• 1000	• 5	• negative
	• 2	• 1, 10, 50, 100, 200, 250	• 1000	• 5	• negative
	• 3	• 1, 10, 50, 100, 200, 250	• 1000	• 5	• positive
		• 100	• 1000	• 5	• negative
	• 4	• 1, 10, 50, 100, 200, 250	• 1000	• 5	• positive
25x25	• 1	• 10, 100	• 1000	• 5	• positive
		• 1, 50, 200, 250, 300, 400, 500, 600	• 1000	• 5	• negative
	• 2	• 10, 100, 300, 500	• 1000	• 5	• positive
		• 1, 50, 200, 250, 400, 600	• 1000	• 5	• negative
	• 3	• 50, 300, 500	• 1000	• 5	• positive
		• 1, 10, 100, 200, 250, 400, 600	• 1000	• 5	• negative
	• 4	• 50, 100, 200, 300, 500, 600	• 1000	• 5	• positive
		• 1, 10, 250	• 1000	• 5	• negative
30x30	• 1	• 200, 400	• 1000	• 5	• negative
		• 1, 10, 50, 100, 300, 500, 600, 700, 800	• 1000	• 5	• positive
	• 2	• 100, 500	• 1000	• 5	• negative
		• 1, 10, 50, 200, 300, 400, 600, 700, 800	• 1000	• 5	• positive
	• 3	• 10, 50, 400	• 1000	• 5	• negative
		• 1, 100, 200, 300, 500, 600, 700, 800	• 1000	• 5	• positive
	• 4	• 10, 200, 600	• 1000	• 5	• negative
		• 1, 50, 100, 300, 400, 500, 700, 800	• 1000	• 5	• positive

continued on following page

Table 20. Continued

The Cellular Automata Size	The Number of Inhomogeneous Cells	The Number of Cells That Are in the Initial State of the Log. "1"	The Length of the Formed Sequence	The Block Length	The Test Result (Positive / Negative)
		• The Fourth Pseudorandom Number Generator			
16x16		• 1, 50, 100	• 800	• 6	• negative
		• 10, 200	• 800	• 6	• positive
		• The Fifth Pseudorandom Number Generator			
16x16 inv		• 1, 50, 100	• 800	• 6	• negative
		• 10, 200	• 800	• 6	• positive
		• The Sixth Pseudorandom Number Generator			
10x10	• 1	• 1, 10	• 800	• 6	• positive
		• 50	• 800	• 6	• negative
	• 2, 3, 4	• 1, 10, 50	• 800	• 6	• positive
20x20	• 1	• 1, 10, 50, 100, 200, 300	• 800	• 6	• positive
	• 2	• 10, 50, 100, 200, 300	• 800	• 6	• positive
	• 3	• 1, 10, 200, 300	• 800	• 6	• positive
	• 4	• 1, 10, 50, 200, 300	• 800	• 6	• positive

cells (more than 3 inhomogeneous cells). The results of the passage of the fifteenth NIST test in the Table 22 are presented.

The sixteenth NIST test was carried out as well as for the fifteenth NIST test for the sequences with the number of bits equal to 100,000 or more. The sixteenth NIST test results do not differ from the fifteenth NIST test results. The results of the passage of the sixteenth NIST test in the Table 23 are presented.

The NIST tests showed that all the pseudorandom number generators under certain the initial conditions can pass all the NIST tests. According to the main initial settings, a developer may pick up necessary the pseudorandom number generator. The main parameters are:

1. The cellular automata size;
2. The number and Location of the cellular automata cells that are in the initial state of a logical "1";
3. The initial position of the active cell and of the inhomogeneous cells;
4. The number of inhomogeneous cells;
5. The neighborhood structure;
6. The geometric coating of cellular automata.

Table 21. The results of the passage of the fourteenth NIST test by all the designed pseudorandom number generators

The Cellular Automata Size	The Number of Inhomogeneous Cells	The Number of Cells That Are in the Initial State of the Log. "1"	The Length of the Formed Sequence	The Test Result (Positive / Negative)
• The First Pseudorandom Number Generator				
10x10		• 1, 10, 50	• 10000	• positive
15x15		• 1, 10, 50, 100	• 10000	• positive
20x20		• 1	• 10000	• negative
		• 10, 50, 100, 200, 250	• 10000	• positive
25x25		• 1, 10	• 10000	• negative
		• 50, 100, 200, 250, 300, 400, 500, 600	• 10000	• positive
30x30		• 1, 10	• 10000	• negative
		• 50, 100, 200, 250, 300, 400, 500, 600, 700, 800	• 10000	• positive
• The Second Pseudorandom Number Generator				
10x10		• 1, 10, 50	• 10000	• positive
15x15		• 1	• 10000	• negative
		• 10, 50 100	• 10000	• positive
20x20		• 1	• 10000	• negative
		• 10, 50 100, 200, 250	• 10000	• positive
25x25		• 1, 10	• 10000	• negative
		• 50, 100, 200, 250, 300, 400, 500, 600	• 10000	• positive
30x30		• 1, 10, 50	• 10000	• negative
		• 100, 200, 300, 400, 500, 600, 700, 800	• 10000	• positive
• The Third Pseudorandom Number Generator				
10x10	• 1	• 1, 10 50	• 10000	• positive
	• 2	• 1, 10 50	• 10000	• negative
	• 3	• 1, 50	• 10000	• positive
		• 10	• 10000	• negative
	• 4	• 1, 10, 50	• 10000	• positive
15x15	• 1, 2, 3, 4	• 1, 10, 50, 100	• 10000	• positive
20x20	• 1	• 1, 10, 50, 100, 200, 250	• 10000	• negative
	• 2, 3, 4	• 1, 10, 50, 100, 200, 250	• 10000	• positive
25x25	• 1, 2, 3, 4	• 1, 10, 50, 100, 200, 250, 300, 400, 500, 600	• 10000	• positive
30x30	• 1	• 1, 10, 50, 100, 250, 300, 400, 500, 600, 700, 800	• 10000	• positive
		• 200	• 10000	• negative
	• 2	• 1, 10, 50, 100, 200, 250, 300, 400, 500, 600, 700, 800	• 10000	• positive
	• 3	• 1, 10, 50, 100, 200, 250, 300, 400, 500, 600, 700, 800	• 10000	• positive
		• 600	• 10000	• negative
	• 4	• 1, 10, 50, 100, 200, 250, 300, 400, 500, 600, 700, 800	• 10000	• positive

continued on following page

Table 21. Continued

The Cellular Automata Size	The Number of Inhomogeneous Cells	The Number of Cells That Are in the Initial State of the Log. "1"	The Length of the Formed Sequence	The Test Result (Positive / Negative)
• The Fourth Pseudorandom Number Generator				
16x16		• 1, 10, 50, 100, 200	• 80000	• positive
• The Fifth Pseudorandom Number Generator				
16x16 inv		• 1, 10, 50, 100, 200	• 80000	• positive
• The Sixth Pseudorandom Number Generator				
10x10	• 1, 2, 3, 4	• 1, 10, 50	• 80000	• positive
20x20	• 1, 2, 3	• 1, 10, 50, 100, 200, 300	• 80000	• positive
	• 4	• 1, 10, 200	• 80000	• positive
		• 50, 100, 300	• 80000	• negative

Table 22. The results of the passage of the fifteenth NIST test by all the developed pseudorandom number generators

The Cellular Automata Size	The Number of Inhomogeneous Cells	The Number of Cells That Are in the Initial State of the Log. "1"	The Length of the Formed Sequence	The Test Result (Positive / Negative)
• The First Pseudorandom Number Generator				
10x10		• 1, 10, 50	• 1000000	• negative
15x15		• 1, 50	• 1000000	• negative
		• 10, 100	• 1000000	• positive
20x20		• 1, 100, 200, 250	• 1000000	• negative
		• 50	• 1000000	• positive
25x25		• 1, 10, 50, 200, 600	• 1000000	• negative
		• 100, 250, 300, 400, 500	• 1000000	• positive
30x30		• 1, 10, 50, 400, 700, 800	• 1000000	• negative
		• 100, 200, 300, 500, 600	• 1000000	• positive
• The Second Pseudorandom Number Generator				
10x10		• 1, 10, 50	• 1000000	• positive
15x15		• 10, 50	• 1000000	• positive
		• 1, 100	• 1000000	• negative
20x20		• 1	• 1000000	• negative
		• 10, 50, 100, 200, 250	• 1000000	• positive
25x25		• 50, 100	• 1000000	• negative
		• 1, 200, 250, 300, 400, 500, 600	• 1000000	• positive
30x30		• 100, 200, 400, 600	• 1000000	• positive
		• 1, 10, 50, 250, 300, 500, 700, 800	• 1000000	• negative

continued on following page

Table 22. Continued

The Cellular Automata Size	The Number of Inhomogeneous Cells	The Number of Cells That Are in the Initial State of the Log. "1"	The Length of the Formed Sequence	The Test Result (Positive / Negative)
• The Third Pseudorandom Number Generator				
10x10	• 1	• 1, 10, 50	• 1000000	• negative
	• 2	• 1, 10, 50	• 1000000	• negative
	• 3	• 1, 50	• 1000000	• negative
		• 10	• 1000000	• positive
	• 4	• 10, 50	• 1000000	• negative
		• 1	• 1000000	• positive
15x15	• 1	• 1, 50	• 1000000	• positive
		• 10, 100	• 1000000	• negative
	• 2	• 1, 10, 50, 100	• 1000000	• positive
	• 3	• 1	• 1000000	• positive
		• 10, 50, 100	• 1000000	• negative
	• 4	• 1, 10, 50, 100	• 1000000	• negative
20x20	• 1	• 1, 10, 50, 100, 200, 250	• 1000000	• negative
	• 2	• 1, 50, 100, 200, 250	• 1000000	• negative
		• 10	• 1000000	• positive
	• 3	• 1, 10, 200, 250	• 1000000	• positive
		• 50, 100	• 1000000	• negative
	• 4	• 1, 10, 100, 200, 250	• 1000000	• positive
		• 10, 50	• 1000000	• negative
25x25	• 3	• 50, 100, 300, 600	• 1000000	• positive
		• 1, 10, 200, 250, 400, 500	• 1000000	• negative
	• 4	• 1, 10, 50, 300, 400, 500	• 1000000	• positive
		• 100, 200, 250, 600	• 1000000	• negative
30x30	• 1	• 1, 50, 500, 700, 800	• 1000000	• positive
		• 10, 100, 200, 300, 400, 600	• 1000000	• negative
	• 3	• 10, 200, 300, 600	• 1000000	• positive
		• 1, 50, 100, 400, 500, 600, 700, 800	• 1000000	• negative
	• 4	• 10, 50, 100, 200, 300, 800	• 1000000	• positive
		• 1, 50, 400, 500, 600, 700	• 1000000	• negative
• The Fourth Pseudorandom Number Generator				
16x16		• 1, 10, 50, 100, 200	• 8000000	• positive
• The Fifth Pseudorandom Number Generator				
16x16 inv		• 1, 10, 100, 200	• 8000000	• positive
		• 50	• 8000000	• negative

continued on following page

Table 22. Continued

The Cellular Automata Size	The Number of Inhomogeneous Cells	The Number of Cells That Are in the Initial State of the Log. "1"	The Length of the Formed Sequence	The Test Result (Positive / Negative)
		• The Sixth Pseudorandom Number Generator		
10x10	• 1	• 1	• 8000000	• positive
		• 10, 50	• 8000000	• negative
	• 2	• 1	• 80000000	• negative
	• 3	• 50	• 1600000	• positive
	• 4	• 10	• 1600000	• negative
		• 50	• 1600000	• positive
20x20	• 1	• 10, 100, 300	• 1000000	• negative
		• 200	• 1342176	• positive
	• 2	• 1, 10, 50, 100	• 1342176	• positive
		• 200, 300	• 1342176	• negative
	• 3	• 10, 100, 300	• 1342176	• positive
		• 300	• 1342176	• negative
	• 4	• 1, 200, 300	• 1342176	• negative
		• 10, 50, 100	• 1342176	• positive

The results allow choosing the right structure of the pseudorandom number generator. The investigations allow us to study the dynamics of the operation of the cellular automata of different configurations.

ANALYSIS OF THE PSEUDORANDOM BIT SEQUENCE GENERATORS BASED ON A GRAPHICAL TESTS

ENT and NIST tests set the value of the degree of similarity of the properties analyzed and truly random sequence. Decision that bite sequence is random, accepted on base of received numerical characteristics. These numerical characteristics make an analysis on base of appropriate static criteria. The static characteristics are determined on the base of special functions from the set of quantitative data. These functions are difficult enough.. The obtained evaluation values are virtually impossible to define groups of bits, in which there are malfunctions that from the presence of defects PRNG are obtained. The ENT and NIST tests don't allow to find and fix a wick sides

Table 23. The results of the passage of the sixteenth NIST test by all the developed pseudorandom number generators

The Cellular Automata Size	The Number of Inhomogeneous Cells	The Number of Cells That Are in the Initial State of the Log. "1"	The Length of the Formed Sequence	The Test Result (Positive / Negative)
• The First Pseudorandom Number Generator				
10x10		• 1, 10	• 1000000	• negative
		• 50	• 1000000	• positive
15x15		• 1, 50	• 1000000	• negative
		• 10, 100	• 1000000	• positive
20x20		• 1, 200, 250	• 1000000	• negative
		• 10, 50, 100	• 1000000	• positive
25x25		• 1, 50, 200	• 1000000	• negative
		• 10, 100, 250, 300, 400, 500, 600	• 1000000	• positive
30x30		• 1, 10, 50, 400, 800	• 1000000	• negative
		• 100, 200, 300, 500, 600, 700	• 1000000	• positive
• The Second Pseudorandom Number Generator				
10x10		• 1, 10, 50	• 1000000	• positive
15x15		• 10, 50	• 1000000	• positive
		• 1, 100	• 1000000	• negative
20x20		• 1	• 1000000	• negative
		• 10, 50, 100, 200, 250	• 1000000	• positive
25x25		• 1, 50, 100, 600	• 1000000	• negative
		• 10, 200, 250, 300, 400, 500	• 1000000	• positive
30x30		• 100, 200, 400, 600	• 1000000	• positive
		• 1, 10, 50, 250, 300, 500, 700, 800	• 1000000	• negative
• The Third Pseudorandom Number Generator				
10x10	• 1, 2	• 1, 10, 50	• 1000000	• negative
	• 3	• 1, 50	• 1000000	• negative
		• 10	• 1000000	• positive
	• 4	• 10, 50	• 1000000	• negative
		• 1	• 1000000	• positive
15x15	• 1	• 1, 50	• 1000000	• positive
		• 10, 100	• 1000000	• negative
	• 2	• 1, 10, 50, 100	• 1000000	• positive
	• 3	• 1, 100	• 1000000	• positive
		• 10, 50	• 1000000	• negative
	• 4	• 10, 50, 100	• 1000000	• negative
		• 1	• 1000000	• positive

continued on following page

Table 23. Continued

The Cellular Automata Size	The Number of Inhomogeneous Cells	The Number of Cells That Are in the Initial State of the Log. "1"	The Length of the Formed Sequence	The Test Result (Positive / Negative)
20x20	• 1	• 1, 10, 50, 100, 200, 250	• 1000000	• negative
	• 2	• 1, 50, 200	• 1000000	• negative
		• 10, 100, 250	• 1000000	• positive
	• 3	• 1, 10, 200, 250	• 1000000	• positive
		• 50, 100	• 1000000	• negative
	• 4	• 1, 10, 50, 100, 200, 250	• 1000000	• positive
		• 10	• 1000000	• negative
25x25	• 3	• 50, 100, 300, 600	• 1000000	• positive
		• 1, 10, 200, 250, 400, 500	• 1000000	• negative
	• 4	• 1, 10, 50, 300, 400, 500	• 1000000	• positive
		• 100, 200, 250, 600	• 1000000	• negative
30x30	• 1	• 1, 50, 500, 700, 800	• 1000000	• positive
		• 10, 100, 200, 300, 400, 600	• 1000000	• negative
	• 3	• 10, 200, 300, 600	• 1000000	• positive
		• 1, 50, 100, 400, 500, 600, 700, 800	• 1000000	• negative
	• 4	• 10, 50, 100, 200, 300, 800	• 1000000	• positive
		• 1, 500, 600, 700	• 1000000	• negative
• The Fourth Pseudorandom Number Generator				
16x16		• 1, 10, 50, 100, 200	• 80000000	• positive
• The Fifth Pseudorandom Number Generator				
16x16 inv		• 1, 10, 100, 200	• 80000000	• positive
		• 50	• 80000000	• negative
• The Sixth Pseudorandom Number Generator				
10x10	• 1	• 1	• 80000000	• positive
	• 2	• 1	• 80000000	• positive
		• 50	• 80000000	• negative
	• 3	• 50	• 80000000	• positive
	• 4	• 10	• 80000000	• negative
		• 50	• 80000000	• positive
20x20	• 1	• 10, 50, 300	• 1000000	• negative
		• 100	• 1342176	• positive
	• 2	• 1, 10, 50, 100	• 1342176	• positive
		• 200, 300	• 1342176	• negative
	• 3	• 10, 100, 300	• 1342176	• positive
		• 50, 200	• 1342176	• negative
	• 4	• 1, 200, 300	• 1342176	• negative
		• 10, 50, 100	• 1342176	• positive

in the generator structure. That's why are developed whole sets of graphical tests, which allow visually display the static properties of the sequences (Chugunkov, 2012). Results of these tests displayed as distribution graphs of the generated numerical values. With help of these graphs, the specialists make a conclusion about the properties of the test numbers (bits) sequence.

Researchers and developers make decision not always clear. Each developer on base of personal experience and knowledge make the decision about the properties of a bit sequence character. However, using a graphical test can often determine the presence of a defect generator immediately. These defects can be seen by unarmed eye on the displayed charts. That is why graphical tests necessarily need to use for analyze of the PRNG quality.

The graphical tests include: (Chugunkov, 2012):

1. The Histogram of a distribution of the elements of sequences.
2. The points distribution on the plane.
3. The series test.
4. Spectral test.
5. The Monotony check.
6. The autocorrelation function (ACF).
7. The linear complexity Profile.

Let us consider the first test, which allows building the distribution histograms of the elements of sequence. With help of this test developer of RPNG can have opportunity to estimate an uniform distribution of the numbers in the test sequence. This test allows to estimate the frequency of occurrence of the individual number.

Histogram can be built in simple way. The generated sequence of numbers are being selected. Each number is presented as selected amount of discharges (for example, an eight bits form each generated number). If the sequence is generated as bite sequence, it broke into m – bite groups.

Each such group codes a number. In obtained sequence are counted, how much meets the S_i number. After that, the graphic is build. The x-axis shows the number of all kinds the numbers, which may be presented by m-bite code. Amount of these numbers complies 2^m. The ordinate axis shows the number of which corresponds to the number of occurrences of each sequence in (Figure 17).

Figure 17. The generalized distribution histogram of sequence elements

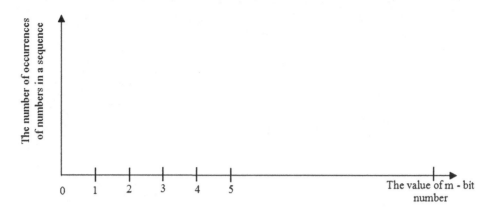

The sequence is considered as random or the sequence satisfies the properties of randomness, if in sequence all the elements are m-bit numbers. However, their frequency of occurrence in the sequence should be equal for all the numbers and the variation of frequencies should aspire to 0. In another case the generated sequence is not random.

All the proposed pseudorandom number generators based on the cellular automata were exposed to the first test with the construction of a histogram distribution of elements in a sequence. The first was tested the first pseudorandom number generator. In that pseudorandom number generator additional bit is formed by additional cellular automata, which change it state through N×M time steps. The results of passing of the first graphical test by the first pseudorandom number generator based on cellular automata with the size of 10 to 10 are shown in Figure 18.

The obtained histograms show that the number 170 is most common in the first pseudorandom number generator. This is represented by the maximum value of the area of histogram. For the first histogram is the number in the sequences is encountered 961 times, and the minimum number is 132, and it appears 410 times. The presence of a jump in the histogram requires an additional analysis of the obtained values. Therefore, an analysis of the distribution of the number 170 on the duration of the of time intervals of its occurrence was held. The histogram of distribution of its appearance in

Figure 18. The histograms of the distribution of the sequence of elements for the first pseudorandom number generator based on the cellular automata with size 10×10

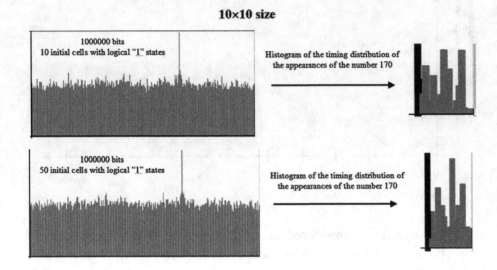

time to the right of each histogram is represented. These histograms showed the presence of various of time intervals, which indicates the absence of dependencies between these elements.

Histograms of distribution of the sequence of numbers that are generated by the first pseudorandom number generator for sizes 15×15, 20×20, 25×25, 30×30, are shown in Figure 19 – Figure 22.

Histograms of distribution of the sequence of numbers for the first pseudorandom number generator have shown that there is a number that occurs most of all the initial settings. The appearance of this number caused by use of local transmission function of the active state in accordance with which the next active cell is selected. However, this number appears is sequence at different time intervals, which indicates the absence periodicity.

A second pseudorandom number generator also is tested with the help of graphical test. Histograms of distribution of for the second pseudorandom number generator with help of the different sizes and the different initial settings are shown in Figure 23 - Figure 27.

Figure 19. The histograms of the distribution of the sequence of elements for the first pseudorandom number generator based on the cellular automata with size 15×15

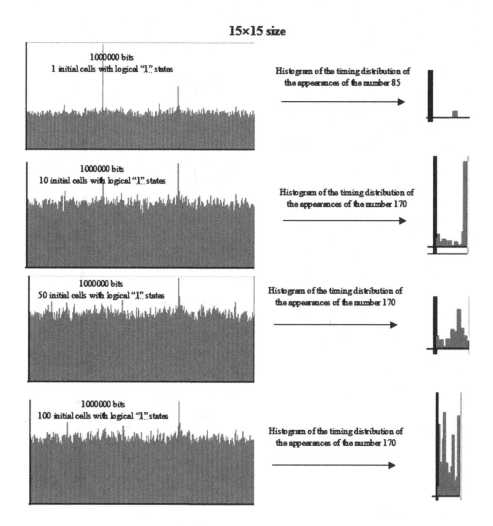

Test results have shown fairly good distribution of the numbers in the sequence. The greatest number of times the number 170 is encountered. Therefore, the sequence of the distribution of this number in all of the generated sequence was considered. The histogram of the distribution of the greatest

Figure 20. The histograms of the distribution of the sequence of elements for the first pseudorandom number generator based on the cellular automata with size 20×20

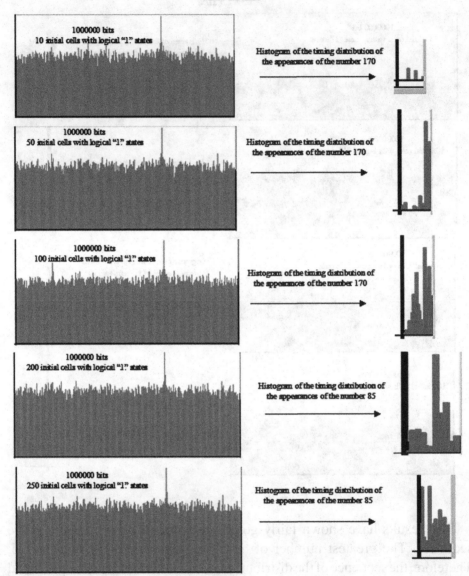

Figure 21. The histograms of the distribution of the sequence of elements for the first pseudorandom number generator based on the cellular automata with size at 25×25 (partly)

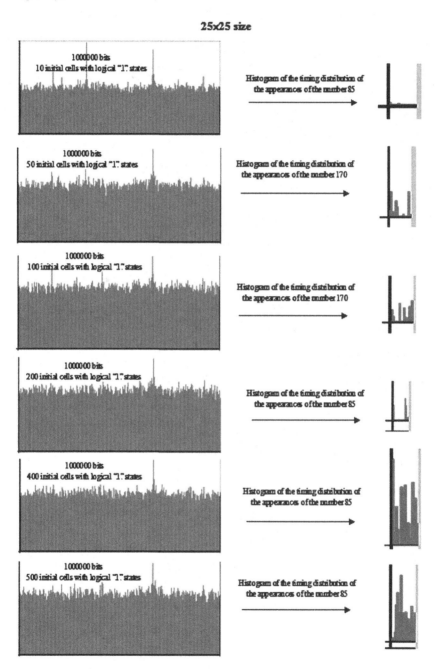

Figure 22. The histograms of the distribution of the sequence of elements for the first pseudorandom number generator based on the cellular automata with size at 30×30

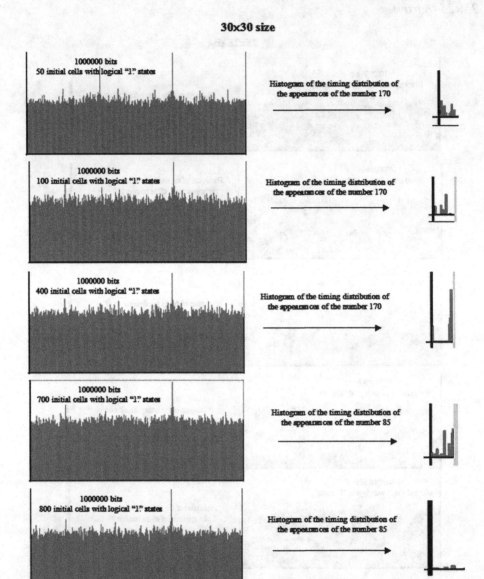

Figure 23. The histograms of the distribution of the sequence of elements for the second pseudorandom number generator based on the cellular automata with size at 10×10

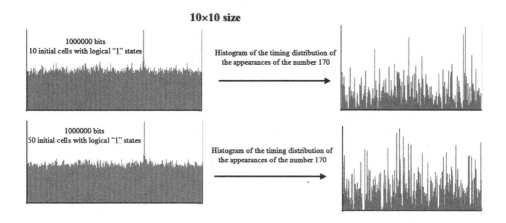

Figure 24. The histograms of the distribution of the sequence of elements for the second pseudorandom number generator based on the cellular automata with size at 15×15

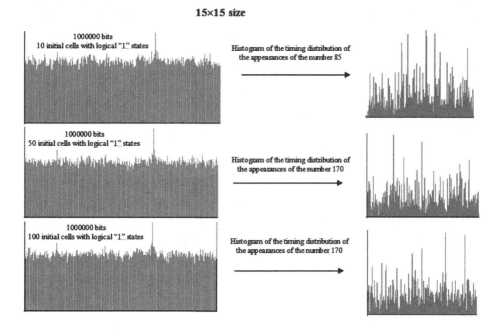

Figure 25. The histograms of the distribution of the sequence of elements for the second pseudorandom number generator based on the cellular automata with size at 20×20

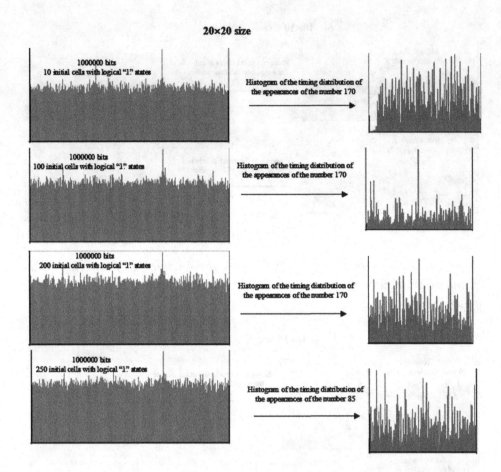

number were built. The histograms represent amount of numbers between the adjacent occurrences of the maximum numbers. As we seen from the graphs that the maximum numbers is randomly in the sequence are distributed. The number in the sequence is almost impossible to predict.

Let us consider testing of the third pseudorandom number generator. The histograms of distribution of the third pseudorandom number generator are presented in Figure 28 - Figure 32.

Figure 26. The histograms of the distribution of the sequence of elements for the second pseudorandom number generator based on the cellular automata with size at 25×25 (partly)

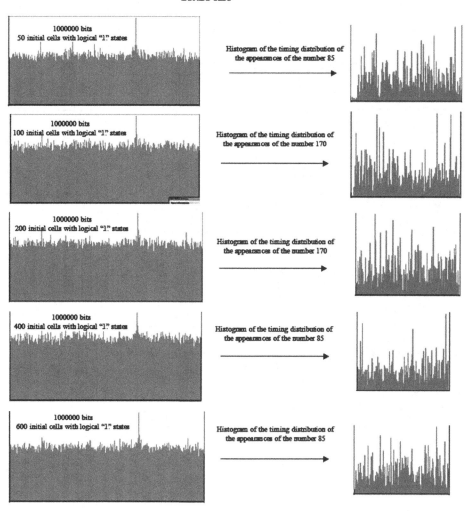

Figure 27. The histograms of the distribution of the sequence of elements for the second pseudorandom number generator based on the cellular automata with size at 30×30 (partly)

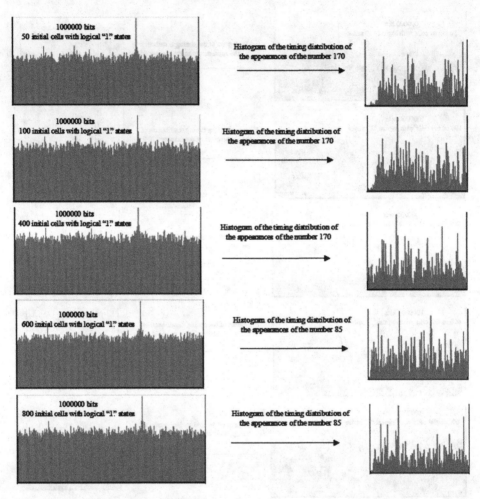

266

Figure 28. The histograms of the distribution of the sequence of elements for the third pseudorandom number generator based on the cellular automata with size at 10×10

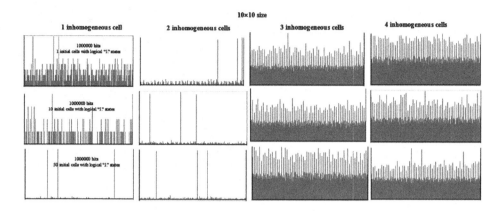

Figure 29. The histograms of the distribution of the sequence of elements for the third pseudorandom number generator based on the cellular automata with size at 15×15

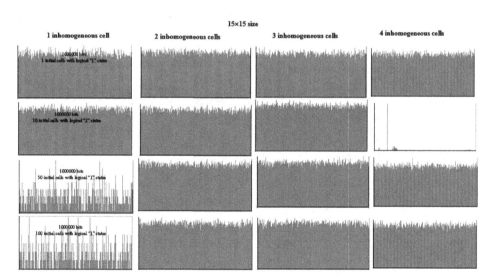

Figure 30. The histograms of the distribution of the sequence of elements for the third pseudorandom number generator based on the cellular automata with size at 20×20

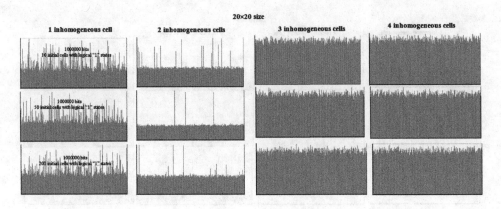

Figure 31. The histograms of the distribution of the sequence of elements for the third pseudorandom number generator based on the cellular automata with size at 25×25 (partly)

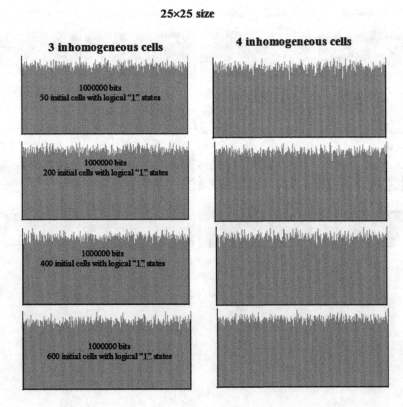

Figure 32. The histograms of the distribution of the sequence of elements for the third pseudorandom number generator based on the cellular automata with size at 30×30 (partly)

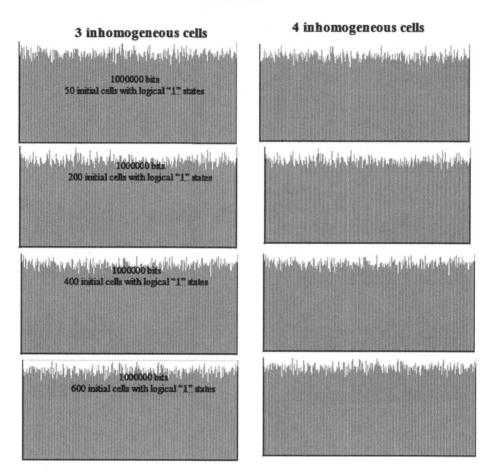

The graphical test showed a good distribution of the numbers in the sequence. Especially when a 3 heterogeneous cell are used. The graphical test showed coincidence between the results with ENT tests and NISN tests.

The test results of the fourth and fifth pseudorandom number generators in Figure 33 are presented.

Figure 33. The histograms of the distribution of the sequence of elements for the fourth and fifth pseudorandom number generators based on the cellular automata with size at 16×16 (partly)

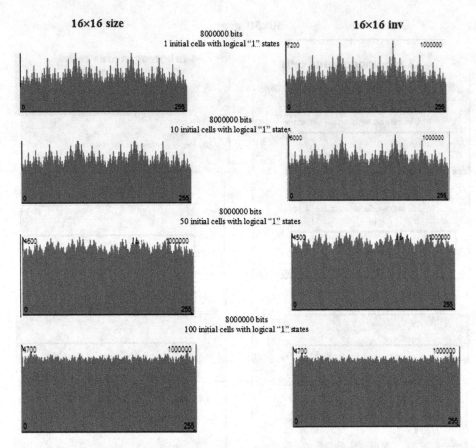

The fourth and fifth generators also showed positive results for the initial settings with a large number of initial cells, which are set to logic "1" state. It is seen from the diagrams.

The results of of passing the test by the sixth pseudorandom number generator in the Figure 34 and Figure 35 are presented.

All the generators have shown a good distribution of numbers for different the initial settings. This gives us the right to assert that the generators have a high quality of performance and they form a pseudo-random sequence.

The second test is also very popular. It allows you to determine the presence of dependencies between elements of generated the bit sequence. The essence of the test is to create a field that has size $2^m \times 2^m$ (were m – number of bits

Figure 34. The histograms of the distribution of the sequence of elements for the sixth pseudorandom number generator based on the cellular automata with size at 10×10 (partly)

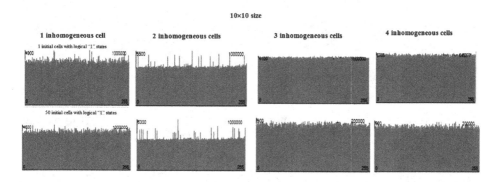

Figure 35. The histograms of the distribution of the sequence of elements for the sixth pseudorandom number generator based on the cellular automata with size at 20×20 (partly)

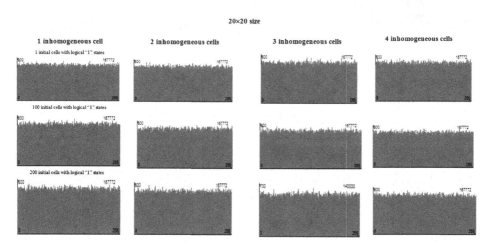

which are used to encode the numbers in the sequence). In this area the points are depicted. Each point is specified by coordinates that are adjacent numbers of the generated sequence (S_{i-1}, S_i). In fact, every number in the sequence is the X coordinate of a point in the plane, and the Y coordinate for the previous adjacent point of the plane.

The resulting graphic picture is analyzed by the developer. If there are no dependencies between the elements of the sequence, then the points on

271

Figure 36. The histograms of distribution of sequence elements for the first pseudorandom number generator based on the cellular automata of all sizes (in part)

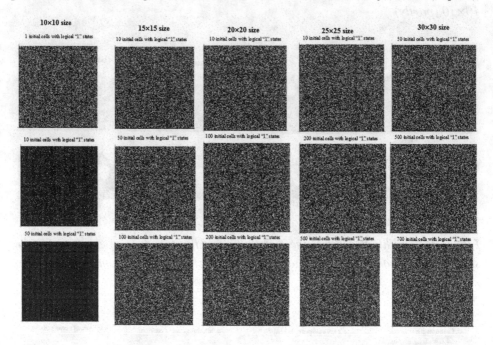

Figure 37. The histograms of distribution of sequence elements for the second pseudorandom number generator based on the cellular automata of all sizes (in part)

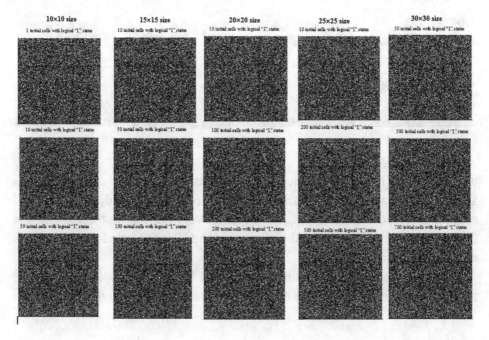

the area are chaotically located. When present at the coordinate field of conspicuous graphic dependences as any periodic patterns or fills, then the sequence is not random are make concluded.

This test can be improved, if we consider the distribution of points in space. Using this test it is possible to determine the statistical relationships that can not be determined by other not graphical tests. Many generators successfully pass the tests of the DIEHARD, NIST and others. But the graphics tests determine the presence in them of dependencies between elements of the sequence.

The test of the numbers distribution on the plane were also all the generators for a different initial systems. A graphical representation of test results for the first pseudorandom number generator with sizes 10×10, 15×15, 20×20, 25×15, 30×30 in Figure 36 are presented. The bit sequence 1000000 bits was used. They were divided into bytes that the decimal numbers encode. As can be seen from the distribution on the plane all the sequences give a good result. If we use a shorter length sequence with the same initial conditions,

Figure 38. The histograms of distribution of sequence elements for the third pseudorandom number generator based on the cellular automata with a size 10×10

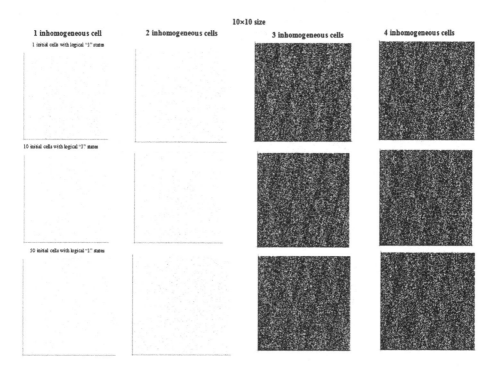

10×10 size

| 1 inhomogeneous cell | 2 inhomogeneous cells | 3 inhomogeneous cells | 4 inhomogeneous cells |

1 initial cells with logical "1" states

10 initial cells with logical "1" states

50 initial cells with logical "1" states

Figure 39. The histograms of distribution of sequence elements for the third pseudorandom number generator based on the cellular automata with a size 15×15

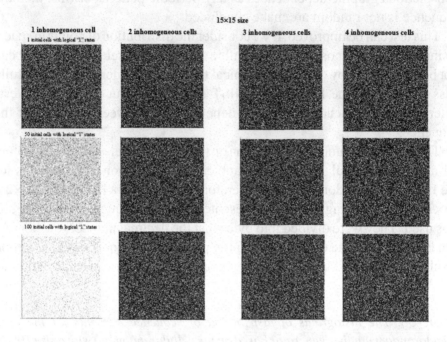

Figure 40. The histograms of distribution of sequence elements for the third pseudorandom number generator based on the cellular automata with a size 20×20

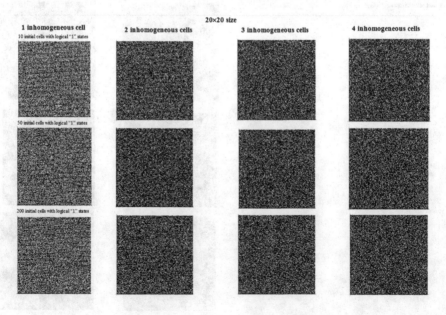

we can see that the distribution of points are grouped near several points in the plane for a small number of primary cells with a logic "1" state. With an increase in the number of cells that are at logic "1" state and becomes aligned distribution uniform in the whole plane for bit sequences with a small number of bits.

Figure 41. The histograms of distribution of sequence elements for the third pseudorandom number generator based on the cellular automata with a size 25×25 (in part)

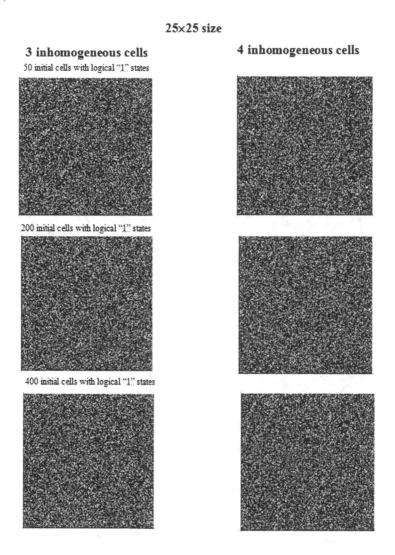

The results of passing the test of the second pseudorandom number generator on the Figure 37 are shown.

Histograms of the distribution of points on a plane for a third pseudorandom number generator and also for sizes 10×10, 15×15, 20×20, 25×25, 30×30 on the Figure 38 - Figure 42 are shown.

Figure 42. The histograms of distribution of sequence elements for the third pseudorandom number generator based on the cellular automata with a size 30×30 (in part)

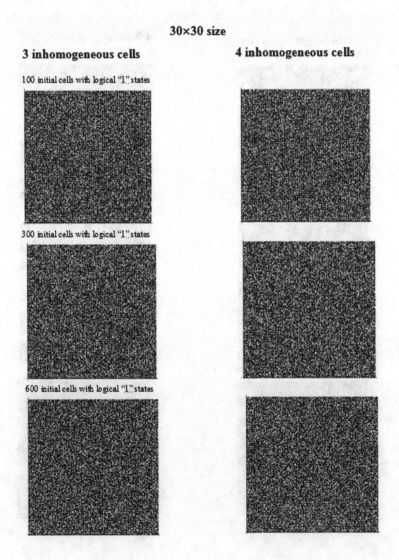

Figure 43. The histograms of distribution of the sequence elements on a plane for the fourth and fifth pseudorandom number generators based on the cellular automata with size 16×16 (in part)

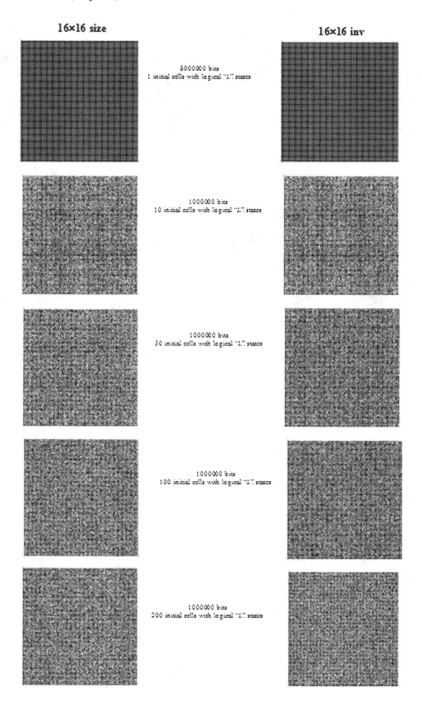

Figure 44. The histograms of distribution of the sequence elements on a plane for the sixth pseudorandom number generator based on the cellular automata with size 10×10 (in part)

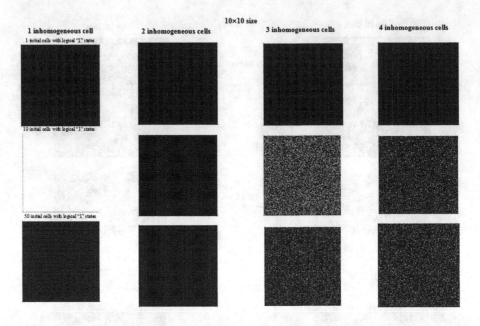

Figure 45. The histograms of distribution of the sequence elements on a plane for the sixth pseudorandom number generator based on the cellular automata with size 20×20 (in part)

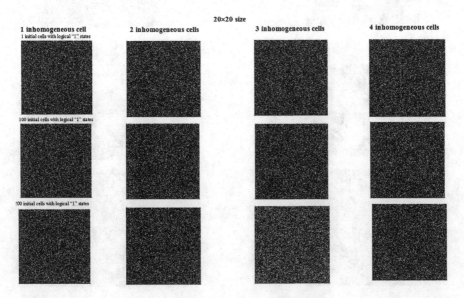

The results of analysis of the fourth and fifth pseudorandom number generators on the test of a distribution on a plane in the Figure 43 are shown.

In this example, the first graph shows the distribution of 8000000 bits and the remaining pictures for the bit sequence of 1000000 bits are shown. The test shows a positive result.

The sixth pseudorandom number generator based on the hexagonal coating with inhomogeneous cells for sizes 10×10 and 20×20 in the Figure 44 and Figure 45 for the second graphical test are shown.

The second graphical test showed a good distribution on a plane of a numbers for all bit sequences of the pseudorandom number generator. This confirms the high quality of the proposed generators.

REFERENCES

Chugunkov, E.V. (2012). *Methods and tools to evaluate the quality of pseudorandom sequence generators, focused on solving problems of information security: Textbook*. NEYAU MIFI.

Knuth, D. E. (1969). The Art of Computer Programming: Vol. 2. *Seminumerical Algorithms*. Reading, MA: Addison-Wesley.

Richard, W. (1980). *Hamming. Coding and Information Theory*. Prentice-Hall.

NIST Special Publications 800-22. (2001). *A statistical test suite for random and pseudorandom number generators for cryptographic applications*. NIST.

NIST Special Publications 800-22. (2010). *A statistical test suite for random and pseudorandom number generators for cryptographic applications. Revision 1*. NIST.

Walker, J. (2008). *ENT. A Pseudorandom Number Sequence Test Program*. Retrieved January 28th, from http://www.fourmilab.ch/random

Conclusion

In this book, the known pseudorandom number generators were analysed. An assessment of the advantages and disadvantages was held. Much attention was paid to the analysis of different architectures cellular automata, as well as the pseudorandom number generators based CA are considered. The analysis showed that there are a number of problems that are inherent to the pseudorandom number generator based CA. These disadvantages do not allow to state that pseudorandom number generator based on CA have the characteristics of high quality.

For searching the best model of the pseudorandom number generator based on CA, in book the various options PRNG based on CA are proposed. Using new architecture a high quality generator been achieved. This is confirmed by the testing. With the tests the initial setup of pseudorandom number generator are defined, which do not give good pseudorandom sequence at the output. With the help of this book, the developer can choose the optimal pseudorandom number generator structure and the best initial installations. In addition, the developer can choose the pseudorandom number generator with the desired speed. A material of book contains a small part of the experimental studies. However, the book helps to develop and to investigate other the pseudorandom number generator structure based CA. The structures of combined pseudorandom number generators are proposed. Their study will be carried out more. The technique of the pseudorandom number generator research based on the CA is developed.

Search of the pseudorandom number generator based on the CA with a good performance given the opportunity to explore different configuration of cellular automata that use asynchronous and synchronous operating principles. These results complement modern theory of cellular automata and pseudorandom number generator theory.

Related Readings

To continue IGI Global's long-standing tradition of advancing innovation through emerging research, please find below a compiled list of recommended IGI Global book chapters and journal articles in the areas of pseudorandom number generators, fuzzy sets, and fuzzy numbers. These related readings will provide additional information and guidance to further enrich your knowledge and assist you with your own research.

Acherjee, B., Maity, D., Kuar, A. S., Mitra, S., & Misra, D. (2017). Optimization of Laser Transmission Welding Parameters Using Chicken Swarm Optimization Algorithm: Chicken Swarm Algorithm Optimization of Laser Transmission Welding. In R. Das & M. Pradhan (Eds.), *Handbook of Research on Manufacturing Process Modeling and Optimization Strategies* (pp. 142–161). Hershey, PA: IGI Global. doi:10.4018/978-1-5225-2440-3.ch007

Adak, A. K. (2017). Interval-Valued Intuitionistic Fuzzy Partition Matrices. In A. Adak, D. Manna, & M. Bhowmik (Eds.), *Emerging Research on Applied Fuzzy Sets and Intuitionistic Fuzzy Matrices* (pp. 64–81). Hershey, PA: IGI Global. doi:10.4018/978-1-5225-0914-1.ch003

Aggarwal, S., & Azim, S. (2017). Outliers, Missing Values, and Reliability: An Integrated Framework for Pre-Processing of Coding Data. In A. Sangaiah, X. Gao, & A. Abraham (Eds.), *Handbook of Research on Fuzzy and Rough Set Theory in Organizational Decision Making* (pp. 316–330). Hershey, PA: IGI Global. doi:10.4018/978-1-5225-1008-6.ch014

Akula, V. S. (2015). Rule-Based Systems for Medical Diagnosis. In A. Kumar (Ed.), *Fuzzy Expert Systems for Disease Diagnosis* (pp. 21–44). Hershey, PA: IGI Global. doi:10.4018/978-1-4666-7240-6.ch002

Ali, M., Smarandache, F., & Vladareanu, L. (2017). Neutrosophic Sets and Logic. In A. Adak, D. Manna, & M. Bhowmik (Eds.), *Emerging Research on Applied Fuzzy Sets and Intuitionistic Fuzzy Matrices* (pp. 18–63). Hershey, PA: IGI Global. doi:10.4018/978-1-5225-0914-1.ch002

Alnafie, E., Hamdadou, D., & Bouamrane, K. (2016). Towards a New Multicriteria Decision Support Method Using Fuzzy Measures and the Choquet Integral. *International Journal of Fuzzy System Applications*, 5(1), 57–86. doi:10.4018/IJFSA.2016010104

Alouane-Ksouri, S., & Hidri, M. S. (2015). Fuzzy Learning of Co-Similarities from Large-Scale Documents. *International Journal of Fuzzy System Applications*, 4(4), 70–86. doi:10.4018/ijfsa.2015100104

Ayshee, T. F., Raka, S. A., Hasib, Q. R., Rahman, R. M., & Hossain, M. (2015). Sign Language Recognition for Bengali Characters. *International Journal of Fuzzy System Applications*, 4(4), 1–14. doi:10.4018/IJFSA.2015100101

Banimelhem, O., Taqieddin, E., Mowafi, M. Y., Awad, F., & Al-Maaqbeh, F. (2015). Fuzzy Logic-Based Cluster Heads Percentage Calculation for Improving the Performance of the LEACH Protocol. *International Journal of Fuzzy System Applications*, 4(4), 100–118. doi:10.4018/IJFSA.2015100106

Barik, S. K., & Biswal, M. P. (2016). Possibilistic Linear Programming Problems involving Normal Random Variables. *International Journal of Fuzzy System Applications*, 5(3), 1–13. doi:10.4018/IJFSA.2016070101

BenAli-Sougui, I., Hidri, M. S., & Grissa-Touzi, A. (2016). No-FSQL: A Graph-based Fuzzy NoSQL Querying Model. *International Journal of Fuzzy System Applications*, 5(2), 54–63. doi:10.4018/IJFSA.2016040104

Bharathi, C. R., & Shanthi, V. (2015). Hybrid Approach for Analyzing Acute Spots of Clinical Speech Data Using Fuzzy Inference System. In A. Kumar (Ed.), *Fuzzy Expert Systems for Disease Diagnosis* (pp. 93–137). Hershey, PA: IGI Global. doi:10.4018/978-1-4666-7240-6.ch005

Bhattacharya, A. B., & Bhattacharya, A. (2015). Implementation of Fuzzy Technology in Complicated Medical Diagnostics and Further Decision. In A. Kumar (Ed.), *Fuzzy Expert Systems for Disease Diagnosis* (pp. 62–91). Hershey, PA: IGI Global. doi:10.4018/978-1-4666-7240-6.ch004

Bhowmik, M., & Pal, M. (2017). Fuzzy Sets, Intuitionistic Fuzzy Sets: Separation of Generalized Interval-Valued Intuitionistic Fuzzy Sets. In A. Adak, D. Manna, & M. Bhowmik (Eds.), *Emerging Research on Applied Fuzzy Sets and Intuitionistic Fuzzy Matrices* (pp. 1–17). Hershey, PA: IGI Global. doi:10.4018/978-1-5225-0914-1.ch001

Bose, G. K., & Pain, P. (2017). Surface Response Methodology Approach for Multi-Objective Optimization During Electrochemical Grinding of Al2O3/Al Interpenetrating Phase Composite. In R. Das & M. Pradhan (Eds.), *Handbook of Research on Manufacturing Process Modeling and Optimization Strategies* (pp. 162–192). Hershey, PA: IGI Global. doi:10.4018/978-1-5225-2440-3.ch008

Bose, M., & Mali, K. (2016). High Order Time Series Forecasting using Fuzzy Discretization. *International Journal of Fuzzy System Applications*, 5(4), 147–164. doi:10.4018/IJFSA.2016100107

Chaudhuri, A. (2016). Fuzzy Rough Support Vector Machine for Data Classification. *International Journal of Fuzzy System Applications*, 5(2), 26–53. doi:10.4018/IJFSA.2016040103

Chhabra, K., Agrawal, D., & Subbarao, S. S. (2017). Modeling of Polypropylene Modified Bitumen Mix Design Results Using Regression Analysis. In R. Das & M. Pradhan (Eds.), *Handbook of Research on Manufacturing Process Modeling and Optimization Strategies* (pp. 256–275). Hershey, PA: IGI Global. doi:10.4018/978-1-5225-2440-3.ch012

Chkiwa, M., Jedidi, A., & Gargouri, F. (2017). Semantic / Fuzzy Information Retrieval System. *International Journal of Information Technology and Web Engineering*, 12(1), 37–56. doi:10.4018/IJITWE.2017010103

Cuka, M., Elmazi, D., Inaba, T., Oda, T., Ikeda, M., & Barolli, L. (2017). An Integrated Fuzzy-Based System for Cluster-Head Selection and Sensor Speed Control in Wireless Sensor Networks. *International Journal of Distributed Systems and Technologies*, 8(2), 1–14. doi:10.4018/IJDST.2017040101

Das, B. (2017). A Three-Level Supply Chain Model with Necessity Measure. In A. Adak, D. Manna, & M. Bhowmik (Eds.), *Emerging Research on Applied Fuzzy Sets and Intuitionistic Fuzzy Matrices* (pp. 305–321). Hershey, PA: IGI Global. doi:10.4018/978-1-5225-0914-1.ch014

Das, M. K., Barman, T. K., Sahoo, P., & Kumar, K. (2017). Process Optimization in Non-Conventional Processes: Experimentation With Plasma Arc Cutting. In R. Das & M. Pradhan (Eds.), *Handbook of Research on Manufacturing Process Modeling and Optimization Strategies* (pp. 82–119). Hershey, PA: IGI Global. doi:10.4018/978-1-5225-2440-3.ch005

Das, S., Ghosh, S., Pal, J., & Bhattacharya, D. K. (2017). Use of Fuzzy Set Theory in DNA Sequence Comparison and Amino Acid Classification. In A. Adak, D. Manna, & M. Bhowmik (Eds.), *Emerging Research on Applied Fuzzy Sets and Intuitionistic Fuzzy Matrices* (pp. 235–253). Hershey, PA: IGI Global. doi:10.4018/978-1-5225-0914-1.ch010

Das, T. K. (2017). Decision Making by Using Intuitionistic Fuzzy Rough Set. In A. Adak, D. Manna, & M. Bhowmik (Eds.), *Emerging Research on Applied Fuzzy Sets and Intuitionistic Fuzzy Matrices* (pp. 268–286). Hershey, PA: IGI Global. doi:10.4018/978-1-5225-0914-1.ch012

Dash, N., Priyadarshini, R., Mishra, B. K., & Misra, R. (2017). Bio-Inspired Computing through Artificial Neural Network. In A. Sangaiah, X. Gao, & A. Abraham (Eds.), *Handbook of Research on Fuzzy and Rough Set Theory in Organizational Decision Making* (pp. 246–274). Hershey, PA: IGI Global. doi:10.4018/978-1-5225-1008-6.ch011

Dey, A., & Pal, M. (2015). Multi-Fuzzy Complex Numbers and Multi-Fuzzy Complex Sets. *International Journal of Fuzzy System Applications*, 4(2), 15–27. doi:10.4018/IJFSA.2015040102

Dey, A., & Pal, M. (2016). Multi-Fuzzy Complex Nilpotent Matrices. *International Journal of Fuzzy System Applications*, 5(4), 52–76. doi:10.4018/IJFSA.2016100103

Dhingra, S., Thirugnanam, M., Dodwad, P., & Madan, M. (2017). Automated Framework for Software Process Model Selection Based on Soft Computing Approach. In A. Sangaiah, X. Gao, & A. Abraham (Eds.), *Handbook of Research on Fuzzy and Rough Set Theory in Organizational Decision Making* (pp. 395–418). Hershey, PA: IGI Global. doi:10.4018/978-1-5225-1008-6.ch018

Dutta, P. (2016). Dempster Shafer Structure-Fuzzy Number Based Uncertainty Modeling in Human Health Risk Assessment. *International Journal of Fuzzy System Applications*, *5*(2), 96–117. doi:10.4018/IJFSA.2016040107

Edalatpanah, S. A. (2017). Modified Iterative Methods for Solving Fully Fuzzy Linear Systems. In A. Adak, D. Manna, & M. Bhowmik (Eds.), *Emerging Research on Applied Fuzzy Sets and Intuitionistic Fuzzy Matrices* (pp. 322–339). Hershey, PA: IGI Global. doi:10.4018/978-1-5225-0914-1.ch015

Erozan, İ., Ustun, O., & Torkul, O. (2015). An Improved Fuzzy C-Means Algorithm for Cell Formation Problems with Alternative Routes. *International Journal of Fuzzy System Applications*, *4*(4), 15–30. doi:10.4018/IJFSA.2015100102

Faquir, S., Yahyaouy, A., Tairi, H., & Sabor, J. (2015). Implementing a Fuzzy Logic Based Algorithm to Predict Solar and Wind Energies in a Hybrid Renewable Energy System. *International Journal of Fuzzy System Applications*, *4*(3), 10–24. doi:10.4018/IJFSA.2015070102

Faquir, S., Yahyaouy, A., Tairi, H., & Sabor, J. (2017). Prediction of Solar and Wind Energies by Fuzzy Logic Control. In D. Li (Ed.), *Theoretical and Practical Advancements for Fuzzy System Integration* (pp. 351–379). Hershey, PA: IGI Global. doi:10.4018/978-1-5225-1848-8.ch013

Farahani, H., Rahmany, S., & Basiri, A. (2015). Determining of Level Sets for a Fuzzy Surface Using Gröbner Basis. *International Journal of Fuzzy System Applications*, *4*(2), 1–14. doi:10.4018/IJFSA.2015040101

Fei, W. (2015). A Note on Using Trapezoids for Representing Granular Objects: Applications to Learning and OWA Aggregation. *International Journal of Fuzzy System Applications*, *4*(4), 119–121. doi:10.4018/IJFSA.2015100107

Fei, W. (2015). Interval-Valued Bimatrix Game Method for Engineering Project Management. *International Journal of Fuzzy System Applications*, *4*(3), 1–9. doi:10.4018/IJFSA.2015070101

Ferdousi, F., & Sangaiah, A. K. (2017). Investment Climate Factors with Reference to Firm Performance in Bangladesh: A Prospective Cohort Study. In A. Sangaiah, X. Gao, & A. Abraham (Eds.), *Handbook of Research on Fuzzy and Rough Set Theory in Organizational Decision Making* (pp. 419–433). Hershey, PA: IGI Global. doi:10.4018/978-1-5225-1008-6.ch019

Gadekallu, T. R., & Khare, N. (2017). Cuckoo Search Optimized Reduction and Fuzzy Logic Classifier for Heart Disease and Diabetes Prediction. *International Journal of Fuzzy System Applications*, 6(2), 25–42. doi:10.4018/IJFSA.2017040102

Ganesan, T., Vasant, P., & Elamvazuthi, I. (2017). Multiobjective Optimization of Solar-Powered Irrigation System with Fuzzy Type-2 Noise Modelling. In A. Adak, D. Manna, & M. Bhowmik (Eds.), *Emerging Research on Applied Fuzzy Sets and Intuitionistic Fuzzy Matrices* (pp. 189–214). Hershey, PA: IGI Global. doi:10.4018/978-1-5225-0914-1.ch008

Garg, H., Agarwal, N., & Tripathi, A. (2017). Generalized Intuitionistic Fuzzy Entropy Measure of Order α and Degree β and Its Applications to Multi-Criteria Decision Making Problem. *International Journal of Fuzzy System Applications*, 6(1), 86–107. doi:10.4018/IJFSA.2017010105

Gasmi, M., & Bourahla, M. (2017). Reasoning with Vague Concepts in Description Logics. *International Journal of Fuzzy System Applications*, 6(2), 43–58. doi:10.4018/IJFSA.2017040103

Gholizadeh, R., Barahona, M. J., & Khalilpour, M. (2016). Fuzzy E-Bayesian and Hierarchical Bayesian Estimations on the Kumaraswamy Distribution Using Censoring Data. *International Journal of Fuzzy System Applications*, 5(2), 74–95. doi:10.4018/IJFSA.2016040106

Ghosal, K., Haldar, P., & Sutradhar, G. (2015). Application of Fuzzy Expert System in Medical Treatment. In A. Kumar (Ed.), *Fuzzy Expert Systems for Disease Diagnosis* (pp. 200–246). Hershey, PA: IGI Global. doi:10.4018/978-1-4666-7240-6.ch008

Göçken, T. (2017). Direct Solution of Fuzzy Project Crashing Problem with Fuzzy Decision Variables using Tabu Search and Simulated Annealing Algorithms. *International Journal of Fuzzy System Applications*, 6(1), 17–35. doi:10.4018/IJFSA.2017010102

González-López, V. A., Gholizadeh, R., & Shirazi, A. M. (2016). Optimization of Queuing Theory Based on Vague Environment. *International Journal of Fuzzy System Applications*, 5(1), 1–26. doi:10.4018/IJFSA.2016010101

Goyal, M., Tripathi, A., & Yadav, D. (2016). Intuitionistic Group Decision Making to Identify the Status of Students Knowledge Acquisition in E-Learning Systems. *International Journal of Fuzzy System Applications*, 5(3), 14–29. doi:10.4018/IJFSA.2016070102

Gupta, P., & Pradhan, M. K. (2017). Fault Detection Through Vibration Signal Analysis of Rolling Element Bearing in Time Domain. In R. Das & M. Pradhan (Eds.), *Handbook of Research on Manufacturing Process Modeling and Optimization Strategies* (pp. 208–234). Hershey, PA: IGI Global. doi:10.4018/978-1-5225-2440-3.ch010

Gupta, P., & Tiwari, P. (2016). Decision Making Approach using Weighted Coefficient of Correlation along with Generalized Parametric Fuzzy Entropy Measure. *International Journal of Fuzzy System Applications*, 5(3), 30–41. doi:10.4018/IJFSA.2016070103

Gupta, R., & Naqvi, S. K. (2017). The Fuzzy-AHP and Fuzzy TOPSIS Approaches to ERP Selection: A Comparative Analysis. In A. Sangaiah, X. Gao, & A. Abraham (Eds.), *Handbook of Research on Fuzzy and Rough Set Theory in Organizational Decision Making* (pp. 188–218). Hershey, PA: IGI Global. doi:10.4018/978-1-5225-1008-6.ch009

Hadjileontiadou, S. J., Dias, S. B., Diniz, J. A., & Hadjileontiadis, L. J. (2015). Placing the Framework within the Educational Context. In *Fuzzy Logic-Based Modeling in Collaborative and Blended Learning* (pp. 1–17). Hershey, PA: IGI Global. doi:10.4018/978-1-4666-8705-9.ch001

Hadjileontiadou, S. J., Dias, S. B., Diniz, J. A., & Hadjileontiadis, L. J. (2015). Understanding Online Learning Environments (OLEs). In *Fuzzy Logic-Based Modeling in Collaborative and Blended Learning* (pp. 18–50). Hershey, PA: IGI Global. doi:10.4018/978-1-4666-8705-9.ch002

Hadjileontiadou, S. J., Dias, S. B., Diniz, J. A., & Hadjileontiadis, L. J. (2015). Computer-Supported Collaborative Learning: A Holistic Perspective. In *Fuzzy Logic-Based Modeling in Collaborative and Blended Learning* (pp. 51–88). Hershey, PA: IGI Global. doi:10.4018/978-1-4666-8705-9.ch003

Hadjileontiadou, S. J., Dias, S. B., Diniz, J. A., & Hadjileontiadis, L. J. (2015). Towards Blending Potentialities within a Learning Management System: Definitions, Issues, and Trends. In *Fuzzy Logic-Based Modeling in Collaborative and Blended Learning* (pp. 89–118). Hershey, PA: IGI Global. doi:10.4018/978-1-4666-8705-9.ch004

Hadjileontiadou, S. J., Dias, S. B., Diniz, J. A., & Hadjileontiadis, L. J. (2015). Personal/Cloud Learning Environment, Semantic Web 3.0, and Ontologies. In *Fuzzy Logic-Based Modeling in Collaborative and Blended Learning* (pp. 119–146). Hershey, PA: IGI Global. doi:10.4018/978-1-4666-8705-9.ch005

Hadjileontiadou, S. J., Dias, S. B., Diniz, J. A., & Hadjileontiadis, L. J. (2015). Placing the Framework within the Fuzzy Logic World. In *Fuzzy Logic-Based Modeling in Collaborative and Blended Learning* (pp. 148–167). Hershey, PA: IGI Global. doi:10.4018/978-1-4666-8705-9.ch006

Hadjileontiadou, S. J., Dias, S. B., Diniz, J. A., & Hadjileontiadis, L. J. (2015). Fuzzy Logic Essentials. In *Fuzzy Logic-Based Modeling in Collaborative and Blended Learning* (pp. 168–208). Hershey, PA: IGI Global. doi:10.4018/978-1-4666-8705-9.ch007

Hadjileontiadou, S. J., Dias, S. B., Diniz, J. A., & Hadjileontiadis, L. J. (2015). Fuzzy Logic-Based Inference Systems. In *Fuzzy Logic-Based Modeling in Collaborative and Blended Learning* (pp. 209–239). Hershey, PA: IGI Global. doi:10.4018/978-1-4666-8705-9.ch008

Hadjileontiadou, S. J., Dias, S. B., Diniz, J. A., & Hadjileontiadis, L. J. (2015). Connecting the Educational and Fuzzy Worlds. In *Fuzzy Logic-Based Modeling in Collaborative and Blended Learning* (pp. 241–259). Hershey, PA: IGI Global. doi:10.4018/978-1-4666-8705-9.ch009

Hadjileontiadou, S. J., Dias, S. B., Diniz, J. A., & Hadjileontiadis, L. J. (2015). FIS-Based Collaborative/Metacognitive Data Modeling. In *Fuzzy Logic-Based Modeling in Collaborative and Blended Learning* (pp. 260–302). Hershey, PA: IGI Global. doi:10.4018/978-1-4666-8705-9.ch010

Hadjileontiadou, S. J., Dias, S. B., Diniz, J. A., & Hadjileontiadis, L. J. (2015). ANFIS-Based Collaborative/Metacognitive Data Modeling. In *Fuzzy Logic-Based Modeling in Collaborative and Blended Learning* (pp. 303–325). Hershey, PA: IGI Global. doi:10.4018/978-1-4666-8705-9.ch011

Hadjileontiadou, S. J., Dias, S. B., Diniz, J. A., & Hadjileontiadis, L. J. (2015). FIS/IFIS Modeling in Professional and Collaborative Learning: A Systemic Approach. In *Fuzzy Logic-Based Modeling in Collaborative and Blended Learning* (pp. 326–354). Hershey, PA: IGI Global. doi:10.4018/978-1-4666-8705-9.ch012

Hadjileontiadou, S. J., Dias, S. B., Diniz, J. A., & Hadjileontiadis, L. J. (2015). Embracing Macro-, Meso-, and Micro-Levels of Analysis of FIS-Based LMS Users' Quality of Interaction. In *Fuzzy Logic-Based Modeling in Collaborative and Blended Learning* (pp. 355–387). Hershey, PA: IGI Global. doi:10.4018/978-1-4666-8705-9.ch013

Hadjileontiadou, S. J., Dias, S. B., Diniz, J. A., & Hadjileontiadis, L. J. (2015). FCM-Based Modeling of LMS Users' Quality of Interaction. In *Fuzzy Logic-Based Modeling in Collaborative and Blended Learning* (pp. 388–420). Hershey, PA: IGI Global. doi:10.4018/978-1-4666-8705-9.ch014

Hadjileontiadou, S. J., Dias, S. B., Diniz, J. A., & Hadjileontiadis, L. J. (2015). Towards a Hybrid Modeling. In *Fuzzy Logic-Based Modeling in Collaborative and Blended Learning* (pp. 422–442). Hershey, PA: IGI Global. doi:10.4018/978-1-4666-8705-9.ch015

Hadjileontiadou, S. J., Dias, S. B., Diniz, J. A., & Hadjileontiadis, L. J. (2015). Concluding Remarks and Probing Further. In *Fuzzy Logic-Based Modeling in Collaborative and Blended Learning* (pp. 443–459). Hershey, PA: IGI Global. doi:10.4018/978-1-4666-8705-9.ch016

Hiziroglu, A., & Senbas, U. D. (2016). An Application of Fuzzy Clustering to Customer Portfolio Analysis in Automotive Industry. *International Journal of Fuzzy System Applications*, 5(2), 13–25. doi:10.4018/IJFSA.2016040102

Hosseinzadeh, A., & Edalatpanah, S. A. (2017). Classification Techniques in Data Mining: Classical and Fuzzy Classifiers. In A. Adak, D. Manna, & M. Bhowmik (Eds.), *Emerging Research on Applied Fuzzy Sets and Intuitionistic Fuzzy Matrices* (pp. 153–188). Hershey, PA: IGI Global. doi:10.4018/978-1-5225-0914-1.ch007

Hudedagaddi, D. P., & Tripathy, B. K. (2017). Clustering Approaches in Decision Making Using Fuzzy and Rough Sets. In A. Sangaiah, X. Gao, & A. Abraham (Eds.), *Handbook of Research on Fuzzy and Rough Set Theory in Organizational Decision Making* (pp. 116–136). Hershey, PA: IGI Global. doi:10.4018/978-1-5225-1008-6.ch006

Jagadeesan, A., & Patil, A. (2017). Sentimental Analysis of Online Reviews Using Fuzzy Sets and Rough Sets. In A. Sangaiah, X. Gao, & A. Abraham (Eds.), *Handbook of Research on Fuzzy and Rough Set Theory in Organizational Decision Making* (pp. 376–394). Hershey, PA: IGI Global. doi:10.4018/978-1-5225-1008-6.ch017

John Robinson, P. (2016). Multiple Attribute Group Decision Analysis for Intuitionistic Triangular and Trapezoidal Fuzzy Numbers. *International Journal of Fuzzy System Applications*, 5(3), 42–76. doi:10.4018/IJFSA.2016070104

Joshi, B. P. (2016). Interval-Valued Intuitionistic Fuzzy Sets based Method for Multiple Criteria Decision-Making. *International Journal of Fuzzy System Applications, 5*(4), 192–210. doi:10.4018/IJFSA.2016100109

Kaliyaperumal, P. (2017). Fuzzy Dynamic Programming Problem for Single Additive Constraint with Additively Separable Return by Means of Trapezoidal Membership Functions. In A. Sangaiah, X. Gao, & A. Abraham (Eds.), *Handbook of Research on Fuzzy and Rough Set Theory in Organizational Decision Making* (pp. 168–187). Hershey, PA: IGI Global. doi:10.4018/978-1-5225-1008-6.ch008

Kamalanathan, S., Lakshmanan, S. R., & Arputharaj, K. (2017). Fuzzy-Clustering-Based Intelligent and Secured Energy-Aware Routing. In A. Sangaiah, X. Gao, & A. Abraham (Eds.), *Handbook of Research on Fuzzy and Rough Set Theory in Organizational Decision Making* (pp. 24–37). Hershey, PA: IGI Global. doi:10.4018/978-1-5225-1008-6.ch002

Kamali, A., & Moradi, H. R. (2016). Characterization of Fuzzy δg*-Closed Sets in Fuzzy Topological Spaces. *International Journal of Fuzzy System Applications, 5*(2), 1–12. doi:10.4018/IJFSA.2016040101

Kamath, S. (2015). Fuzzy Logic for Breast Cancer Diagnosis Using Medical Thermogram Images. In A. Kumar (Ed.), *Fuzzy Expert Systems for Disease Diagnosis* (pp. 168–199). Hershey, PA: IGI Global. doi:10.4018/978-1-4666-7240-6.ch007

Kanthi, M. (2015). Fuzzy Logic-Based Intelligent Control System for Active Ankle Foot Orthosis. In A. Kumar (Ed.), *Fuzzy Expert Systems for Disease Diagnosis* (pp. 248–279). Hershey, PA: IGI Global. doi:10.4018/978-1-4666-7240-6.ch009

Kharola, A. (2016). Design of a Hybrid Adaptive Neuro Fuzzy Inference System (ANFIS) Controller for Position and Angle control of Inverted Pendulum (IP) Systems. *International Journal of Fuzzy System Applications, 5*(1), 27–42. doi:10.4018/IJFSA.2016010102

Kharola, A., & Patil, P. P. (2017). A Comparative Study for Position Regulation and Anti-Swing Control of Highly Non-Linear Double Inverted Pendulum (DIP) System Using Different Soft Com. *International Journal of Fuzzy System Applications, 6*(2), 59–81. doi:10.4018/IJFSA.2017040104

Kharola, A., & Patil, P. P. (2017). Neural Fuzzy Control of Ball and Beam System. *International Journal of Energy Optimization and Engineering*, *6*(2), 64–78. doi:10.4018/IJEOE.2017040104

Kohli, S. (2015). Developing and Validating Fuzzy-Based Trust Measures for Online Medical Diagnosis and Symptoms Analysis. In A. Kumar (Ed.), *Fuzzy Expert Systems for Disease Diagnosis* (pp. 302–332). Hershey, PA: IGI Global. doi:10.4018/978-1-4666-7240-6.ch011

Kumar, A. V., & Kalpana, M. (2015). Emerging Application of Fuzzy Expert System in Medical Domain. In A. Kumar (Ed.), *Fuzzy Expert Systems for Disease Diagnosis* (pp. 1–20). Hershey, PA: IGI Global. doi:10.4018/978-1-4666-7240-6.ch001

Kumar, A. V., & Kalpana, M. (2015). Fuzzy Expert System to Diagnose Diabetes Using S Weights for S Fuzzy Assessment Methodology. In A. Kumar (Ed.), *Fuzzy Expert Systems for Disease Diagnosis* (pp. 280–301). Hershey, PA: IGI Global. doi:10.4018/978-1-4666-7240-6.ch010

Kumar, H. (2017). Some Recent Defuzzification Methods. In D. Li (Ed.), *Theoretical and Practical Advancements for Fuzzy System Integration* (pp. 31–48). Hershey, PA: IGI Global. doi:10.4018/978-1-5225-1848-8.ch002

Kumar, H., Chauhan, N. K., & Yadav, P. K. (2016). Dynamic Tasks Scheduling Algorithm for Distributed Computing Systems under Fuzzy Environment. *International Journal of Fuzzy System Applications*, *5*(4), 77–95. doi:10.4018/IJFSA.2016100104

Kumar, K. (2017). Optimizing the Electrical Discharge Drilling Process for High Aspect Micro Hole Drilling in Die Steel. In R. Das & M. Pradhan (Eds.), *Handbook of Research on Manufacturing Process Modeling and Optimization Strategies* (pp. 120–141). Hershey, PA: IGI Global. doi:10.4018/978-1-5225-2440-3.ch006

Kumar, M. (2017). Modeling and Simulation of Surface Texture for End-Milling Process: Modeling End-Milling Process. In R. Das & M. Pradhan (Eds.), *Handbook of Research on Manufacturing Process Modeling and Optimization Strategies* (pp. 19–39). Hershey, PA: IGI Global. doi:10.4018/978-1-5225-2440-3.ch002

Kumar, M. (2017). P-F Fuzzy Rings and Normal Fuzzy Ring: Fuzzy Ring. In A. Adak, D. Manna, & M. Bhowmik (Eds.), *Emerging Research on Applied Fuzzy Sets and Intuitionistic Fuzzy Matrices* (pp. 82–111). Hershey, PA: IGI Global. doi:10.4018/978-1-5225-0914-1.ch004

Kumar, P. S. (2016). PSK Method for Solving Type-1 and Type-3 Fuzzy Transportation Problems. *International Journal of Fuzzy System Applications*, 5(4), 121–146. doi:10.4018/IJFSA.2016100106

Liao, X. (2015). Decision Method of Optimal Investment Enterprise Selection under Uncertain Information Environment. *International Journal of Fuzzy System Applications*, 4(1), 33–42. doi:10.4018/IJFSA.2015010102

Loharkar, P. K., & Pradhan, M. K. (2017). Modeling and Analysis of Cold Drawing Process: Parameters and Methods. In R. Das & M. Pradhan (Eds.), *Handbook of Research on Manufacturing Process Modeling and Optimization Strategies* (pp. 40–53). Hershey, PA: IGI Global. doi:10.4018/978-1-5225-2440-3.ch003

Manna, D. (2017). Semiring of Generalized Interval-Valued Intuitionistic Fuzzy Matrices. In A. Adak, D. Manna, & M. Bhowmik (Eds.), *Emerging Research on Applied Fuzzy Sets and Intuitionistic Fuzzy Matrices* (pp. 132–152). Hershey, PA: IGI Global. doi:10.4018/978-1-5225-0914-1.ch006

Mohammadian, M. (2015). Intelligent Decision Making and Risk Analysis of B2c E-Commerce Customer Satisfaction. *International Journal of Fuzzy System Applications*, 4(1), 60–75. doi:10.4018/IJFSA.2015010104

Molina, T., García-Alcaraz, J. L., Loya, V. M., Tanino, N. S., & Tlapa, D. (2017). Impact of Human Resources on Quality After Just-in-Time Implementation. In R. Das & M. Pradhan (Eds.), *Handbook of Research on Manufacturing Process Modeling and Optimization Strategies* (pp. 235–255). Hershey, PA: IGI Global. doi:10.4018/978-1-5225-2440-3.ch011

Mondal, S. P. (2017). Non-Linear Intuitionistic Fuzzy Number and Its Application in Partial Differential Equation. In A. Adak, D. Manna, & M. Bhowmik (Eds.), *Emerging Research on Applied Fuzzy Sets and Intuitionistic Fuzzy Matrices* (pp. 215–234). Hershey, PA: IGI Global. doi:10.4018/978-1-5225-0914-1.ch009

Mondal, S. P. (2017). Solution of Basic Inventory Model in Fuzzy and Interval Environments: Fuzzy and Interval Differential Equation Approach. In A. Sangaiah, X. Gao, & A. Abraham (Eds.), *Handbook of Research on Fuzzy and Rough Set Theory in Organizational Decision Making* (pp. 65–95). Hershey, PA: IGI Global. doi:10.4018/978-1-5225-1008-6.ch004

Mondal, S. P., Vishwakarma, D. K., & Saha, A. K. (2017). Intuitionistic Fuzzy Difference Equation. In A. Adak, D. Manna, & M. Bhowmik (Eds.), *Emerging Research on Applied Fuzzy Sets and Intuitionistic Fuzzy Matrices* (pp. 112–131). Hershey, PA: IGI Global. doi:10.4018/978-1-5225-0914-1.ch005

Moradi, H. R. (2015). Bounded and Semi Bounded Inverse Theorems in Fuzzy Normed Spaces. *International Journal of Fuzzy System Applications*, 4(2), 47–55. doi:10.4018/IJFSA.2015040104

Nagarajan, S. K. (2017). Genetic-Based Estimation of Biomass Using Geographical Information System: Study Area Vellore. In A. Sangaiah, X. Gao, & A. Abraham (Eds.), *Handbook of Research on Fuzzy and Rough Set Theory in Organizational Decision Making* (pp. 275–304). Hershey, PA: IGI Global. doi:10.4018/978-1-5225-1008-6.ch012

Nan, J., Wang, T., & An, J. (2016). Intuitionistic Fuzzy Distance Based TOPSIS Method and Application to MADM. *International Journal of Fuzzy System Applications*, 5(1), 43–56. doi:10.4018/IJFSA.2016010103

Nan, J., Wang, T., & An, J. (2017). Intuitionistic Fuzzy Distance-Based Intuitionistic Fuzzy TOPSIS Method and Application to MADM. In D. Li (Ed.), *Theoretical and Practical Advancements for Fuzzy System Integration* (pp. 72–96). Hershey, PA: IGI Global. doi:10.4018/978-1-5225-1848-8.ch004

Narayanan, S. J., Bhatt, R. B., & Paramasivam, I. (2016). An Improved Second Order Training Algorithm for Improving the Accuracy of Fuzzy Decision Trees. *International Journal of Fuzzy System Applications*, 5(4), 96–120. doi:10.4018/IJFSA.2016100105

Nematian, J., & Ghotb, S. S. (2017). Mathematical Programming for Modelling Green Supply Chains Under Randomness and Fuzziness. *International Journal of Fuzzy System Applications*, 6(1), 56–85. doi:10.4018/IJFSA.2017010104

Ng, P. S., & Zhang, F. (2016). An Improved Hybrid Model for Order Quantity Allocation and Supplier Risk Exposure. *International Journal of Fuzzy System Applications*, 5(3), 120–147. doi:10.4018/IJFSA.2016070107

Nine, M. S., Azad, A. K., Abdullah, S., & Rahman, R. M. (2015). Fuzzy Dynamic Load Balancing in Virtualized Data Centers of SaaS Cloud Provider. *International Journal of Fuzzy System Applications*, *4*(3), 50–71. doi:10.4018/IJFSA.2015070104

Ojokoh, B. A., Omisore, O. M., Samuel, O. W., & Otunniyi, T. (2015). A Fuzzy-Based Recommender System for Electronic Products Selection using Users Requirements and Other Users Opinion. *International Journal of Fuzzy System Applications*, *4*(1), 76–87. doi:10.4018/IJFSA.2015010105

Osman, T., Mahjabeen, M., Psyche, S. S., Urmi, A. I., Ferdous, J. S., & Rahman, R. M. (2017). Application of Fuzzy Logic for Adaptive Food Recommendation. *International Journal of Fuzzy System Applications*, *6*(2), 110–133. doi:10.4018/IJFSA.2017040106

P., J. R., & E. C., H. A. (2017). MAGDM Problems with Correlation Coefficient of Triangular Fuzzy IFS. In D. Li (Ed.), *Theoretical and Practical Advancements for Fuzzy System Integration* (pp. 154-192). Hershey, PA: IGI Global. doi:10.4018/978-1-5225-1848-8.ch007

Pakniyat, A., Hosseini, R., & Mazinai, M. (2016). A Fuzzy Expert System for Star Classification Based on Photometry. *International Journal of Fuzzy System Applications*, *5*(3), 109–119. doi:10.4018/IJFSA.2016070106

Perumal, B., & Aramudhan, M. (2016). A Multi-Objective Fuzzy Ant Colony Optimization Algorithm for Virtual Machine Placement. *International Journal of Fuzzy System Applications*, *5*(4), 165–191. doi:10.4018/IJFSA.2016100108

Pradheep Kumar, K., & Venkata Subramanian, D. (2017). Fuzzy-Based Querying Approach for Multidimensional Big Data Quality Assessment. In A. Sangaiah, X. Gao, & A. Abraham (Eds.), *Handbook of Research on Fuzzy and Rough Set Theory in Organizational Decision Making* (pp. 1–23). Hershey, PA: IGI Global. doi:10.4018/978-1-5225-1008-6.ch001

Qian, Q., & Liu, W. (2016). Quality Credit Supervision Research Based on Minimum Dataset: With the Licensed Enterprises in Kunming of China for Case. *International Journal of Fuzzy System Applications*, *5*(2), 64–73. doi:10.4018/IJFSA.2016040105

Raheja, S. (2017). Intuitionistic Fuzzy Set Theory with Fair Share CPU Scheduler: A Dynamic Approach. In D. Li (Ed.), *Theoretical and Practical Advancements for Fuzzy System Integration* (pp. 126–153). Hershey, PA: IGI Global. doi:10.4018/978-1-5225-1848-8.ch006

Raheja, S., Dadhich, R., & Rajpal, S. (2015). Designing of Vague Logic Based Fair-Share CPU Scheduler: VFS CPU Scheduler. *International Journal of Fuzzy System Applications*, 4(3), 25–49. doi:10.4018/IJFSA.2015070103

Rahimi, S. A. (2017). Application of Fuzzy Soft Set in Patients' Prioritization. In D. Li (Ed.), *Theoretical and Practical Advancements for Fuzzy System Integration* (pp. 221–244). Hershey, PA: IGI Global. doi:10.4018/978-1-5225-1848-8.ch009

Robinson, J. P. (2016). Contrasting Correlation Coefficient with Distance Measure in Interval Valued Intuitionistic Trapezoidal Fuzzy MAGDM Problems. *International Journal of Fuzzy System Applications*, 5(4), 16–51. doi:10.4018/IJFSA.2016100102

Robinson, J. P., & Henry Amirtharaj, E. C. (2015). MAGDM Problems with Correlation Coefficient of Triangular Fuzzy IFS. *International Journal of Fuzzy System Applications*, 4(1), 1–32. doi:10.4018/IJFSA.2015010101

S., S. G., K., M., Jayaprakash, A., & Sathasivam, S. (2017). Optimized-Fuzzy-Logic-Based Bit Loading Algorithms. In A. Sangaiah, X. Gao, & A. Abraham (Eds.), *Handbook of Research on Fuzzy and Rough Set Theory in Organizational Decision Making* (pp. 305-315). Hershey, PA: IGI Global. doi:10.4018/978-1-5225-1008-6.ch013

Sahu, A. K., Sahu, A. K., & Sahu, N. K. (2017). Benchmarking of Advanced Manufacturing Machines Based on Fuzzy-TOPSIS Method. In D. Li (Ed.), *Theoretical and Practical Advancements for Fuzzy System Integration* (pp. 309–350). Hershey, PA: IGI Global. doi:10.4018/978-1-5225-1848-8.ch012

Sahu, A. K., Sahu, N. K., & Sahu, A. K. (2015). Benchmarking CNC Machine Tool Using Hybrid-Fuzzy Methodology: A Multi-Indices Decision Making (MCDM) Approach. *International Journal of Fuzzy System Applications*, 4(2), 28–46. doi:10.4018/IJFSA.2015040103

Sahu, A. K., Sahu, N. K., & Sahu, A. K. (2017). Appraise the Economic Values of Logistic Handling System under Mixed Information. In D. Li (Ed.), *Theoretical and Practical Advancements for Fuzzy System Integration* (pp. 278–308). Hershey, PA: IGI Global. doi:10.4018/978-1-5225-1848-8.ch011

Sahu, A. K., Sahu, N. K., & Sahu, A. K. (2017). Fuzziness: A Mathematical Tool. In D. Li (Ed.), *Theoretical and Practical Advancements for Fuzzy System Integration* (pp. 1–30). Hershey, PA: IGI Global. doi:10.4018/978-1-5225-1848-8.ch001

Sahu, A. K., Sahu, N. K., & Sahu, A. K. (2017). Performance Estimation of Firms by G-L-A Supply Chain under Imperfect Data. In D. Li (Ed.), *Theoretical and Practical Advancements for Fuzzy System Integration* (pp. 245–277). Hershey, PA: IGI Global. doi:10.4018/978-1-5225-1848-8.ch010

Sahu, N. K., Sahu, A. K., & Sahu, A. K. (2017). Fuzzy-AHP: A Boon in 3PL Decision Making Process. In D. Li (Ed.), *Theoretical and Practical Advancements for Fuzzy System Integration* (pp. 97–125). Hershey, PA: IGI Global. doi:10.4018/978-1-5225-1848-8.ch005

Sajja, P. S. (2015). Knowledge Representation Using Fuzzy XML Rules in Web-Based Expert System for Medical Diagnosis. In A. Kumar (Ed.), *Fuzzy Expert Systems for Disease Diagnosis* (pp. 138–167). Hershey, PA: IGI Global. doi:10.4018/978-1-4666-7240-6.ch006

Sampath, S., & Ramya, B. (2017). Credibility Hypothesis Testing of Variance of Fuzzy Normal Distribution. In D. Li (Ed.), *Theoretical and Practical Advancements for Fuzzy System Integration* (pp. 193–220). Hershey, PA: IGI Global. doi:10.4018/978-1-5225-1848-8.ch008

Sampath, S., & Renitta, L. P. (2016). Chance Hypotheses Testing. *International Journal of Fuzzy System Applications, 5*(3), 77–108. doi:10.4018/IJFSA.2016070105

Sangaiah, A. K., & Jain, V. (2017). Fusion of Fuzzy Multi-Criteria Decision Making Approaches for Discriminating Risk with Relate to Software Project Performance: A Prospective Cohort Study. In A. Sangaiah, X. Gao, & A. Abraham (Eds.), *Handbook of Research on Fuzzy and Rough Set Theory in Organizational Decision Making* (pp. 38–64). Hershey, PA: IGI Global. doi:10.4018/978-1-5225-1008-6.ch003

Sasirekha, S., & Swamynathan, S. (2017). Fuzzy Rule Based Environment Monitoring System for Weather Controlled Laboratories using Arduino. *International Journal of Intelligent Information Technologies, 13*(1), 50–66. doi:10.4018/IJIIT.2017010103

Selvachandran, G., & John, S. J. (2017). Possibility Interval-Valued Vague Soft Expert Sets and Its Similarity Measure. *International Journal of Fuzzy System Applications, 6*(1), 108–121. doi:10.4018/IJFSA.2017010106

Senapati, T. (2017). On Bipolar Fuzzy B-Subalgebras of B-Algebras. In A. Adak, D. Manna, & M. Bhowmik (Eds.), *Emerging Research on Applied Fuzzy Sets and Intuitionistic Fuzzy Matrices* (pp. 254–267). Hershey, PA: IGI Global. doi:10.4018/978-1-5225-0914-1.ch011

Siddiquee, M. R., Haider, N., & Rahman, R. M. (2015). Movie Recommendation System Based on Fuzzy Inference System and Adaptive Neuro Fuzzy Inference System. *International Journal of Fuzzy System Applications*, *4*(4), 31–69. doi:10.4018/IJFSA.2015100103

Singh, C., & Singh, S. R. (2017). Supply Chain Model with Two Storage Facility for Stock Dependent Demand Incorporating Learning and Inflationary Effect under Crisp and Fuzzy Environment. *International Journal of Fuzzy System Applications*, *6*(2), 82–109. doi:10.4018/IJFSA.2017040105

Singh, P. (2017). An Efficient Method for Forecasting Using Fuzzy Time Series. In A. Adak, D. Manna, & M. Bhowmik (Eds.), *Emerging Research on Applied Fuzzy Sets and Intuitionistic Fuzzy Matrices* (pp. 287–304). Hershey, PA: IGI Global. doi:10.4018/978-1-5225-0914-1.ch013

Sinha, G. R. (2015). Fuzzy-Based Medical Image Processing. In A. Kumar (Ed.), *Fuzzy Expert Systems for Disease Diagnosis* (pp. 45–61). Hershey, PA: IGI Global. doi:10.4018/978-1-4666-7240-6.ch003

Subramaniam, P. R. (2017). An Adaptive Fuzzy-Based Service-Oriented Approach with QoS Support for Vehicular Ad Hoc Networks. In A. Sangaiah, X. Gao, & A. Abraham (Eds.), *Handbook of Research on Fuzzy and Rough Set Theory in Organizational Decision Making* (pp. 137–167). Hershey, PA: IGI Global. doi:10.4018/978-1-5225-1008-6.ch007

Subramaniam, P. R., Venugopal, C., & Sangaiah, A. K. (2017). A Fuzzy-Based Calorie Burn Calculator for a Gamified Walking Activity Using Treadmill. In A. Sangaiah, X. Gao, & A. Abraham (Eds.), *Handbook of Research on Fuzzy and Rough Set Theory in Organizational Decision Making* (pp. 96–115). Hershey, PA: IGI Global. doi:10.4018/978-1-5225-1008-6.ch005

Subramanian, T., & Savarimuthu, N. (2016). Cloud Service Evaluation and Selection Using Fuzzy Hybrid MCDM Approach in Marketplace. *International Journal of Fuzzy System Applications*, *5*(2), 118–153. doi:10.4018/IJFSA.2016040108

Sundaram, S., Madhavachari, L. S., & Balu, R. (2015). Chance Single Sampling Plan for Variables. *International Journal of Fuzzy System Applications*, *4*(1), 43–59. doi:10.4018/IJFSA.2015010103

Suresh, R., & Joshi, A. G. (2017). Investigations on Machinability Characteristics of Hardened AISI H13 Steel With Multilayer Coated Carbide Tool Using Statistical Techniques. In R. Das & M. Pradhan (Eds.), *Handbook of Research on Manufacturing Process Modeling and Optimization Strategies* (pp. 194–207). Hershey, PA: IGI Global. doi:10.4018/978-1-5225-2440-3. ch009

Taeib, A., & Chaari, A. (2015). Optimal Tuning Strategy for MIMO Fuzzy Predictive Controllers. *International Journal of Fuzzy System Applications*, *4*(4), 87–99. doi:10.4018/IJFSA.2015100105

Tiwari, A., & Pradhan, M. K. (2017). Modelling and Optimization of End Milling Process Using TLBO and TOPSIS Algorithm: Modelling and Optimization of End Milling Process. In R. Das & M. Pradhan (Eds.), *Handbook of Research on Manufacturing Process Modeling and Optimization Strategies* (pp. 54–81). Hershey, PA: IGI Global. doi:10.4018/978-1-5225-2440-3.ch004

Tiwari, S., & Pradhan, M. K. (2017). Optimisation of Machining Parameters in Electrical Discharge Machining of LM25-RHA Composites. In R. Das & M. Pradhan (Eds.), *Handbook of Research on Manufacturing Process Modeling and Optimization Strategies* (pp. 1–18). Hershey, PA: IGI Global. doi:10.4018/978-1-5225-2440-3.ch001

Tripathy, B., Mohanty, R., Sooraj, T. R., & Arun, K. R. (2017). Parameter Reduction in Soft Set Models and Application in Decision Making. In A. Sangaiah, X. Gao, & A. Abraham (Eds.), *Handbook of Research on Fuzzy and Rough Set Theory in Organizational Decision Making* (pp. 331–354). Hershey, PA: IGI Global. doi:10.4018/978-1-5225-1008-6.ch015

Tuan, T. M., Duc, N. T., Van Hai, P., & Son, L. H. (2017). Dental Diagnosis from X-Ray Images using Fuzzy Rule-Based Systems. *International Journal of Fuzzy System Applications*, *6*(1), 1–16. doi:10.4018/IJFSA.2017010101

Tyagi, K., & Tripathi, A. (2017). Rough Fuzzy Automata and Rough Fuzzy Grammar. *International Journal of Fuzzy System Applications*, *6*(1), 36–55. doi:10.4018/IJFSA.2017010103

Uppala, A. K., Ranka, R., Thakkar, J. J., Kumar, M. V., & Agrawal, S. (2017). Selection of Green Suppliers Based on GSCM Practices: Using Fuzzy MCDM Approach in an Electronics Company. In A. Sangaiah, X. Gao, & A. Abraham (Eds.), *Handbook of Research on Fuzzy and Rough Set Theory in Organizational Decision Making* (pp. 355–375). Hershey, PA: IGI Global. doi:10.4018/978-1-5225-1008-6.ch016

Venugopal, C. (2017). Fuzzy-Based Matrix Converter Drive for Induction Motor. In A. Sangaiah, X. Gao, & A. Abraham (Eds.), *Handbook of Research on Fuzzy and Rough Set Theory in Organizational Decision Making* (pp. 219–245). Hershey, PA: IGI Global. doi:10.4018/978-1-5225-1008-6.ch010

Vijayachitra, S. (2015). Diagnosis of Angina Using Neuro-Fuzzy Technique. In A. Kumar (Ed.), *Fuzzy Expert Systems for Disease Diagnosis* (pp. 333–368). Hershey, PA: IGI Global. doi:10.4018/978-1-4666-7240-6.ch012

Yu, G., Li, D., & Qiu, J. (2017). Interval-Valued Intuitionistic Fuzzy Multi-Attribute Decision Making Based on Satisfactory Degree. In D. Li (Ed.), *Theoretical and Practical Advancements for Fuzzy System Integration* (pp. 49–71). Hershey, PA: IGI Global. doi:10.4018/978-1-5225-1848-8.ch003

Zoulfaghari, H., Nematian, J., & Nezhad, A. A. (2016). A Resource-Constrained Project Scheduling Problem with Fuzzy Activity Times. *International Journal of Fuzzy System Applications*, 5(4), 1–15. doi:10.4018/IJFSA.2016100101

Index

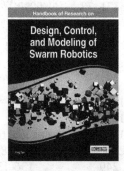

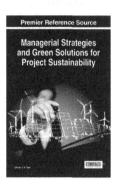

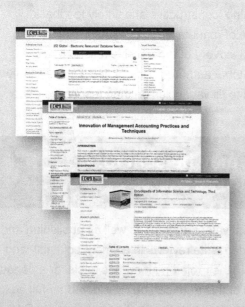

Printed in the United States
By Bookmasters